THE EVERYTHING®
GUIDE TO
FOOD REMEDIES

Dear Reader,

After choosing to study and work in the field of nutrition and wellness, I quickly learned that the focus was less about food and more about isolated nutrients, replacers, and pills. As a result, my excitement about wellness dwindled and my frustration with health issues in our society grew . . . until I began to travel and rediscovered real food.

Traveling taught me to look at food from a cultural perspective. It brought me back to my roots of eating homegrown and homemade. It inspired me to cook, to reach into my past and the past of other cultures, and to adopt food practices while keeping the challenges of today in mind.

Most importantly, it taught me that real food, grown and nurtured, whether plant or animal, is medicine. Food provides the vitamins, minerals, and secret miracle substances we need to fight disease. It is all right there in each fresh, delicious, natural bite. We just have to eat it.

This book combines my desire for health, my fascination with food and its nutrients, and my love of cooking. I hope you will find the information and inspiration you need to eat, enjoy, and be well.

In Health,

Lori Rice

Welcome to the EVERYTHING® Series!

These handy, accessible books give you all you need to tackle a difficult project, gain a new hobby, comprehend a fascinating topic, prepare for an exam, or even brush up on something you learned back in school but have since forgotten.

You can choose to read an *Everything*® book from cover to cover or just pick out the information you want from our four useful boxes: e-questions, e-facts, e-alerts, and e-ssentials.

We give you everything you need to know on the subject, but throw in a lot of fun stuff along the way, too.

We now have more than 400 *Everything*® books in print, spanning such wide-ranging categories as weddings, pregnancy, cooking, music instruction, foreign language, crafts, pets, New Age, and so much more. When you're done reading them all, you can finally say you know *Everything*®!

QUESTION

Answers to
common questions

FACT

Important snippets
of information

ALERT

Urgent
warnings

ESSENTIAL

Quick
handy tips

PUBLISHER Karen Cooper

DIRECTOR OF ACQUISITIONS AND INNOVATION Paula Munier

MANAGING EDITOR, EVERYTHING® SERIES Lisa Laing

COPY CHIEF Casey Ebert

ASSISTANT PRODUCTION EDITOR Jacob Erickson

ACQUISITIONS EDITOR Katrina Schroeder

SENIOR DEVELOPMENT EDITOR Brett Palana-Shanahan

EDITORIAL ASSISTANT Ross Weisman

EVERYTHING® SERIES COVER DESIGNER Erin Alexander

LAYOUT DESIGNERS Colleen Cunningham, Elisabeth Lariviere, Ashley Vierra, Denise Wallace

NUTRITION STATS Lorena Novak Bull, RD

Visit the entire Everything® series at *www.everything.com*

THE
EVERYTHING®
GUIDE TO
FOOD
REMEDIES

An A–Z guide to healing with food

Lori Rice, MS

Aadamsmedia

Avon, Massachusetts

*To my best friend, my husband, whose
strengths, abilities, and perseverance inspire
me every day.*

An Everything® Series Book.
Everything® and everything.com® are registered trademarks of F+W Media, Inc.

Published by Adams Media, a division of F+W Media, Inc.
57 Littlefield Street, Avon, MA 02322 U.S.A.
www.adamsmedia.com

ISBN 10: 1-4405-1100-4
ISBN 13: 978-1-4405-1100-4
eISBN 10: 1-4405-1157-8
eISBN 13: 978-1-4405-1157-8

Printed in the United States of America.

10 9 8 7 6 5 4 3 2 1

Library of Congress Cataloging-in-Publication Data
is available from the publisher.

This publication is designed to provide accurate and authoritative information with regard to the subject matter covered. It is sold with the understanding that the publisher is not engaged in rendering legal, accounting, or other professional advice. If legal advice or other expert assistance is required, the services of a competent professional person should be sought.
　　　　　—From a *Declaration of Principles* jointly adopted by a Committee of the American Bar Association and a Committee of Publishers and Associations

Many of the designations used by manufacturers and sellers to distinguish their products are claimed as trademarks. Where those designations appear in this book and Adams Media was aware of a trademark claim, the designations have been printed with initial capital letters.

This book is intended as general information only, and should not be used to diagnose or treat any health condition. In light of the complex, individual, and specific nature of health problems, this book is not intended to replace professional medical advice. The ideas, procedures, and suggestions in this book are intended to supplement, not replace, the advice of a trained medical professional. Consult your physician before adopting any of the suggestions in this book, as well as about any condition that may require diagnosis or medical attention. The author and publisher disclaim any liability arising directly or indirectly from the use of this book.

This book is available at quantity discounts for bulk purchases.
For information, please call 1-800-289-0963.

Contents

Introduction **xi**

01 The Healing Power of Food / 1

Food as Medicine **2**

The Positive Side of Nutrition Research **3**

Nutrients Versus Real Food **3**

Popular Foods with Healing Power **4**

Selecting Healing Foods **6**

Cooking and Eating Healing Foods **7**

Medical Considerations **8**

02 Acne / 9

What Causes Acne? **10**

Nutrients That May Prevent
or Alleviate Acne **11**

Quick, Budget Recipes **12**

Advanced Recipes **15**

03 Alzheimer's Disease / 17

What Is Alzheimer's Disease? **18**

Nutrients That May Prevent
Alzheimer's Disease **18**

Foods That Contain These Nutrients **19**

▶ Quick, Budget Recipes **20**

▶ Advanced Recipes **23**

04 Anemia / 25

What Is Anemia? **26**

Nutrients That Prevent or
Treat Anemia **26**

Foods That Contain These Nutrients **27**

▶ Quick, Budget Recipes **29**

▶ Advanced Recipes **32**

05 Arthritis / 35

Types of Arthritis **36**

Nutrients That Alleviate Arthritis **36**

Foods That Contain These Nutrients **37**

▶ Quick, Budget Recipes **40**

▶ Advanced Recipes **43**

06 Asthma / 45

What Is Asthma? **46**

Nutrients That Alleviate
the Symptoms of Asthma **46**

Foods That Contain These Nutrients **47**

▶ Quick, Budget Recipes **49**

▶ Advanced Recipes **52**

07 Cancer / 55

What Is Cancer? **56**

Nutrients That May Prevent Cancer **56**

Foods That Contain These Nutrients **57**

▶ Quick, Budget Recipes **59**

▶ Advanced Recipes **62**

08 Candida / 65

What Is Candida? **66**

Nutrients That Relieve
Candida Symptoms **66**

Foods That Contain These Nutrients **67**

▶ Quick, Budget Recipes **68**

▶ Advanced Recipes **71**

09 **Cataracts / 73**

What Are Cataracts? **74**

Nutrients That May Prevent Cataracts **74**

Foods That Contain These Nutrients **75**

▶ Quick, Budget Recipes **77**

▶ Advanced Recipes **80**

10 **Celiac Disease / 83**

What Is Celiac Disease? **84**

Nutrients That Increase the
Symptoms of Celiac Disease **84**

Foods That Contain These Nutrients **84**

▶ Quick, Budget Recipes **87**

▶ Advanced Recipes **90**

11 **Chronic Fatigue Syndrome / 93**

What Is Chronic Fatigue Syndrome? **94**

Nutrients That Alleviate CFS **94**

Foods That Contain These Nutrients **95**

▶ Quick, Budget Recipes **98**

▶ Advanced Recipes **101**

12 **Cold and Flu / 103**

Symptoms and Causes of
Cold and Flu **104**

Nutrients That Prevent or
Alleviate Cold and Flu **104**

Foods That Contain These Nutrients **105**

▶ Quick, Budget Recipes **107**

▶ Advanced Recipes **110**

13 **Cold Sores / 113**

What Is a Cold Sore? **114**

Nutrients That Prevent or
Alleviate Cold Sores **114**

Foods That Contain These Nutrients **115**

▶ Quick, Budget Recipes **116**

▶ Advanced Recipes **119**

14 **Constipation / 121**

What Is Constipation? **122**

Nutrients That Alleviate Constipation **122**

Foods That Contain These Nutrients **123**

▶ Quick, Budget Recipes **124**

▶ Advanced Recipes **127**

15 **Depression / 129**

What Is Depression? **130**

Nutrients That Prevent
or Alleviate Depression **130**

Foods That Contain These Nutrients **131**

▶ Quick, Budget Recipes **133**

▶ Advanced Recipes **136**

16 **Diabetes / 139**

What Is Diabetes? **140**

Nutrients That Control
or Prevent Diabetes **140**

Foods That Contain These Nutrients **141**

▶ Quick, Budget Recipes **142**

▶ Advanced Recipes **145**

17 Diarrhea / 147

What Causes Diarrhea? **148**

Nutrients That Prevent or Alleviate Diarrhea **148**

Foods That Contain These Nutrients **148**

▶ Quick, Budget Recipes **150**

▶ Advanced Recipes **153**

18 Fibromyalgia / 155

What Is Fibromyalgia? **156**

Nutrients That Prevent or Alleviate Fibromyalgia **156**

Foods That Contain These Nutrients **157**

▶ Quick, Budget Recipes **158**

▶ Advanced Recipes **161**

19 Headaches / 163

Types of Head Pain **164**

Nutrients That Alleviate Head Pain **164**

Foods That Contain These Nutrients **164**

▶ Quick, Budget Recipes **166**

▶ Advanced Recipes **169**

20 Heartburn / 171

What Is Heartburn? **172**

Nutrients That Alleviate Heartburn **172**

Foods That Contain These Nutrients **172**

▶ Quick, Budget Recipes **174**

▶ Advanced Recipes **177**

21 High Blood Pressure / 179

What Is High Blood Pressure? **180**

Nutrients That Prevent or Reduce High Blood Pressure **180**

Foods That Contain These Nutrients **181**

▶ Quick, Budget Recipes **182**

▶ Advanced Recipes **185**

22 High Cholesterol / 187

What Is High Cholesterol? **188**

Nutrients That Prevent or Control High Cholesterol **188**

Foods That Contain These Nutrients **189**

▶ Quick, Budget Recipes **190**

▶ Advanced Recipes **193**

23 Insomnia / 195

What Is Insomnia? **196**

Nutrients That Alleviate Insomnia **196**

Foods That Contain These Nutrients **196**

▶ Quick, Budget Recipes **198**

▶ Advanced Recipes **201**

24 Irritable Bowel Syndrome / 203

What Is Irritable Bowel Syndrome? **204**

Nutrients That Alleviate IBS **204**

Foods That Contain These Nutrients **205**

▶ Quick, Budget Recipes **206**

▶ Advanced Recipes **209**

25 Menopause / 211

What Is Menopause? **212**

Nutrients That Alleviate Symptoms of Menopause **212**

Foods That Contain These Nutrients **213**

▶ Quick, Budget Recipes **214**

▶ Advanced Recipes **217**

26 **Muscle Cramps / 219**

Types and Causes of Muscle Cramps **220**

Nutrients That Prevent or
Alleviate Muscle Cramping **221**

Foods That Contain These Nutrients **221**

▶ Quick, Budget Recipes **223**

▶ Advanced Recipes **226**

27 **Nausea and Motion
Sickness / 229**

What Causes Nausea
and Motion Sickness? **230**

Nutrients That Alleviate Nausea
and Motion Sickness **230**

Foods That Contain These Nutrients **231**

▶ Quick, Budget Recipes **232**

▶ Advanced Recipes **235**

28 **Premenstrual Syndrome / 237**

What Is Premenstrual Syndrome? **238**

Nutrients That Alleviate
the Symptoms of PMS **238**

Foods That Contain These Nutrients **238**

▶ Quick, Budget Recipes **240**

▶ Advanced Recipes **243**

29 **Psoriasis / 245**

What Is Psoriasis? **246**

Nutrients That Alleviate Psoriasis **246**

Foods That Contain These Nutrients **247**

▶ Quick, Budget Recipes **248**

▶ Advanced Recipes **251**

30 **Stress and Anxiety / 253**

What Causes Stress and Anxiety? **254**

Nutrients That Alleviate
Stress and Anxiety **254**

Foods That Contain These Nutrients **255**

▶ Quick, Budget Recipes **256**

▶ Advanced Recipes **259**

31 **Urinary Tract Infections / 261**

What Is a Urinary Tract Infection? **262**

Nutrients That Prevent or
Alleviate UTIs **262**

Foods That Contain These Nutrients **263**

▶ Quick, Budget Recipes **264**

▶ Advanced Recipes **267**

32 **Varicose Veins / 269**

What Are Varicose Veins? **270**

Nutrients That Improve Circulation
and Prevent Varicose Veins **270**

Foods That Contain These Nutrients **271**

▶ Quick, Budget Recipes **272**

▶ Advanced Recipes **275**

Appendix A: Print Resources / **277**

Appendix B: Web-Based
Resources / **279**

Index / **281**

Acknowledgments

I would like to thank my husband for supporting me in my work, my dad who taught me the beauty of growing my own food, and my mom who taught me how to prepare and preserve it.

Introduction

SAFFRON BOOSTS YOUR MOOD. Pumpkin seeds promote a healthy prostate. Sea scallops improve cardiovascular health. When it comes to food, health, and preventing disease, research continues to reveal how food can influence well-being.

Food contains nutrients, and nutrients prevent and alleviate aches, pains, diseases, and disorders. Despite what the miracle-cure marketing campaigns tell you, before the pills and the powders there was food. The truth is that food and its valuable nutrients are the real miracle. These aren't just fads that will come and go, but real food with real healing power. When fresh, natural, and fashioned into delicious recipes, food is not only beneficial to health but quite enjoyable to the taste buds as well.

In this A to Z guide, readers will find helpful tips on what foods to eat for which ailments along with more than 150 recipes utilizing these foods, such as:

- Kale Berry Smoothie
- Tropical Oatmeal
- Savory Barley Salad
- Avocado Banana Salad
- Curry Chicken Salad

If you have a specific ailment in mind, you can easily flip right to the chapter to find the exact information you need. You can also start from the beginning and work your way through the information to create a shopping list and menu that will keep you happy, healthy, and eating well.

Worried about the time demands of the recipes or the price of healthy ingredients? Don't be. Each chapter provides quick, budget-friendly recipes that are easy to make or that include less-expensive ingredients. These are followed by recipes that involve more ingredients and advanced cooking techniques, perfect for special occasions. In addition, you will find an abundance of tips for shopping, preparation, and substitutions.

With *The Everything® Guide to Food Remedies* you will soon be cooking your way to better health, one meal at a time!

CHAPTER 1

The Healing
Power of Food

The human body heals itself and nutrition provides the resources to accomplish the task.

—Roger Williams, PhD

The healing power of food has been well documented throughout history. Cultures throughout the world have used foods—fruits, vegetables, herbs, and animal products—to ward off disease and prevent ailments, aches, and pains. Now we live in a time when advances in technology allow us to take a closer look at food and discover why and how it heals. As a consumer, you have the ability to take this valuable knowledge and use it to guide your eating while reaping the benefits of improved health and wellness.

Food as Medicine

Think back to a time when there were no medicines, no pharmaceutical companies, and very little of the hard science you are familiar with today. Having difficulty? That's not surprising, because you have likely not lived during such an era. However, there was a time in history when food was the only medicine.

The history of the healing power of food dates back more than 4,000 years. References regarding food and herbs for healing can be found in the Bible. Greek and Chinese cultures have a long history of utilizing food and its nutrients as cures and relief for ailments and disease. It was the people of these times who saw the effects that food can have on healing the body even if they didn't know exactly why or how it happened.

ESSENTIAL

While research findings validate the necessity to eat fresh and natural foods for health, sometimes they can lead to a new product that attempts to isolate the active nutrient in these foods. When consumers are led to believe that a pill or powder filled with a foodlike substance or isolated nutrient is better than the food itself, perhaps science has been taken a little too far.

Many of the reputed benefits of food from the past are now strongly supported by scientific evidence. The well-known Nurses' Health Studies are considered some of the largest and longest-running research studies evaluating factors that influence women's health. Through these studies scientists have learned things such as eating cruciferous and green leafy vegetables can help maintain cognitive function as you age, and the consumption of nuts and whole grains reduces risk for coronary heart disease. Other scientific research has shown that strawberries may contain nutrients that damage or kill leukemia cells, antioxidants have the potential to inhibit enzymes that cause inflammation, and mushrooms have antimicrobial powers to fight off infection.

The Positive Side of Nutrition Research

As time has passed and technology has advanced, nutritional researchers have not forgotten the powers of food. What has changed, however, is that now the tools exist to evaluate exactly what makes food such a healing force. Not only are new powers of foods being discovered, but now the active components of these foods are being identified, giving people the ability to eat well and reduce disease.

For example, growing and eating garlic for its medicinal properties dates back several thousand years. Today's researchers have been able to determine that the sulfur-containing compounds of garlic, as well as its vitamin and mineral content, produce valuable health benefits. Research has linked garlic to a reduced risk of cardiovascular disease and some cancers, and it carries the potential to reduce the pain and inflammation of arthritis.

Similarly, fruits and vegetables have long been recommended as part of a healthy diet, and for good reason. Not only do they provide fiber linked to gastrointestinal health, but the skin and flesh of these fresh foods contain incredible substances called phytochemicals (plant chemicals) that can reduce disease. It is evident that the color of a fruit or vegetable and its species of plant origin influence exactly what ailment or condition the food will benefit.

Nutrients Versus Real Food

Today, the terms "nutraceutical," meaning a nutrient-rich food or food component, and "functional food," describing a food that has nutrients added to it to increase health benefit, are used widely in the food and nutrition industry. As research continues to identify the specific components of foods responsible for health, the drive increases to isolate these nutrients, add them to other commonly eaten, less-nutritious packaged foods (thus making functional foods), and create supplements and pills. This often results in a marketing campaign promising a miracle cure for what ails you.

The problem is that an isolated nutrient is often less effective than a nutrient that comes from real food. There are issues with an isolated nutrient being absorbed after digestion, dangers of toxicity when high doses of a vitamin or mineral are consumed, and risks of unhealthy interactions with high doses of other nutrients. These risks of overconsumption are not often an issue when obtaining nutrients through whole, complex foods. Healthy foods give you a balanced supply of nutrients when you eat a varied diet.

FACT

Currently food manufacturers do not have to put any distinction on food labels between naturally occurring fiber and isolated fiber. Isolated fiber is the fiber that is added to foods that would not normally be sources of fiber. Consumers are led to believe that these isolated fibers will give them the same benefits as natural fiber, but often these added fibers are not the right viscous consistency to lower cholesterol or blood sugar.

Nutritional science continues to uncover links between nutrients and health, but there seems to be little or no benefit when the nutrient is in the form of a supplement. For example, recent research has linked adequate vitamin D levels to brain health and reducing risk of dementia. Yet researchers did not find the same outcome in a group that used vitamin D supplements instead of food, and recommended that people increase their intake of food rich in vitamin D rather than add supplements to their diet.

While vitamins and minerals are known to protect against disease, they are best consumed in their natural form—in food. Food is the original source of healing nutrients. So if it is known that vitamins and minerals protect against disease, yet supplements aren't the answer, what is the answer? Food. Food is the original source of healing nutrients.

Popular Foods with Healing Power

Almost every type of real food—fruits, vegetables, herbs, animal products, nuts, grains, and seeds—contains at least one valuable nutrient that may reduce the risk of disease or alleviate the symptoms of a condition. This makes the options almost endless when it comes to food choices, but there are a few specific foods that often stand in the spotlight.

Salmon

Salmon isn't the only cold-water fatty fish that supplies valuable omega-3 fatty acids, but it is by far the most talked about. Wild-caught Alaskan salmon is the best choice. It is rich in omega-3 fatty acids and low in mercury. Omega-3 fatty acids are linked to a reduced inflammation that may lower the risk for such diseases as heart disease, cancer, and arthritis. They also promote brain health. Albacore tuna and lake trout are also sources of omega-3 fatty acids.

Garlic

Garlic contains sulfur compounds and is considered a phytochemical, which was defined earlier as a term for plant chemicals that provide a variety of health benefits. Garlic has antimicrobial and antibacterial properties. Garlic intake has been associated with reduced cholesterol and a lower risk for cardiovascular disease as well as reduced inflammation and a lower risk for some cancers. Onions are in the same food category as garlic, called allium vegetables.

FACT

As of 2008 there are several clinical trials in humans studying the effects of curcumin against various diseases including colon cancer, pancreatic cancer, psoriasis, and Alzheimer's disease. The results of a 2004 UCLA Veterans Affairs study suggest that curcumin may inhibit the destructive beta-amyloid in the brains of Alzheimer's patients as well as break up existing plaque from the disease.

Curry

Well known as the characteristic flavor ingredient in Indian, Thai, and some Caribbean dishes, curry has received much attention for its potential health benefits. Curry contains the spice turmeric, which contains curcumin. Curcumin has antioxidant activity that can protect against disease and has been linked to reduced inflammation. Because of its antioxidant activity and anti-inflammatory properties, further research is being conducted regarding curcumin's ability to reduce the risk or progression of Alzheimer's disease.

Berries and Cherries

Blackberries, blueberries, cranberries, and raspberries as well as cherries pack valuable healing nutrients. Anthocyanins give these fruits their deep purple, blue, and red colors, and are flavonoids that fall into the category of phytochemicals. These substances protect against damage to cells (oxidation) and thus reduce the risk for some diseases, such as cancer.

Selecting Healing Foods

Most foods contain the maximum healing nutrients when in their natural state. However, the nutrients your body obtains from a specific food are dependent on a number of variables. The growing practices such as the use of composted manure or pesticides, the ripeness when harvested, storage after harvest, and damage during transport can all make a fruit or vegetable more or less nutritious.

ESSENTIAL

The organic standards in the United States do not address food quality, just the methods of production and handling. Valid research comparing organic and conventional food is scant, although some studies suggest that organic foods contain higher levels of some trace minerals.

This is why the claim that local and organic foods are more nutritious is still a topic of scientific debate. It makes sense that a local product picked the same morning that travels a short distance would offer the most nutrients. However, when considering only nutritional value, it is not always a sure thing that local and organic will come out on top. For example, perhaps organic practices were used to grow the food, but it was damaged during transport, causing a loss of nutrients.

Your choice and source of food are decisions you will have to make for yourself. Considerations pertaining to your budget, the environment, and your local economy will all play a role in your decision. That being said, here are a few guidelines you can use to increase the likelihood that you will get the most nutritious foods, specifically produce, for your dollar:

- If you are purchasing from a local farmers' market or grocery store, get to know the grower and supplier. Find out where your food is coming from, how it is grown, when it is picked, and how it is transported.
- Buy ripe, undamaged produce and use it as soon as possible.
- Buy foods that are in season when you can. However, there are many foods, such as papayas, mangoes, guavas, seeds, and nuts, that offer health benefits but may not be grown locally. In this case, embrace global access to food or take advantage of the availability of these foods when you travel.
- Consider growing your own food. It may seem overwhelming at first, but amazing things can be done even with small balcony and urban gardens. At the very least, a pot full of herbs can be beneficial to your health and add flavor to your foods.

When it comes to animal products, research has indicated that some sources do have enhanced nutritional value. Evaluations have shown that eggs from pastured hens contain more omega-3 fatty acids than those from hens raised on factory farms. Beef from grass-fed cows that eat little to no grain is lower in total fat, and has more vitamin A, vitamin E, and omega-3 fatty acids than beef from grain-fed cows. In addition, beef and dairy products from grass-fed cows contain more conjugated linoleic acid (ALA), which has possible anticancer and antioxidant properties.

Cooking and Eating Healing Foods

It is true that heating foods during cooking can destroy some of the valuable nutrients that fresh food provides. For example, vitamin C and folate are unstable to heat. When these foods are cooked, especially for longer periods of time, their nutrient content is decreased.

On the other hand, cooking isn't all bad. For example, boiling spinach for a short period of time, about one minute, may reduce the vitamin C content, but it also reduces the oxalate content. Oxalates may interfere with the absorption of calcium, so fewer oxalates are a good thing. In addition, while long periods of heat can destroy some of the beta carotene in carrots, lightly steaming them may help to improve its absorption by the body.

You will find tips throughout this book for cooking methods to preserve nutrients, but the best advice for cooking and eating healing foods is to vary the foods you eat and your preparation methods. Enjoy fresh fruits and vegetables raw, but don't be afraid to toss them in a stir-fry or steam and mix them with whole-grain pasta from time to time. Variety in both cooking and food choice is the best way to eat for health and healing.

Medical Considerations

It is important to note that the recommendations in this book are most often focused on prevention. Eating certain foods and specific nutrients can decrease your risk of developing common diseases and conditions.

In some cases, foods can also help to alleviate symptoms. However, once you have been diagnosed with a disease or disorder, it is important to work with your health care provider in order to control it. This is especially true if you are taking a medication. Unfortunately, some foods can interact with medication and cause adverse health effects. While your long-term goal may be to control your condition and eliminate the need for such drugs, it is important to devise a plan with a medical professional who knows you and your health history to reach that goal.

CHAPTER 2

Acne

A skin condition that often occurs in the teenage and young adult years, acne is difficult to cope with, and to prevent and treat. While a relationship between acne and food is sometimes classified as a myth, many patients do recognize some foods as triggers, and a healthy diet promotes healthy skin.

What Causes Acne?

According to the American Academy of Dermatology, there is no exact cause for acne. However, it is believed that four key factors play a role in its development: excess oil, clogged pores, bacteria, and inflammation. Sebum oil production is meant to prevent skin from drying. During adolescence, though, the production increases and this can lead to clogged pores and inflammation. The results can range from simple whiteheads to severe acne lesions.

The bacteria *Propionibacterium acnes* is a normal part of healthy human skin. This bacteria uses sebum oil for growth, so when sebum oil production increases during adolescence so does the bacteria. Hence the increase in acne with adolescence. People with acne have more *Propionibacterium acnes* in their skin than people without acne.

Many of the traditional food links to acne are considered myths by health professionals. You have likely heard the recommendation to stop eating fried foods or chocolate in order to prevent a breakout. There is no proof that any foods "cause" acne; acne is usually the result of stress, chronic inflammation, and blood sugar problems. There are, however, some foods that can trigger or aggravate these conditions and can be avoided to prevent worsening the condition. These foods include:

- **High-fat foods.** High-fat foods can cause blood sugar levels to fluctuate severely, thereby leading to more acne.
- **Dairy products.** Dairy products are often high-fat foods, which as mentioned above can cause blood sugar spikes. Milk also contains hormones that can lead to increased sebum oil production by the body.
- **Caffeine.** Caffeine in foods triggers your body to release stress hormones, which increase stress levels.
- **Alcohol.** Drinking alcohol can lead to a release of hormones that trigger sebum oil production.
- **Refined carbohydrates and high-sugar foods.** The sugars in these carbohydrates cause blood sugar spikes.

While there may not be scientific evidence linking a specific food to acne, there are many nutrients and foods that can promote healthy skin.

Nutrients That May Prevent or Alleviate Acne

There are several nutrients that can help alleviate acne including vitamins C and E. Vitamin C helps to support a healthy immune system, which can defend against bacteria and viruses. It also promotes wound healing and repairs tissue. Vitamin E assists in the repair of skin damage. All of these factors may play a role in the development of acne.

Try guavas, red sweet peppers, kiwis, and oranges for vitamin C. If guava is available fresh in your area, experiment with using it in homemade juices. Kiwi makes a convenient, transportable snack when you slice it in half and eat it out of the skin with a spoon.

ESSENTIAL

Saying that guava is high in vitamin C is an understatement when compared to the orange. Oranges get a lot of attention for vitamin C content; however, guavas have this citrus fruit beat. One cup of guava contains about 375 milligrams of vitamin C compared to just 83 milligrams in the same amount of orange segments.

Vitamin E is found in a variety of seeds and nuts, such as sunflower seeds, almonds, hazelnuts, peanuts, and peanut butter. Avocados, tomatoes, and turnip greens also contain vitamin E. Seeds and nuts are ideal snacks and also great toppers for cereals and salad. Enjoy more greens with your meals by serving roasted chicken breasts or fillets of grilled fish over a bed of sautéed spinach and turnip greens instead of on a bed of rice.

Red Bell Pepper Spinach Pasta Salad

A cold pasta salad is a great way to incorporate a few veggies that are rich in vitamin C. This one is dressed simply with olive oil and lemon juice, but feel free to substitute your favorite vinaigrette.

INGREDIENTS | SERVES 4

3 cups dry whole-wheat rigatoni

1 red bell pepper, sliced

3 green onions, sliced

1 cup cherry tomatoes, halved

1 cup fresh spinach, chopped

¼ cup grated Parmesan cheese

3 tablespoons olive oil

1 tablespoon lemon juice

½ teaspoon salt

¼ teaspoon black pepper

Fresh Grated Parmesan

You are likely familiar with grated Parmesan in a can, but have you ever purchased a wedge of fresh Parmesan for cooking? Fresh Parmesan adds much more flavor and is reasonably priced, and a little of it goes a long way. Simply grate it right before using. You will be surprised by the flavor and by just how long one small wedge will last.

1. Bring about 5 cups of water to a boil; add the pasta and stir. Cook until tender, but firm. Drain and rinse with cold water. Set aside.

2. In a bowl, combine the bell pepper, onions, tomatoes, and spinach. Stir in the Parmesan cheese. Add the olive oil, lemon juice, salt, and pepper. Stir to coat the vegetables.

3. Add the pasta to the vegetables and toss to coat evenly. Add more salt and pepper to taste. Refrigerate for at least 30 minutes before serving.

PER SERVING Calories: 290 | Fat: 13g | Sodium: 395mg | Carbohydrates: 38g | Fiber: 2g | Protein: 10g

Kiwi Orange Salad

This simple recipe stacks colorful fruit and is drizzled with a sweet glaze. It can be used as either a sweet starter to a meal or a light dessert.

INGREDIENTS | SERVES 4

2 oranges

2 kiwis

½ cup orange juice

¼ cup fresh basil leaves, chopped

Fruit Sauces

Turning juice into a sauce to drizzle over fruit, a salad, or fish is as simple as cooking it to evaporate the water and intensify the flavor. Most juices will reduce by half, so keep in mind how much you need and begin with double that amount. Pomegranate juice, cherry juice, and orange juice make delicious glazes.

1. Carefully peel the oranges with a knife. You need to remove both the peel and the white fibrous layer so that the orange flesh is visible. Slice each into 8 slices, discarding the ends. (Save them for a snack for later.)

2. Peel the kiwi fruit and cut each into 4 slices, discarding the ends.

3. Place the orange juice in a saucepan and bring to a boil. Reduce heat slightly and cook for about 7 to 10 minutes, stirring often. Continue to cook until the juice thickens.

4. On 4 plates, arrange the stacked fruit. Begin with 1 slice of orange, then put 2 slices of kiwi side by side on the orange slice. Add another slice of orange and 2 slices of kiwi.

5. Sprinkle on a tablespoon of chopped basil and drizzle with ¼ of the orange glaze. Repeat for the other 3 plates. Serve immediately.

PER SERVING Calories: 80 | Fat: 0g | Sodium: 2mg | Carbohydrates: 20g | Fiber: 3g | Protein: 2g

Guava Juice

Guava is rich in vitamin C, and if you have access to the fresh fruit, it makes a wonderful juice. The juice will be thick, so add ice and water, and then sweeten to taste with a small amount of raw sugar or honey, or add an orange to the mix.

INGREDIENTS | SERVES 1

2 guava fruits
½ cup cold water
2 teaspoons demerara sugar

1. Wash the guavas and cut them into quarters, or into pieces small enough to feed into your electric juicer. Use the plunger to push the pieces through the juicer and collect the juice in a glass at the spout.

2. Stir in cold water and the sugar. Serve immediately. If the pulp and juice separate, stir well before serving.

PER SERVING Calories: 98 | Fat: 1g | Sodium: 4mg | Carbohydrates: 22g | Fiber: 6g | Protein: 3g

Roasted Tomato Marinara

It may seem silly to make your own marinara sauce when you can buy it at the store, but the homemade flavor makes it well worthwhile. There is nothing quite like a slow-roasted tomato taste.

INGREDIENTS | MAKES 2 CUPS

8 medium tomatoes

3 tablespoons olive oil

4 cloves garlic

2 teaspoons salt

1 teaspoon black pepper

1 tablespoon muscovado sugar

2 teaspoons dried basil

2 teaspoons dried oregano

Adding Spices

If you prefer, you can add the spices to the tomatoes before roasting. Be sure to have extra on hand, because you may decide that your sauce needs some more flavor once you purée the roasted tomatoes. If you like a spicy marinara, add ¼ teaspoon of crushed red pepper when heating the sauce.

1. Preheat the oven to 400°F. Wash the tomatoes and remove the stems. Cut into quarters and place on a baking sheet.

2. Coat the tomatoes with the olive oil. Add the garlic cloves and stir again. Add more oil if necessary, as the size of tomatoes can vary. Sprinkle with salt and pepper and bake for 35 to 45 minutes or until the tomatoes become shriveled and are cooked through.

3. Transfer the tomatoes and garlic to a blender and purée until smooth. Pour the mixture into a saucepan on medium heat. Add the sugar, basil, and oregano. Simmer, partially covered, stirring occasionally, for 7 to 10 minutes. Taste and add more salt if desired.

PER ½ CUP SERVING Calories: 150 | Fat: 11g | Sodium: 1177mg | Carbohydrates: 14g | Fiber: 3g | Protein: 3g

Vitamin C Salad

This bright and colorful salad combines some of the best sources for vitamin C. A sprinkle of nuts and seeds adds a little vitamin E. Try topping it with the orange vinaigrette from the Spinach Salad with Strawberries (Chapter 4).

INGREDIENTS | SERVES 2

1 cup romaine lettuce, chopped

1 cup fresh spinach, chopped

½ red bell pepper, sliced

½ green bell pepper, sliced

1 orange, sliced into segments

1 kiwi, sliced

2 tablespoons almonds, chopped

2 tablespoons sunflower seeds

Salt and pepper, to taste

1. Toss together the lettuce and spinach and divide equally on 2 plates. Top with the sliced bell peppers, followed by the orange segments and kiwi slices.

2. Sprinkle on almonds and sunflower seeds. Add salt and pepper to taste, and top with your favorite vinaigrette before serving.

PER SERVING Calories: 190 | Fat: 10g | Sodium: 17mg | Carbohydrates: 24g | Fiber: 7g | Protein: 6g

Other Fruits Rich in Vitamin C

When you need a change, but don't want to miss out on valuable vitamin C, there are plenty of fruit substitutions you can make in this salad recipe. Grapefruit segments, sliced tomatoes, sliced strawberries, and cantaloupe chunks all contain vitamin C, and provide fresh flavor mixed with a little creativity.

CHAPTER 3

Alzheimer's Disease

In 2010, the Alzheimer's Association reported that Alzheimer's disease affects over 5 million people in the United States. While this seems like a daunting figure, it is important to note that researchers continue to find links between food, brain health, and the risk of developing this cognitive disorder, so statistics in the future might not be so grim.

What Is Alzheimer's Disease?

Alzheimer's disease is a form of dementia. "Dementia" is the term given to memory loss when it is severe enough to impact a person's daily living. Alzheimer's causes a destruction of the brain cells that influence thinking and behavior. Unfortunately, it is a progressive disease, which means that it gets worse over time and there is no cure.

While the exact cause is not known, it is suspected that oxidation can decrease mental capacity, including the ability to think, remember, and reason. Findings such as these suggest that dietary factors may influence and prevent Alzheimer's.

Nutrients That May Prevent Alzheimer's Disease

According to a July 2010 report from the U.S. Department of Agriculture's Agricultural Research Service, there are specific nutrients that play a role in brain health and in preventing dementia and the development of Alzheimer's. These include omega-3 fatty acids, vitamin D, and B-complex vitamins B_{12}, B_6, and folate.

FACT

In a research study published in the *Archives of Neurology*, higher intakes of salad dressing, nuts, fish, tomatoes, poultry, cruciferous vegetables, fruits, and dark green leafy vegetables along with lower intakes of high-fat dairy, red meat, organ meat, and butter were associated with a lower risk for Alzheimer's disease.

The omega-3 fatty acid docosahexaenoic acid (DHA) is present in the brain and appears to play a role in memory, language, and thinking. Vitamin D is involved in cognitive processing, and B-complex vitamins are important for function and growth of brain and nerve cells and tissues. In addition, B vitamins have been found to reduce the presence of homocysteine in the body. High levels of homocysteine and low concentration of B vitamins have been associated with dementia and impaired cognition.

Foods That Contain These Nutrients

The omega-3 fatty acids associated with brain health are those that come specifically from cold-water oily fish such as wild salmon, albacore tuna, mackerel, sardines, and lake trout. A different type of omega-3 fatty acid can be found in walnuts and flaxseed. This is converted to DHA in the body, the same fatty acid that comes from fish. While fish sources come more highly recommended when it comes to Alzheimer's prevention, walnuts and flax-seeds are still healthy foods and can be considered a source of omega-3s.

QUESTION

Can I reduce my risk for Alzheimer's with fried fish?
No, according to a study reported by the Agricultural Research Service. The study showed that people who ate oily fish more than two times per week reduced Alzheimer's risk by as much as 40 percent. This was compared to those who ate it less than once per month. These same results were not evident with eating fried fish.

The same fish that provide omega-3 fatty acids also supply vitamin D. Egg yolks are also a source of vitamin D. Clams, beef, salmon, and chicken are sources of vitamin B_{12}.

Eat your greens for folate. Spinach, collard greens, turnip greens, romaine lettuce, and asparagus are all rich sources. Also, beans and legumes provide a protein-packed source of the vitamin. Try lentils, pinto beans, black beans, chickpeas, and kidney beans. Get your vitamin B_6 with potatoes, bananas, chickpeas, and chicken breast.

Tips for Incorporating These Foods

A salad made with spinach and romaine and topped with a protein source such as chicken, salmon, chickpeas, or kidney beans is a meal for brain health. Or you can lightly sauté greens with garlic and olive oil to provide a quick side dish to any meal. Toss in some chickpeas or black beans to the greens for even more brain power. You can also use beans to create healthful bean salads. Use cold chickpeas or black beans and toss them with fresh spinach, olive oil, salt, and pepper for a filling, high-protein lunch.

Cilantro Lime Bean Salad

This salad combines a variety of folate-rich beans. The light, fresh flavors are ideal for a summer side dish. Use rinsed and drained canned beans, or cook dried beans ahead of time.

INGREDIENTS | SERVES 6

1 cup black beans, rinsed and drained

1 cup chickpeas, rinsed and drained

1 cup kidney beans, rinsed and drained

1 green bell pepper, chopped

¼ cup white onion, chopped

1 fresh jalapeño, diced

¼ cup lime juice

2 tablespoons olive oil

1 tablespoon fresh cilantro

1 teaspoon salt

½ teaspoon black pepper

1. In a large bowl, combine all of the beans. Stir in the bell pepper, onion, and jalapeño.

2. Add the lime juice, olive oil, and cilantro. Stir gently to incorporate all of the ingredients, but be careful not to break up the soft beans.

3. Add the salt and pepper. Cover and refrigerate for at least 30 minutes before serving.

PER SERVING Calories: 170 | Fat: 5g | Sodium: 594mg | Carbohydrates: 24g | Fiber: 8g | Protein: 8g

Asparagus Chickpea Salad

In this recipe feel free to use cooked chickpeas or canned. You can use leftover asparagus or follow the directions to steam it. Grilled asparagus can also add a wonderful flavor to this salad.

INGREDIENTS | SERVES 4

½ pound asparagus

1½ cups cooked chickpeas

2 tablespoons fresh parsley, chopped

3 tablespoons olive oil

3 tablespoons fresh lemon juice

1 teaspoon salt

½ teaspoon black pepper

1. Bring about 3 cups of water to a boil in a steaming pot or under a steaming basket. Prepare asparagus by trimming off about 1 inch of the bottom ends and chopping into ½- to 1-inch pieces.

2. Reduce the heat under the water; place asparagus in the steaming basket and cover with a lid. Cook 3 to 4 minutes, just until tender. Remove from heat.

3. Combine the rinsed and drained chickpeas and asparagus in a large bowl. Sprinkle in the parsley.

4. In a small bowl, whisk together the olive oil, lemon juice, salt, and pepper. Pour over the salad and toss to coat. Refrigerate 30 minutes before serving.

PER SERVING Calories: 121 | Fat: 2g | Sodium: 741mg | Carbohydrates: 21g | Fiber: 6g | Protein: 7g

Spicy Sautéed Greens

You can use any combination of dark leafy greens in this quick side dish. If you use spinach, add it at the very end of cooking just to wilt it, as it is not as hearty as the other greens and doesn't stand up well to long cooking.

INGREDIENTS | SERVES 8

2 tablespoons olive oil

½ onion, thinly sliced

3 cloves garlic, minced

½ pound kale, chopped

½ pound mustard greens, chopped

1 pound collard greens, chopped

½ cup chicken stock

½ teaspoon crushed red pepper

1 teaspoon salt

½ teaspoon black pepper

1. Heat olive oil in a skillet over medium-high heat and add the onion and garlic. Cook for 2 minutes.

2. Add the kale, mustard greens, and collard greens, and toss to coat in the oil. Pour in the chicken stock and reduce heat to simmer. Cover with a lid and allow to cook for 10 minutes.

3. Remove lid and stir in the crushed red pepper, salt, and black pepper. Serve warm.

PER SERVING Calories: 74 | Fat: 4g | Sodium: 354mg | Carbohydrates: 9g | Fiber: 4g | Protein: 4g

Plating Greens

Sautéed greens make a nice side to serve as a base for meat or fish instead of the basic rice pilaf. Simply spread the kale in the center of the plate, and then lay a salmon fillet or chicken breast over it. You can even serve greens topped with a piece of Sweet Soy Grilled Tofu (Chapter 25).

Simple Lemon Salmon with Dill

Salmon is easy to prepare, but fresh, wild salmon can sometimes be expensive. Make the most of your investment and add simple flavors such as lemon and dill, which bring out the best in salmon. Serve this dish with Quinoa and Summer Squash (Chapter 10) for a special occasion.

INGREDIENTS | SERVES 4

4 fresh salmon fillets
¼ cup olive oil
2 tablespoons fresh lemon juice
2 teaspoons lemon zest
1 tablespoon fresh dill, chopped
½ teaspoon sea salt
½ teaspoon black pepper
½ fresh lemon, quartered, for garnish

1. Preheat the oven to 400°F. Lightly grease a shallow baking dish with olive oil. Place the salmon, skin side down, in the dish.

2. In a small dish, combine the olive oil, lemon juice, lemon zest, and dill. Use a brush to coat the salmon with the lemon mixture. Bake for about 15 to 20 minutes, or until the salmon flakes with a fork.

3. Sprinkle the salmon with salt and pepper. Serve warm with a fresh lemon wedge.

PER SERVING Calories: 237 | Fat: 18g | Sodium: 341mg | Carbohydrates: 0g | Fiber: 0g | Protein: 17g

Grilled Skirt Steak Salad

This salad is full of vitamin B$_{12}$ and folate, not to mention bursting with flavor! It is best to use a simple dressing by drizzling it with a little olive oil and balsamic vinegar just before serving.

INGREDIENTS | SERVES 4

2 pounds grass-fed skirt steak

2 teaspoons salt

1 teaspoon black pepper

4 cups romaine lettuce, chopped

4 cups spinach, chopped

2 red bell peppers, sliced

½ cup blue cheese, crumbled

Finding Grass-Fed Beef

Grass-fed beef is becoming more popular, which means that it is easier to find, especially in health food markets. You can also check out the website *www.eatwild.com* to locate sources in your area. It is likely that you can buy it direct from the farm, which will also support your local farmers.

1. Preheat your grill or a grill pan. Coat the steak with salt and pepper and place on the grill. Grill for about 2 to 3 minutes on each side. Place on a cutting board and allow to rest.

2. Mix together and arrange the lettuce and spinach on 4 plates. Top with sliced bell pepper and crumbled blue cheese.

3. Thinly slice the steak and divide the slices, laying an even amount over each bed of lettuce. Drizzle with desired dressing and serve.

PER SERVING (WITHOUT DRESSING) Calories: 458 | Fat: 24g | Sodium: 1544mg | Carbohydrates: 6g | Fiber: 3g | Protein: 52g

CHAPTER 4

Anemia

Anemia can make you sluggish and irritable. While individual cases vary, many can be linked to a deficiency in one specific nutrient. Increasing your intake of the nutrient through food can often correct the problem and restore your energy.

What Is Anemia?

Anemia is a lack of iron in the blood that can make you feel tired and drained of energy. Anemia is linked to a problem with hemoglobin, a protein in the red blood cells that is rich in iron. Hemoglobin helps to carry oxygen to different areas of the body. When you have a reduced number of red blood cells or these cells do not contain enough hemoglobin, less oxygen is in the blood that is distributed throughout your body. This causes the tiredness associated with anemia.

There are different types of anemia, which have different causes. Often anemia can occur when there is blood loss, as during a trauma or during surgery. Other conditions are inherited or develop over time.

FACT

According to the Centers for Disease Control and Prevention, iron-deficiency anemia is of greatest concern for females aged twelve to forty-nine, and older adults who reside in nursing homes. Twelve percent of females in that age group are iron-deficient, and approximately 19 percent of nursing home residents are anemic.

In more severe cases of anemia, the body cannot produce enough red blood cells, as in aplastic anemia, or there is an excessive amount of red blood cell destruction, as in hemolytic anemia. These severe types of anemia require medical attention and often treatments such as blood transfusions. Mild to moderate cases of anemia can be prevented or treated with food and are often referred to as iron-deficiency anemia.

Nutrients That Prevent or Treat Anemia

Iron is the key nutrient that influences the amount of hemoglobin in the blood. More hemoglobin provides better oxygen delivery throughout the body. However, not all iron is created equal. The body absorbs iron from animal sources and from plant sources differently.

Heme iron comes from animal sources, and is more readily absorbed by the body. *Nonheme* iron comes from plant-based sources. Assistance from other nutrients is necessary for nonheme iron to be absorbed and for anemic conditions to improve.

ALERT

While there are nutrients and foods that can help iron absorption, there are also some that reduce it—for example, the overconsumption of polyphenols from tea and coffee, phytates and oxalates from whole grains and dark greens or supplements, and excess calcium. These substances bind to iron and can prevent absorption.

You can increase the absorption of nonheme iron by also consuming vitamin C, or ascorbic acid. Eating a heme iron source such as a meat with a nonheme iron source such as beans or dark greens also increases absorption.

Foods That Contain These Nutrients

While many people first think of meat and meat products as a source of iron, there are many non-meat options that can improve or prevent anemia. It may be necessary to balance your intake of these foods with meat and improve your intake of vitamin C to maximize the absorption of these sources.

ESSENTIAL

There is some controversy among nutrition professionals regarding whole grains and iron. Some support traditional practices of soaking whole grains before cooking to reduce the negative effects of phytates, which can bind to minerals and prevent absorption. Others believe that soaking is unnecessary in diets that are not heavily composed of grains and that also contain plenty of fruits and vegetables.

Animal-based foods that provide heme iron include egg yolks, chicken, lean beef, pork, salmon, and tuna. Plant-based foods include dried beans, dried fruits such as prunes or raisins, almonds, Brazil nuts, and dark leafy greens such as broccoli, kale, spinach, and collard greens. Whole grains, including wheat, millet, oats, and brown rice also contain iron.

Tips for Incorporating These Foods

By carefully combining the different types of foods you eat, you can enhance iron absorption and improve or correct anemic conditions. When eating plant-based sources of iron, include additional foods that contain vitamin C—for example, a green salad topped with strawberries, beans with a tomato sauce, or oatmeal with a glass of orange or grapefruit juice. When eating foods from animals, include an iron-rich plant source as well to increase your absorption—for example, cook pork with beans in the slow cooker and serve it over brown rice.

Spinach Salad with Strawberries and Orange Vinaigrette

The vitamin C from the strawberries and orange juice in this recipe will help you absorb the iron from the spinach. For even more iron, add roasted chicken breast or a few slices of grilled flank steak.

INGREDIENTS | SERVES 4

6 cups fresh spinach

¾ cup fresh strawberries, sliced

½ red onion, thinly sliced

¼ cup fresh orange juice

2 tablespoons olive oil

½ teaspoon salt

¼ teaspoon garlic powder

¼ teaspoon black pepper

1. In a large salad bowl, add the spinach followed by the strawberries and onion.

2. In a small bowl, whisk together the orange juice, olive oil, salt, garlic powder, and pepper.

3. Pour the dressing over the salad and toss to coat. Serve immediately.

PER SERVING Calories: 93 | Fat: 7g | Sodium: 327mg | Carbohydrates: 7g | Fiber: 2g | Protein: 2g

Add Cheese and Nuts

A strong cheese such as crumbled blue cheese or feta adds a delicious salty contrast to the sweetness of this salad. You only need to add about ¼ cup to the salad before tossing with the dressing. Similarly, unsalted chopped nuts add a nice crunch. Add ¼ cup of pecans or walnuts to the salad before serving.

Scrambled Eggs with Kale

This recipe combines iron from an animal source and from a plant source, boosting your absorption of the mineral. In addition to being good for you, the kale adds a beautiful color to the finished dish. Drink a glass of fresh-squeezed orange juice to enhance iron absorption.

INGREDIENTS | SERVES 4

1 tablespoon extra-virgin olive oil
¼ cup onion, chopped
1½ cups kale, chopped
¼ cup water
½ teaspoon salt
¼ teaspoon black pepper
8 eggs
¼ cup milk

1. Heat the olive oil in a skillet and add in the onion. Cook the onion on medium-high heat for 2 to 3 minutes or until slightly tender.

2. Add the kale and ¼ cup of water. Cover with a lid, reduce heat to medium, and simmer for 10 minutes or until the kale is tender. Remove the lid and allow to cook until the water is evaporated. Add the salt and pepper.

3. Combine the eggs and milk in a bowl and whisk until frothy. For lighter eggs, you can mix the eggs and milk for 15 to 30 seconds in a blender. Set aside.

4. Slowly pour the egg mixture into the skillet, over the kale. Gently turn with a heat-resistant spatula until the eggs are cooked to your desired consistency. Divide into 4 portions and serve hot.

PER SERVING Calories: 199 | Fat: 14g | Sodium: 303mg | Carbohydrates: 5g | Fiber: 1g | Protein: 14g

Black Bean Quesadilla

This is a quick snack or light meal that can be served with Sweet and Spicy Fresh Fruit Salsa (Chapter 6). Pair it with a salad or brown rice for a large meal, or add some shredded chicken to your quesadilla filling for even more iron.

INGREDIENTS | SERVES 1

¼ tablespoon butter, melted

2 whole-wheat tortillas

¼ cup Monterey jack cheese, shredded

½ cup cooked black beans

1 tablespoon onion, minced

1 tablespoon fresh cilantro, chopped

Microwave It First

If you have trouble getting your cheese to melt before your tortilla gets too brown in the skillet, try giving it a head start. Place the tortilla on a microwave safe plate and add the fillings. Microwave it on high for about 20 seconds or until the cheese begins to melt, then slide it into your skillet.

1. Heat a nonstick skillet or griddle pan on medium-high heat. Brush half the butter on one side of one of the tortillas and place the tortilla buttered side down in the skillet.

2. Top the tortilla with half of the cheese, followed by the beans, onion, cilantro, and remaining cheese. Place the other tortilla on top and brush with the remaining butter.

3. Cook for 2 to 3 minutes or until the tortilla begins to brown. Use a large spatula to flip the quesadilla and cook until it is browned on the other side and the cheese is melted.

4. Remove the quesadilla from the skillet and place it on a cutting board. Allow it to rest about 2 minutes and cut into wedges. Serve immediately.

PER SERVING Calories: 418 | Fat: 15g | Sodium: 812mg | Carbohydrates: 54g | Fiber: 14g | Protein: 21g

Cinnamon Steel-Cut Oats with Berries

If you think you don't like oatmeal, give it a second try with steel-cut oats. This variety has more texture and is heartier than traditional rolled oats. In this recipe, it is simmered with cinnamon and topped with berries for added vitamin C.

INGREDIENTS | SERVES 2

½ cup steel-cut oats

1 teaspoon ground cinnamon

½ teaspoon salt (optional)

1 tablespoon maple syrup

1 cup mixed berries

Make Ahead for Busy Mornings

Make a large batch of oats by doubling or tripling the recipe based on your needs. Cook, cool, and store in the refrigerator. Scoop them out into a bowl in the morning, add about 2 tablespoons of water and heat in the microwave, and then add toppings. Use the oats within 4 days.

1. Place oats in a pan and add 2 cups of water and cinnamon. Cook on medium-high heat, stirring often, until grains are tender and oats are thick, about 30 to 40 minutes. Stir in salt if desired.

2. Divide into 2 bowls; drizzle half of the maple syrup on each serving. Chop large berries such as strawberries if necessary, and sprinkle half the berries over each serving of oatmeal. Serve hot.

PER SERVING Calories: 206 | Fat: 3g | Sodium: 2mg | Carbohydrates: 41g | Fiber: 6g | Protein: 6g

Grass-Fed Beef Burgers

Red meat is rich in iron. Grass-fed beef is an excellent red meat choice because it is lower in saturated fat and higher in omega-3 fatty acids than grain-fed beef. These burgers are a healthier way to boost your iron intake.

INGREDIENTS | SERVES 4

1 pound grass-fed ground beef
1 teaspoon garlic powder
1 teaspoon dried basil
1 teaspoon dried oregano
1 teaspoon salt
¼ teaspoon black pepper
¼ teaspoon crushed red pepper
2 tablespoons water
2 tablespoons panko bread crumbs
4 whole-grain buns

1. In a large bowl, combine the ground beef, spices, 2 tablespoons water, and bread crumbs. Mix with a potato masher or with your hands until the spices are incorporated. Divide the mixture into 4 patties.

2. Preheat a nonstick skillet, grill pan, or outdoor grill. Place the burgers on the pan or grill and cook for about 4 minutes on each side, or until they reach your desired doneness. Grass-fed burgers are leaner than traditional burgers and may take less time to cook.

3. Place each burger on a bun and top with lettuce, tomato, onion, ketchup, mustard, barbecue sauce, or other condiments.

PER SERVING Calories: 402 | Fat: 16g | Sodium: 983mg | Carbohydrates: 35g | Fiber: 2g | Protein: 27g

CHAPTER 5

Arthritis

Arthritis is a disease that causes chronic joint pain and stiffness, immobility, and sometimes disability. Because arthritis is an inflammation disease, and food can greatly influence the level of joint pain, choosing the right foods can be pivotal in alleviating the pain and swelling associated with this condition.

Types of Arthritis

There are many forms of arthritis and they can affect individuals of all ages. According to the Arthritis Foundation, the three most often identified and discussed are osteoarthritis, rheumatoid arthritis, and juvenile arthritis.

Women are afflicted with rheumatoid arthritis three times more often than men. The onset can occur at any age, but most often affects those between forty and fifty years old. This form of arthritis is extremely painful and disabling, and if not treated properly can lead to a loss of mobility.

Osteoarthritis is the most common form and results from the breakdown of cartilage in the joints. Without cartilage, the bone rubs on bone, which results in pain and stiffness. *Rheumatoid arthritis* results from the inflammation of the synovium, a layer of tissue around the joint. This inflammation can cause damage to the joint over time and results in chronic pain and disability. *Juvenile arthritis* is any form of arthritis that occurs in children under eighteen years of age.

Nutrients That Alleviate Arthritis

Healthy foods are full of nutrients that combat inflammation and alleviate symptoms of arthritis. Specifically, fatty acids and antioxidants are the most common food components that have been linked to reduced inflammation.

Omega-3 and Omega-6 Fatty Acids

Research suggests that when more omega-6 fatty acids than omega-3 fatty acids are eaten, this results in joint inflammation. You likely eat a high amount of omega-6 fatty acids because they are found in corn, soybean, and sunflower oils. They are also found in many processed snack foods, fried foods, and margarines. Conversely, omega-3 fatty acids are associated with reduced inflammation, but found in fewer foods. Both are essential for proper body function, but better control of inflammation is seen when you aim to eat fewer sources of omega-6 fatty acids and more sources for omega-3 fatty acids.

ESSENTIAL

Reducing your intake of processed, high-calorie foods, and increasing your intake of fresh produce, healthy oils, and fish can help you maintain a healthy weight or lose weight if you need to. If you are overweight or obese, weight loss is important for alleviating arthritis. Fat cells produce cytokines, which are proteins that have been found to promote inflammation.

Antioxidants

Plant-based foods contain antioxidants and phytochemicals that reduce cyclooxygenase-2 (abbreviated as COX-2), a common enzyme associated with arthritis. By inhibiting this enzyme, plant foods help to reduce inflammation. Carotenoids, quercetin, and anthocyanins are antioxidants found in fruits and vegetables that can inhibit enzymes that lead to inflammation. In addition, olive oil contains a polyphenol, a type of antioxidant, called oleocanthal. This component has been found to prevent the production of COX-1 (another enzyme associated with arthritis) and COX-2, which are both considered pro-inflammatory.

Curcumin

Curcumin is a phytochemical found specifically in turmeric. It has anti-inflammatory properties and is associated with reduced joint pain and stiffness.

Foods That Contain These Nutrients

There is an extensive list of foods that can help alleviate the pain and stiffness associated with arthritis. Cold-water fatty fish such as salmon, trout, mackerel, tuna, sardines, and herring provide omega-3 fatty acids. Olive oil and ginger contain polyphenols that act as antioxidants. Curcumin is found in the spice turmeric. Turmeric is used alone in cooking or as part of spice mixes, such as curry, and gives a yellow color to some foods, such as mustard.

When you are taking medications prescribed by your doctor, it is important to know what foods could cause complications when mixed with the medicines. For example, ginger is identified as a blood thinner. If you currently take a blood thinner, be sure to discuss your diet with your doctor before adding large quantities of ginger.

Vegetables beneficial for arthritis pain include carrots, butternut squash, mustard greens, spinach, cherry tomatoes, and broccoli. Dark red and purple berries such as blueberries, raspberries, blackberries, and strawberries combat symptoms, as do other colorful fruits such as cherries (including cherry juices), plums, and cantaloupe.

Tips for Incorporating These Foods

You can reduce omega-6 and increase omega-3 fatty acids in your diet by changing the types of oils you use and by increasing your fish intake. Use olive oil for cooking vegetables and for salad dressings. You can make salad dressings from flaxseed oil or walnut oil. Enjoy at least two meals per week that incorporate a fatty fish such as salmon or trout.

What are the best sources for salmon?
Choose wild-caught Alaskan salmon. Although positive changes are happening, salmon farming can have a negative impact on the environment through pollution and habitat damage. If you choose farmed salmon, stick with Coho or Silver Salmon from the United States, farmed in tank systems.

Choose your fruits and vegetables by color. Eat orange, dark green, red, and purple produce throughout your week and enjoy as much of it as you can in its most natural form—for example, fresh berries added to your yogurt and carrot sticks or cantaloupe for a snack. Get creative with anti-inflammatory spices such as curry and ginger. Sprinkle them into stir-fries or into a chicken or tuna salad.

Fresh Raspberry Salad Dressing

*This recipe combines the antioxidant power of fresh raspberries with extra-virgin olive oil.
It is delicious over dark greens sprinkled with walnuts.*

INGREDIENTS | SERVES 6

1 cup fresh raspberries
2 tablespoons balsamic vinegar
⅓ cup olive oil
½ teaspoon salt
¼ teaspoon black pepper
¼ teaspoon garlic powder

Stock Up on In-Season Produce

Fruits that are in season are better tasting
and more affordable than imported, non-
seasonal fruits. Strawberries and blackberries can easily be substituted for the
raspberries depending on the season and
your location. Consider stocking up on berries when you find a good deal. You can
freeze them and make the dressing with
defrosted berries year round.

1. Place the berries in a bowl and gently break them up
   with a fork until a thick liquid is formed.

2. Whisk in the vinegar and olive oil until everything is
   combined.

3. Continue whisking and add salt, pepper, and garlic
   powder, which can be adjusted to taste.

4. Pour over a mixed green salad, toss, and serve.

PER SERVING OF DRESSING Calories: 121 | Fat: 12g |
Sodium: 99mg | Carbohydrates: 3g | Fiber: 1g | Protein: 0g

Coconut Curry Crusted Trout

Trout has recently become recognized for its omega-3 fatty acid content, adding to the list of healthy, fatty fish that also includes salmon. Here, trout is prepared with a sweet and flavorful coconut-curry crust. The curry powder in this recipe also provides curcumin to further reduce inflammation.

INGREDIENTS | SERVES 4

½ cup coconut milk

3 tablespoons unsweetened shredded coconut

1 teaspoon curry powder

¾ cup panko bread crumbs

½ teaspoon salt

¼ teaspoon black pepper

4 trout fillets

1. Preheat your oven to 350°F and grease a 9" x 13" baking pan.

2. Pour the coconut milk into a shallow bowl. Mix the shredded coconut, curry powder, bread crumbs, salt, and black pepper in a separate shallow bowl.

3. Dip the fillets in coconut milk and then gently place in the bread crumb mixture. Turn to coat the fillet, lightly pressing the coating into the fish.

4. Place the fillets in a single layer in the baking pan. If your fillets have skin, place them skin side down. Bake for 10 to 15 minutes or until the fish flakes with a fork.

PER SERVING Calories: 293 | Fat: 16g | Sodium: 489mg | Carbohydrates: 17g | Fiber: 2g | Protein: 21g

Grilled Plums with Cinnamon Sugar

*The dark color of purple plums comes from anthocyanins, which act as antioxidants.
It is true that heat can destroy some anthocyanin content, but the fruit still contains antioxidant benefit.
Don't be afraid to give your fruit a flavorful twist by grilling it from time to time.*

INGREDIENTS | SERVES 4

4 fresh purple plums
1 tablespoon butter, melted
2 tablespoons muscovado sugar
½ teaspoon ground cinnamon

Less-Refined Cane Sugars

Muscovado sugar, sometimes called mascavo sugar, is common in parts of Southeast Asia and Brazil. The flavor is much more complex and rich than brown sugar and refined white sugar. Because of the limited amount of processing, the muscovado retains some of the mineral content that is lost in refined sugars. It makes an ideal substitute for light or dark brown sugar.

1. Heat a grill or grill pan. Halve each of the plums and remove the pit. Brush the cut side of each plum with melted butter.

2. Place the plums, cut side down, on the grill and allow to cook for 3 to 4 minutes. Once the fruit begins to darken and grill marks are present, flip and place on the grill skin side down.

3. In a small bowl, mix the sugar and cinnamon. Sprinkle the mixture evenly over each plum half.

4. Cook for 3 to 4 minutes more until the plum is cooked through and sugar begins to melt. Remove from the grill and serve warm.

PER SERVING Calories: 73 | Fat: 3g | Sodium: 21mg | Carbohydrates: 12g | Fiber: 1g | Protein: 1g

Curry Chicken Salad

Spice up traditional chicken salad with only a few extra ingredients. This recipe uses curry with inflammation-fighting curcumin and walnuts, which are rich in omega-3 fatty acids. Reducing the mayonnaise brings out more of the flavor of the chicken, and helps create a better omega-3 to omega-6 fatty acid ratio.

INGREDIENTS | SERVES 4

2 roasted or smoked chicken breasts

¼ cup celery, diced

1 tablespoon onion, grated

1 cup grapes, halved

½ cup walnuts, chopped

⅓ to ½ cup mayonnaise

2 teaspoons curry powder

1 teaspoon salt

¼ teaspoon black pepper

1. Chop or shred the chicken into small pieces and place in a medium-size mixing bowl.

2. Add the celery, onion, grapes, and walnuts. Add ⅓ cup of the mayonnaise and mix all ingredients. Judge the consistency, and if you desire, add the remaining mayonnaise.

3. Stir in the curry powder. Taste, and add the salt and pepper if needed. Divide into 4 servings and serve on a fresh tomato slice or whole-grain bread.

PER SERVING Calories: 246 | Fat: 17g | Sodium: 745mg | Carbohydrates: 15g | Fiber: 2g | Protein: 11g

Taste Before Seasoning

If the chicken you are using was seasoned or marinated before cooking, that flavor will transfer to your chicken salad. Always taste before adding salt and pepper. You may not need it at all. You can always add more, but you can't remove it once it's been added.

Roasted Tomato Toasts

This recipe makes a light and refreshing appetizer to start your meal or to serve at a party. Cherry tomatoes, spinach, and olive oil provide anti-inflammatory compounds to combat the symptoms of arthritis.

INGREDIENTS | SERVES 6

1 pint cherry tomatoes, halved

⅓ cup olive oil

1 teaspoon salt

¼ teaspoon black pepper

1 whole-grain baguette

½ cup fresh spinach, chopped

3 green onions, sliced

2 tablespoons fresh lime juice

¼ cup Romano cheese, grated

Tomato Varieties

You can substitute any type of tomato for cherry tomatoes in this recipe. Roma and grape tomatoes work well. You can also add color by including a few yellow cherry tomatoes. When using large tomatoes, allow them to cool slightly and chop them after roasting before you toss them with the other ingredients.

1. Preheat the oven to 400°F. Place the tomatoes on a baking sheet, cut side down, and drizzle with 1 tablespoon of the olive oil. Sprinkle with salt and pepper and bake for about 10 minutes or until they begin to burst and shrivel.

2. Slice the baguette at an angle into 12 even slices. Place in a single layer on a baking sheet and brush with 1 tablespoon of the remaining olive oil. Bake for 3 to 4 minutes just until the breads begin to crisp, but are not browned. Remove and set aside.

3. In a bowl, add the tomatoes and break them up slightly with a fork. Add the spinach, onion, remaining olive oil, and lime juice. Mix all ingredients together and add more salt and pepper to taste.

4. Top each toast with 1/12 of the tomato mixture, and then sprinkle with grated cheese. Return to the oven and bake 7 to 10 minutes or until the toasts are browned and the cheese melted. Serve warm.

PER SERVING Calories: 172 | Fat: 14g | Sodium: 515mg | Carbohydrates: 9g | Fiber: 2g | Protein: 4g

CHAPTER 6

Asthma

More than 300 million people worldwide are afflicted with asthma. Asthma has long been associated with heredity and the environment, but more recent research is showing that the foods you eat can alleviate symptoms of the condition. Some foods contain nutrients that reduce inflammation and stress to the airways, which can result in fewer asthmatic symptoms.

What Is Asthma?

Asthma is a condition that affects the passages that carry air into and out of the lungs. These bronchial tubes, or airways, are sensitive to external substances that enter during breathing. The airways get inflamed and swollen; when they react to these particles the muscles tighten, which narrows the passage for air flow. As a result, less air moves into and out of the lungs, causing coughing and wheezing.

FACT

Several environmental risk factors have been linked to asthma in children, including poor air quality cause by pollutants such as vehicle exhaust, secondhand tobacco smoke, and high ozone levels. Psychological stress, viral infections, and antibiotic use early in life are also thought to increase children's risk of developing asthma.

The symptoms of asthma such as coughing, wheezing, tightness in the chest, and shortness of breath vary from person to person in frequency and severity. For some, these symptoms may simply be bothersome; for others they may interfere with normal daily activities. Severe symptoms can be life threatening so it is important to treat symptoms as soon as they occur. In addition, controlling environmental factors that cause asthmatic symptoms, such as reducing exposure to secondhand smoke, and eating foods that can reduce inflammation and airway stress, are beneficial for those with asthma.

Nutrients That Alleviate the Symptoms of Asthma

There are three main vitamins that act as antioxidants and reduce the inflammation in the lungs that is often brought on by free radicals from air pollutants. These are the same free radicals linked to asthma and its symptoms. The vitamins are beta carotene, a provitamin that is converted to vitamin A in the body; vitamin C; and vitamin E. Phytochemicals in fruits and vegetables also act as antioxidants.

Research has also shown that the omega-3 fatty acids reduce the production of cytokines, which are associated with sensitive lung tissue and inflamed airways. Omega-6 fatty acids, such as those found in refined oils and packaged snack foods, are linked to increased cytokine production.

ALERT

Studies suggest that sulfites can trigger asthma symptoms in some individuals. Foods that contain sulfites include wine, beer, grape juice, some dried fruits, pickles, fresh and frozen shrimp, and vinegar. Monitor your intake of sulfites to determine if they are a trigger for your asthma. Sulfites may also be sprayed on some prepared foods in restaurants before serving to prevent browning.

Foods That Contain These Nutrients

For beta carotene and vitamin A, choose sweet potatoes, kale, carrots, and cantaloupe. When seasoning your foods, use fresh thyme, which is a source of vitamin A. If you prefer dried herbs, dried parsley and dried basil provide vitamin A.

Vitamin C can be found in fruits including guavas, red bell peppers, and kiwis. You will also get a good dose by eating green bell peppers and strawberries. Vitamin E is an active antioxidant that is present in many oils, but you can boost your intake of it and other nutrients such as protein and healthy fat by choosing sunflower seeds, almonds, hazelnuts, turnip greens, and avocados.

Tips for Incorporating These Foods

The easiest way to ensure that you get plenty of the active vitamins from fruits and vegetables is to eat by color. Each week, include a variety of dark green, orange, and red fruits and vegetables in your diet. Choose sweet potatoes or a dark green salad topped with red pepper strips and diced avocado as your side dish for meals. Mix kiwi and strawberries in a yogurt parfait or a smoothie. Eat a small handful of unsalted almonds, hazelnuts, and walnuts for a snack.

QUESTION

Should I eliminate omega-6 fatty acids from my diet?
No, omega-6 fatty acids are essential for health. It is the overconsumption that is a problem. Aim to create a balance between omega-6 fatty acid and omega-3 fatty acid intake. Get your omega-6s from natural sources such as nuts and seeds instead of refined oils and snack foods. Eat more wild salmon and other oily cold-water fish, as well as walnuts and flaxseed, to boost omega-3s.

Set a goal to step outside of your comfort zone with food. Many of the greens offering vitamins that alleviate asthma symptoms are not always common on the dinner table. Kale and turnip greens are delicious sautéed in olive oil and sprinkled with a little sea salt and black pepper. Sometimes you just have to take the first step and try them to learn that you enjoy the flavor.

"Orange" Juice

This recipe offers more than your standard orange juice. It combines a variety of fruits and vegetables that are rich in beta carotene and vitamin C to reduce the lung inflammation caused by free radicals. You will need an electric juicer to make this recipe.

INGREDIENTS | SERVES 1

2 oranges, peeled

1 cup cantaloupe chunks

1 carrot, peeled

Add Some Greens

Collard greens and kale make a delicious addition and blend well with the flavors of sweet juice. They also add even more beta carotene. Add two leaves of collard greens or kale in between larger produce to help push the leaves through the processor.

1. Set up your juicer according to instructions. Place your glass at the bottom of the spout on the machine. Break or chop the produce into pieces small enough to fit through the mouth of the juicer.

2. Turn on the machine and use the stopper to push through the oranges, cantaloupe, and carrot. Collect the juice in your glass, stir, and drink immediately. Add ice if desired.

PER SERVING Calories: 169 | Fat: 1g | Sodium: 27mg | Carbohydrates: 40g | Fiber: 1g | Protein: 3g

Sweet and Spicy Fresh Fruit Salsa

This recipe combines a variety of colorful produce that is full of vitamin C. The jalapeño is optional, so you can make it mild or spicy according to your preferences. Try it with your favorite grilled fish for a light and nutritious meal.

INGREDIENTS | SERVES 4

1 cup strawberries, diced
½ cup kiwi, diced
¼ cup red bell pepper, diced
¼ cup onion, diced
1 clove garlic, minced
1 fresh jalapeño (optional)
3 tablespoons lime juice
Salt and black pepper, to taste

1. Place all of the fruits, bell pepper, onion, and garlic in a bowl. If you are using jalapeño, slice and chop it. If you want less heat, remove the veins and the seeds before chopping. Add the jalapeño to the salsa.

2. Pour the lime juice over the salsa and toss to coat. Taste and add salt and pepper according to your preferences. Refrigerate until ready to serve.

PER SERVING Calories: 38 | Fat: 0g | Sodium: 2mg | Carbohydrates: 9g | Fiber: 2g | Protein: 1g

Avocado Banana Salad

In the United States, vitamin E–rich avocado is most often eaten as a savory, such as in guacamole or on deli sandwiches. In Brazil and other countries, however, it is eaten as a sweet with bananas or sugar as presented in this recipe.

INGREDIENTS | SERVES 2

1 avocado
2 small bananas
2 tablespoons fresh lime juice
1 teaspoon demerara sugar

Choose Fresh

Sulfites are commonly associated with avocados, bananas, and lime juice. However, sulfites are a preservative used in packaged or bottled foods, and as a spray for prepared foods to prevent browning. If you use fresh fruit and juice, and make this recipe yourself, there should be no concern for the presence of this preservative.

1. Peel the avocado and bananas. Chop into bite-size pieces and place in a medium-size bowl.

2. Add the lime juice and sugar, and toss to coat. Serve at room temperature.

PER SERVING Calories: 260 | Fat: 15g | Sodium: 9mg | Carbohydrates: 34g | Fiber: 9g | Protein: 3g

Sautéed Greens Pizza

Greens are often overlooked as a pizza topping. When gently sautéed with olive oil and garlic, they add a wonderful, complex flavor that needs little to accompany it other than a sprinkle of a quality cheese.

INGREDIENTS | SERVES 4

2 tablespoons olive oil

2 cloves garlic, minced

½ cup onion, chopped

1 cup fresh spinach, chopped

1 cup fresh collard greens, chopped

1 cup fresh mustard greens, chopped

1 cup fresh turnip greens, chopped

1 teaspoon smoked paprika

1 teaspoon salt

¼ teaspoon black pepper

1 (14-inch) pizza crust

½ cup aged goat cheese, crumbled

Quality Cheese Is Worth the Cost

The higher quality cheese you use, the better the flavor. Artisanal cheeses are pricier, but the rich flavors allow you to use much less. Shop at a local specialty shop and seek out local producers if possible. This pizza is delicious with aged goat cheese, but also try Gorgonzola or smoked Cheddar.

1. Preheat the oven to 400°F. Heat a large skillet and add the olive oil, garlic, and onion. Cook about 3 minutes on medium-high heat.

2. Add all of the greens and turn to coat in the oil. Cook about 5 minutes more, just until the greens are wilted. Add the paprika, salt, and pepper.

3. Use tongs to evenly spread the cooked greens and onion over the pizza crust. Sprinkle with the crumbled goat cheese.

4. Bake for about 10 to 12 minutes or until the crust begins to brown and toppings are heated through. Remove from oven, slice, and serve hot.

PER SERVING Calories: 466 | Fat: 20g | Sodium: 1284mg | Carbohydrates: 54g | Fiber: 4g | Protein: 17g

Roasted Potatoes and Carrots with Thyme and Rosemary

Roasting vegetables brings out a wonderful flavor, and fresh thyme and rosemary are the ideal herbs to complement it. Using some red or white potatoes in this recipe helps to balance the sweetness of the sweet potatoes and carrots.

INGREDIENTS | SERVES 4

2 large sweet potatoes

2 large white potatoes

4 carrots

2 tablespoons olive oil

1 tablespoon fresh thyme, chopped

1 tablespoon fresh rosemary, chopped

1 teaspoon salt

½ teaspoon black pepper

Cooking with Fresh Herbs

When cooking herbs that have woody stems, such as thyme and rosemary, use only the leaves. Take your thumb and finger and slide them across the stem to release the leaves. Finally, chop the leaves before adding them to the recipe to release the aromatic flavors.

1. Preheat the oven to 425°F. Scrub the potatoes and carrots with a vegetable brush under running water to remove any dirt. Peel the carrots, and then chop the potatoes and carrots into bite-size pieces.

2. Lay the vegetables in a single layer on a baking sheet. Drizzle with the olive oil and sprinkle on the herbs, salt, and pepper. Turn to coat everything evenly.

3. Bake for 35 to 40 minutes or until the vegetables are tender and slightly browned. Cooking time may vary depending on the size of your pieces. Remove from the oven; sprinkle with additional salt if desired and serve hot.

PER SERVING Calories: 270 | Fat: 7g | Sodium: 671mg | Carbohydrates: 51g | Fiber: 8g | Protein: 5g

CHAPTER 7

Cancer

According to the American Cancer Society (ACS), as of 2009 there were over 1.4 million known cases of cancer in the United States. The disease is the second leading cause of death behind heart disease. While the risk of getting cancer is high, the foods you eat can protect you. In fact, the ACS goes so far as to say that one-third of all cancer deaths in the United States could be prevented if Americans ate a more balanced diet rich in plant foods, which is also a diet that helps maintain a healthy weight.

What Is Cancer?

Fundraising efforts for a cure and the prevalence of the disease keep cancer in the public eye. Despite this publicity, the exact causes and precise treatments of cancer seem evasive. It is important to understand what cancer is in order to understand how foods can help prevent it.

Cancer is caused by abnormalities in the genetic material of cells. These abnormalities can be caused by external influences—for example, tobacco smoke, chemicals, radiation, and pollutants. The abnormalities can also be present in a person's body from birth, either by being inherited or from damage to the DNA.

Cancer is a general term used when abnormal cells grow and divide uncontrollably, invade neighboring tissue, and sometimes spread (or metastasize) to other locations. These cells take over healthy tissue and can spread through the blood and lymph system. There are over 100 types of cancer and each affects a different area or tissue of the body. Breast, lung and colorectal cancer are most prevalent among adults; leukemia and cancers of the brain or nervous system are most prevalent in children.

Nutrients That May Prevent Cancer

Cancer-fighting foods often contain multiple nutrients responsible for reducing risk. Beneficial substances in fruits, vegetables, and other foods all work to prevent damage to cells and the development of cancer.

Antioxidants

Antioxidants are some of the most active food components for reducing risk of cancers. Oxidation causes damage to tissues in the body, and this damage can lead to a greater risk for the disease.

While the specific action of antioxidants as they relate to cancer is under constant evaluation, it is currently believed that because these antioxidants ward off the free radicals responsible for oxidation, they protect tissues, therefore reducing risk for cancers. The antioxidants associated with cancer prevention include beta carotene, which is converted to vitamin A, vitamin C, and vitamin E.

ESSENTIAL

Antioxidants reduce cancer risk overall, but they can also help reduce the cancer-causing potential of common foods. For example, when beef is cooked at high heat, there is the potential for development of heterocyclic amines (HCAs), a cancer-causing compound, or carcinogen. Research shows that by adding herbs and spices high in antioxidants to marinades and meats, the HCAs can be reduced.

Phytochemicals

A July 2010 report from the U.S. Department of Agriculture's Agricultural Research Service states that there are multiple phytochemicals that may protect against the inflammation that can increase cancer risk. There are five main phytochemicals in common fruits, vegetables, and herbs that act as anti-inflammatory agents: luteolin, quercetin, hesperetin, eriodictol, and naringenin.

Foods That Contain These Nutrients

Research continues to support a diet high in fruits and vegetables for the prevention of cancer because of the foods' high antioxidant and phytochemical concentration. Some specific foods that have high concentrations of the anti-inflammatory phytochemicals include celery, thyme, green bell peppers, capers, apples, onions, oranges, grapefruits, and lemons. In addition, strawberries have shown potential for fighting leukemia, and lycopene from tomatoes can increase protective antioxidant levels in the prostate gland.

Raw and cooked garlic are associated with reduced risks of stomach and colorectal cancers. Red bell peppers, kiwis, oranges, and Brussels sprouts contain vitamin C, and almonds and peanut butter contain vitamin E. Try spinach and broccoli if you are allergic to nuts.

Tips for Incorporating These Foods

Eating more fruits and vegetables in general is one practice that is strongly associated with reduced cancer risk. Choose those with the most active components and you will boost your benefit. Give salads or steamed and grilled vegetables the most space on your dinner plate, and if you enjoy mushrooms, include them in your meals regularly.

ESSENTIAL

Phytochemicals, carbohydrate compounds, and the fatty acid of mushrooms have been evaluated for their cancer-fighting properties. Mushrooms contain substances that block aromatase, which plays a role in estrogen production, thus creating a link between mushroom intake and reduced risk of breast cancer.

Grill meats with sprigs of fresh rosemary, or allow them to marinate in a sauce that includes fresh rosemary before cooking. Take advantage of seasonal fruits such as blueberries and watermelons, and try more exotic fruits such as papayas and guavas, which are now becoming more available in California, Florida, and other coastal regions of the United States.

Mushroom Spinach Calzones

If you prepare your dough earlier in the week or pick some up from your local pizza restaurant, calzones become a quick weeknight meal. Pair this one with some spicy marinara for dipping and you'll get even more cancer-fighting benefit from the lycopene in tomatoes.

INGREDIENTS | SERVES 2

1 tablespoon olive oil
1 cup fresh spinach, chopped
1 cup white button mushrooms, sliced
2 cloves garlic, minced
1 teaspoon dried basil
½ teaspoon dried oregano
½ teaspoon salt
¼ teaspoon black pepper
⅓ cup part-skim ricotta cheese
2 tablespoons Parmesan cheese, grated
Dough for 2 (8-inch) pizza crusts

White Button Mushrooms

Mushrooms are known cancer-fighters, and don't overlook the standard white button mushrooms. They have anticancer compounds similar to those of more exotic varieties such as shiitake, and they are much more budget friendly.

1. Preheat the oven to 400°F. Heat a skillet on medium-high heat and add olive oil. Add the spinach, mushrooms, and garlic. Cook for 5 to 7 minutes until spinach is wilted and mushrooms have browned.

2. Stir in the basil, oregano, salt, and pepper. Remove skillet from heat and stir in ricotta and Parmesan cheeses. Set aside and allow to cool.

3. Roll out the dough into 2 (8-inch) rounds. Place them on a baking sheet brushed with olive oil. Divide the filling in half and place it on the bottom half of each round of dough.

4. Fold the top of the dough over the filling to meet the bottom side. Pinch the edges together to secure the filling inside. Gently use a fork to poke a few holes in the top to allow steam to escape. Bake for 10 to 15 minutes, or until crust is browned. Serve hot.

PER SERVING Calories: 510 | Fat: 22g | Sodium: 17mg | Carbohydrates: 64g | Fiber: 3g | Protein: 17g

Garlic Rosemary Thyme Marinade

This marinade adds flavor to meat, and research shows that the rosemary can counteract carcinogens that are formed when meat is cooked at high temperatures. If you are not a meat-eater, try using it to marinate portobello mushrooms.

INGREDIENTS | MAKES 1 CUP

3 cloves garlic, minced

2 tablespoons fresh rosemary leaves, chopped

2 tablespoons fresh thyme leaves, chopped

¼ cup fresh lime juice

¼ cup fresh orange juice

½ cup olive oil

1 teaspoon salt

1 teaspoon black pepper

1. Combine all ingredients in a small bowl and whisk together.

2. To use, place your cut of meat, such as flank steak or chicken breast, in a shallow baking dish. Pour the marinade over the meat and turn to coat evenly. Cover and refrigerate until ready to use, but no longer than 2 hours.

PER 1 TABLESPOON Calories: 64 | Fat: 7g | Sodium: 146mg | Carbohydrates: 1g | Fiber: 0g | Protein: 0g

How Long to Marinate

When you use citrus juices in marinades, your meat should only marinate for ½ hour to 2 hours. The acid can begin to cook the meat, so these are not the marinades to use if you plan to leave the meat in the fridge overnight.

Mushroom Fajitas

Mushrooms are a hearty substitute if you don't eat meat or simply want to incorporate more vegetarian meals into your diet. They also provide a variety of cancer-fighting nutrients. In this recipe you can use simple white button mushrooms, or try a combination such as cremini and shiitake mushrooms.

INGREDIENTS | SERVES 4

2 tablespoons olive oil

2 cloves garlic, minced

1 medium onion, sliced

1 green bell pepper, sliced

2 cups mushrooms, sliced

1 teaspoon cumin

1 teaspoon chili powder

1 teaspoon salt

¼ teaspoon black pepper

8 corn tortillas

1 cup Monterey jack cheese, shredded

1. Heat a large skillet and add the olive oil. Add the garlic, onion, bell pepper, and mushrooms. Cook for 5 to 7 minutes or until the mushrooms are cooked through and the onions have begun to soften and become translucent.

2. Stir in the cumin, chili powder, salt, and pepper and cook for 1 minute more.

3. Divide the filling among the 8 tortillas and top each with some of the shredded cheese. Serve with salsa, sour cream, guacamole, or other condiments.

PER SERVING Calories: 305 | Fat: 17g | Sodium: 766mg | Carbohydrates: 29g | Fiber: 5g | Protein: 12g

Some Like It Hot

If you like your fajitas spicy, there are several ways you can increase the heat in this recipe. You can add ¼ teaspoon of dried cayenne or crushed red pepper with the spices. However, if the rest of your family would prefer mild, serve pickled jalapeños or prepared hot sauce as a condiment.

Almond Broccoli Salad

*If you are tired of taking the same potato or pasta salad to parties and potlucks,
then this recipe is for you! It combines fresh broccoli and crunchy almonds with a light touch
of sweetened mayonnaise-based dressing.*

INGREDIENTS | SERVES 8

2 heads fresh broccoli

½ red onion

½ cup celery, sliced

⅓ cup dried cranberries

⅓ cup slivered almonds

¾ cup mayonnaise

1 tablespoon demerara sugar

1½ tablespoons red wine vinegar

½ teaspoon garlic powder

½ teaspoon salt

Demerara Sugar

Demerara is a type of raw sugar that can be found in most supermarkets in the baking section. It has a larger granule and is less refined than white and brown sugar. Demerara can easily be substituted for white sugar in recipes such as this one, and it adds a nice texture and crunch to baked goods.

1. Prepare the broccoli by breaking the florets into bite-size pieces and place them in a large bowl. Slice the red onion very thinly and place in the bowl with the broccoli. Add the celery, cranberries, and almonds.

2. In a small bowl, whisk together the mayonnaise, sugar, vinegar, garlic powder, and salt. Whisk quickly to help dissolve the sugar. If the dressing is too thick, simply add a few more drops of vinegar. If not sweet enough for your tastes, add more sugar.

3. Pour the dressing over the broccoli and stir to coat all ingredients. Cover and place in the refrigerator for at least 30 minutes before serving to allow flavors to blend and sugar to further dissolve. Serve cold.

PER SERVING Calories: 189 | Fat: 10g | Sodium: 358mg | Carbohydrates: 23g | Fiber: 5g | Protein: 6g

Lemon Quinoa Stuffed Tomatoes

Stuffing vegetables is a great way to create a delicious side dish with a beautiful presentation. This dish is served cold with the tomatoes uncooked to preserve the vitamin C content.

INGREDIENTS | SERVES 4

1 cup quinoa

2 cups chicken stock

½ cup green bell pepper, diced

¼ cup feta cheese, crumbled

3 tablespoons fresh lemon juice

1 teaspoon lemon zest

Salt and pepper, to taste

4 tomatoes

Flavor Your Grains

Chicken, vegetable, or beef stock adds delicious flavor to cooked grains. It can be substituted for water when cooking quinoa, couscous, brown rice, and many other whole grains. Be sure to taste the grains before adding any seasoning. The stock often eliminates the need to add extra salt and pepper.

1. Rinse the quinoa well with cold water and drain. Place in a saucepan and add the chicken stock. Bring the quinoa to a boil and then reduce the heat to simmer, and cover. Cook about 15 minutes or until liquid is absorbed and quinoa is softened.

2. Remove the pan from the heat and add bell pepper, feta cheese, lemon juice, lemon zest, and salt and pepper if necessary. Allow to cool completely.

3. Prepare your tomatoes by slicing off the top fourth and using a spoon to gently remove the inside of the tomato to create a bowl. Save the tops and insides to use in soups and pasta sauces.

4. Fill each tomato with a heaping amount of quinoa. Refrigerate for at least 30 minutes and serve cold.

PER SERVING Calories: 220 | Fat: 6g | Sodium: 369mg | Carbohydrates: 35g | Fiber: 5g | Protein: 11g

CHAPTER 8

Candida

A condition that results when the flora of the intestinal tract is out of balance, candida can affect your ability to perform daily activities and your overall wellness. There are many foods associated with promoting and preventing this condition.

What Is Candida?

Candida is the name given to a specific condition when there is an overgrowth of the yeast *Candida albicans* in the body. This yeast is normally present in the body as a healthy microorganism of the intestinal tract, but when conditions are out of balance overgrowth can occur.

The overgrowth can produce toxic byproducts that damage tissues and impact the immune system. This can cause oral thrush, which is an infection of the mouth and throat, and upset stomach. Fatigue, headaches, joint pain, weight gain, and depression are also associated with candida. The condition can develop from a variety of factors, including antibiotics use, diet, stress, or alcohol and drug use.

Nutrients That Relieve Candida Symptoms

Foods that possess antifungal properties are recommended for a diet that reduces the symptoms of candida. The antifungal properties of these foods allows them to combat the overgrowth of the candida. Foods high in antioxidants can help to protect the immune system from the toxic byproducts of candida overgrowth and reduce inflammation in the body. In addition, probiotics and prebiotics can promote the growth of healthy bacteria in the gut.

ESSENTIAL

Not all health professionals consider candida to be a valid medical condition. Symptoms are often attributed to other causes because of the lack of hard scientific evidence. However, candida is widely recognized among naturopathic and homeopathic doctors. Those diagnosed with candida find that changes in food intake improve symptoms associated with the condition.

It is also believed that a pH imbalance in the body plays a role in candida overgrowth. An acidic environment (lower pH) promotes candida, while a slightly alkaline (higher pH) environment will help to keep candida under control. As a result, reducing intake of acidic or acid-forming foods, while increasing the intake of foods that decrease acidity, is recommended to create this more alkaline state within the body.

Foods That Contain These Nutrients

Garlic, onions, pumpkin seeds, olive oil, and virgin coconut oil are recognized for their antifungal properties. The essential oils found in clove and cinnamon are also considered to be antifungal. Ginger contains substances that may decrease inflammation and support a healthy immune system. Cayenne pepper has been found to improve digestion, which can help rid the body of toxins and can also boost your immune system. Almonds have prebiotic substances for intestinal health, and yogurt contains probiotics. Lemon and lime juice and seaweed promote a less acidic, more alkaline environment in the body.

ESSENTIAL

If you don't fully embrace the presence of candida as a medical condition, but experience similar symptoms, you may benefit from the diet recommended. A candida diet promotes eating whole, gluten-free grains, plenty of antioxidant-rich vegetables, seeds, nuts, and herbs while reducing processed foods. These are all healthy changes that can improve energy levels and overall wellness.

Tips for Incorporating These Foods

It is most beneficial to incorporate garlic and onions in their raw form. Use them in fresh salsas, condiments for sandwiches, and salad dressings. Substitute virgin coconut oil for other fats in your oatmeal and even in your baking. Use clove, cinnamon, and ginger to season stir-fry or in desserts. Yogurt topped with chopped almonds makes an ideal breakfast or snack.

Lemon Quinoa Stuffed Cucumbers

The lemon quinoa provides a fresh, summery salad with a delicious tangy flavor that goes well with its cucumber base. Choose broad cucumbers that will hold up well when you scoop out the flesh and fill them with the quinoa.

INGREDIENTS | SERVES 4

1 cup quinoa

½ cup onion, diced

2 cloves garlic, minced

2 Roma tomatoes, diced

3 tablespoons lemon juice

1 tablespoon fresh basil, chopped

1 tablespoon fresh rosemary, chopped

½ teaspoon salt

¼ teaspoon pepper

4 cucumbers

Affordable Quinoa

Quinoa can be a pricey grain when purchased prepackaged. Try buying it in bulk at your local health food store for much more affordable pricing. You can also substitute brown rice for the quinoa in this recipe. It does take longer to cook, about double the time of quinoa.

1. Rinse and drain the quinoa and place in a saucepan. Add 2 cups of water and bring to a boil. Reduce heat and simmer, covered, for about 15 minutes, stirring occasionally.

2. Place the quinoa in a large bowl and add the onion, garlic, tomatoes, lemon juice, basil, and rosemary. Stir well and add the salt and pepper. Cover and place in the refrigerator.

3. Prepare the cucumbers by washing them under running water; pat dry. Peel the cucumbers if they have a waxy skin. Cut them in half lengthwise and use a spoon to gently scrape out the seeds.

4. Place 2 cucumber halves on each plate. Sprinkle with salt and pepper if desired. Remove the quinoa from the fridge and spoon an equal amount into each cucumber boat. Serve immediately.

PER SERVING Calories: 182 | Fat: 3g | Sodium: 297mg | Carbohydrates: 33g | Fiber: 4g | Protein: 7g

Yogurt Herb Spread

Use this flavorful spread in place of mayonnaise on sandwiches or in wraps.
It also makes a tasty dip for fresh, nutrient-rich vegetables.

INGREDIENTS | MAKES 1 CUP

8 ounces plain Greek yogurt

2 cloves garlic, finely minced

1 tablespoon onion, grated

1 tablespoon fresh dill, chopped

1 tablespoon fresh basil, chopped

1 tablespoon fresh parsley, chopped

¼ teaspoon sea salt

¼ teaspoon black pepper

Mix all ingredients in small bowl. Cover and refrigerate at least 30 minutes before serving.

PER 1 TABLESPOON Calories: 10 | Fat: 1g | Sodium: 44mg | Carbohydrates: 1g | Fiber: 0g | Protein: 1g

Make a Spread a Dressing

If you prefer a thinner dip or want to turn this yogurt-based spread into a salad dressing, thin it by adding fresh lime or lemon juice. Whichever you have on hand will work fine and add even tangier flavor. Add it 1 tablespoon at a time until you get your desired consistency.

Cinnamon Spice Almonds

Feel free to adjust the spices for this snack. This recipe focuses on cinnamon and clove for their antifungal properties. Leave out something you don't like; add in something you do. There are as many options as there are spices!

INGREDIENTS | MAKES 3 CUPS

3 cups raw almonds

¼ cup virgin coconut oil, melted

1 teaspoon cinnamon

½ teaspoon powdered cloves

½ teaspoon dried ginger

½ teaspoon nutmeg

1. Preheat the oven to 350°F and set out a large baking sheet. In a bowl, mix the almonds and coconut oil so that each nut is coated evenly.

2. Stir in all of the spices and mix well. Spread the almonds onto a baking sheet in a single layer. Use 2 sheet pans if necessary.

3. Bake for about 15 minutes, stirring about every 5 minutes to prevent burning. Remove from the oven; serve warm or at room temperature.

PER 2 TABLESPOONS Calories: 260 | Fat: 27g | Sodium: 0mg | Carbohydrates: 4g | Fiber: 2g | Protein: 4g

Grilled Eggplant and Summer Squash

This colorful salad is stacked, drizzled with olive oil, and topped with chèvre, fresh cheese made from goat's milk, for a beautiful presentation. Serve it with wild rice or as a side dish with grilled fish.

INGREDIENTS | SERVES 4

1 large eggplant
1 medium zucchini
1 yellow squash
1 onion
⅓ cup olive oil
Salt and pepper, to taste
4 ounces goat cheese
4 leaves fresh basil

Indoor Grilling

Grill pans make a nice substitute for an outdoor grill when the weather isn't cooperating. You won't get that same smoky flavor, but the appearance and texture will be close to the same. Follow the same instructions; just preheat the grill pan and cook until each side is slightly browned with grill marks and the vegetables are tender.

1. Preheat your grill. Slice the eggplant, zucchini, and yellow squash about ½ inch thick, ensuring that you have at least 4 slices of each vegetable. Slice the onion the same way, being careful to keep all of the layers of the slice intact. Using half of the olive oil, coat each slice of vegetable in oil.

2. Place all of the slices on the grill and cook for 4 to 5 minutes on each side, or until the flesh is softened and begins to brown. Remove from the grill.

3. Prepare 4 plates. Each will have 1 slice of eggplant, zucchini, yellow squash, and onion. Begin with the eggplant, top with the onion, add the zucchini, and finally add the yellow squash.

4. Drizzle each with ¼ of the remaining olive oil. Add salt and pepper to taste. Gently break the goat cheese into pea-size pieces and drop onto the stacked vegetables and plate. Top each stack with a leaf of basil and serve.

PER SERVING Calories: 292 | Fat: 24g | Sodium: 109mg | Carbohydrates: 14g | Fiber: 6g | Protein: 8g

Spiced Hot Cereal

This warm and filling cereal combines gluten-free grains spiced with clove and cinnamon.
A bit of coconut milk poured over the top creates a rich and creamy breakfast.

INGREDIENTS | SERVES 2

½ cup amaranth

¼ cup millet

¼ cup quinoa

½ teaspoon cinnamon

½ teaspoon ground cloves

2 tablespoons almonds, chopped

2 teaspoons muscovado sugar

4 tablespoons coconut milk

1. Rinse the grains and drain. Place in a saucepan with 3 cups of water. Bring to a boil over medium-high heat; reduce heat and simmer. Stir occasionally for about 20 to 30 minutes or until the water has been absorbed and the grains are tender.

2. Add the cinnamon and cloves and mix well. You can add the spices just before the grains are done cooking so that the grains will absorb more of the flavor.

3. Divide the cereal into 2 bowls. Top each with 1 tablespoon of almonds, 1 teaspoon of sugar, and 2 tablespoons of the coconut milk. Serve hot.

PER SERVING Calories: 404 | Fat: 15g | Sodium: 10mg | Carbohydrates: 58g | Fiber: 7g | Protein: 12g

CHAPTER 9

Cataracts

According to the National Eye Institute of the National Institutes of Health, cataracts can develop around the ages of forty to fifty, but the effects on vision often go unnoticed until after the age of sixty. While age may contribute to the condition, research has shown that nutrition also has an influence on the development of cataracts.

What Are Cataracts?

A cataract is a clouding of the eye varying in intensity from a slight opacity to the complete obstruction of light. Cataracts cause blurry vision or changes in the clarity and color of vision, often causing a gradual yellowing of the eye that can at times cause a problem perceiving the color blue. Cataracts result when there is clouding on the lens of the eye due to the clumping of proteins. A cataract makes the lens cloudy, and when light travels through the cloudy lens to reach the retina, a blurry image results. Contrast sensitivity can also be lost, meaning that shadows, contours, and colors become less vivid.

FACT

Cataracts can also be caused by exposure to radiation, hypertension, eye injury, or physical trauma, or can be hereditary. Cataracts are also common to certain occupations—glassblowers and airline pilots both have unusually high likelihood of developing cataracts because they are both exposed to unusual amounts of radiation.

Different types of cataracts have different causes, but many people get them simply because of age and oxidative stress. Oxidative stress occurs when free radicals in the body damage cells, including proteins. In addition to aging, cataracts can also be brought about by smoking and diseases such as diabetes, both of which contribute to oxidative stress in the body.

Nutrients That May Prevent Cataracts

Phytochemicals found in fruits and vegetables have been linked to eye health and the prevention of cataracts, specifically lutein and zeaxanthin. These two phytochemicals are carotenoids, and because carotenoids are found in the lens of the eye it is possible that eating plenty of foods that contain them can slow the aging process of the eye.

Antioxidants are important to reduce the oxidative stress that is linked to the development of a cataract. Vitamins C and E are both antioxidants that can reduce your risk of developing cataracts and progression of the condition.

ESSENTIAL

Eat fruits and vegetables every day to protect your eyes from cataracts. A study in the *American Journal of Clinical Nutrition* found that women who ate 2.6 servings of fruits and vegetables daily had a 10 percent reduced risk of cataracts. Those who maintained a higher intake of 3.4 servings per day reduced risk by 10 to 15 percent.

Foods That Contain These Nutrients

Leafy greens such as kale and spinach, as well as chicken eggs, corn, zucchini, and peas, are sources of lutein and zeaxanthin. Wheat germ or whole grains that contain wheat germ provide vitamin E, as do almonds, hazelnuts, turnip greens, and avocados. Raspberries, blueberries, and strawberries are rich in vitamin C.

Tips for Incorporating These Foods

Greens may not be a common item on your dinner table unless you are familiar with Southern cuisine. However, they are inexpensive and very easy to prepare. When sautéed in olive oil with garlic, they make an ideal addition to pasta, quinoa, or other whole grains.

ALERT

Wheat germ contains the fatty acids of the grain and if not stored correctly can spoil, or become rancid. It is important to store wheat germ in an airtight container in the refrigerator or freezer after opening the package. It will stay fresh for about two weeks in the refrigerator and up to two months if stored in the freezer.

Wheat germ can be purchased in the baking aisle of most supermarkets and used with many foods to boost your vitamin E intake. In addition to stirring it into muffin or pancake batters, you can also sprinkle it over a yogurt parfait made with antioxidant-rich berries.

Berries can be expensive when purchased in the supermarket out of season. During the summer months, check out your local farmers' market or seek out a u-pick farm in your area. Stock up when blueberries, strawberries, raspberries, and blackberries are in season and affordable. Freeze them in airtight containers to use throughout the year.

Greens and Cheddar Omelet

This hearty omelet is perfect for either breakfast or dinner. If you find omelet making difficult, simply turn the dish into scrambled eggs and sprinkle the Cheddar cheese on top.

INGREDIENTS | SERVES 1

1 tablespoon olive oil

1 clove garlic, minced

¼ cup fresh spinach, chopped

¼ cup turnip greens, chopped

2 tablespoons onion, minced

¼ teaspoon salt

¼ teaspoon black pepper

2 eggs

1 tablespoon milk

¼ cup Cheddar cheese, shredded

1. In a nonstick skillet, heat the olive oil over medium-high heat. Add the garlic, greens, and onion. Cook for 5 minutes or until greens become tender. Add the salt and pepper. Reduce heat to medium.

2. In a small bowl, whisk together the eggs and milk. Pour the mixture into the hot pan with the greens and cook slowly as you gently scrape the edges in and tip the pan to allow the raw egg to spread to the surface of the pan. Once the center of the egg is firm and barely jiggles, turn off the heat.

3. Sprinkle the cheese over the egg and use a spatula to fold one side of the omelet over to meet the other. Slide onto a plate and serve hot.

PER SERVING Calories: 405 | Fat: 33g | Sodium: 916mg | Carbohydrates: 6g | Fiber: 1g | Protein: 21g

Kale Berry Smoothie

Fresh greens are not a common ingredient in homemade smoothies, but that needs to change! You will think so too once you try this smoothie. A leaf or two of kale adds a rich flavor and plenty of nutrients to promote eye health.

INGREDIENTS | SERVES 2

2 cups milk

1 cup frozen blueberries

1 cup frozen strawberries

2 tablespoons honey

3 kale leaves

Substitutions for Cow's Milk

If you can't tolerate cow's milk or choose not to drink it, there are a variety of substitutions you can make in your smoothie. Soy milk, almond milk, and goat's milk are some examples. Choose unsweetened, natural forms of these milks with few ingredients and additives for the most nutritious options.

1. Place the milk, berries, honey, and kale in a blender or smoothie maker. Process on high until all ingredients are chopped and blended.

2. Check the texture and taste for sweetness. If a thinner smoothie is desired, add more milk, and if you would like a sweeter smoothie, add more honey. Pour into 2 glasses and serve immediately.

PER SERVING Calories: 304 | Fat: 9g | Sodium: 122mg | Carbohydrates: 53g | Fiber: 4g | Protein: 10g

Zucchini, Corn, and Green Bell Peppers

This recipe will remind you of a summer garden's bounty. The fresh flavors make it the perfect side dish for fish or chicken. It can even be tossed with pasta for a vegetarian meal.

INGREDIENTS | SERVES 4

4 small zucchini
1 green bell pepper
2 tablespoons olive oil
1 cup corn kernels
1 teaspoon salt
¼ teaspoon black pepper
1 teaspoon fresh rosemary, chopped

Fresh Corn

Nothing beats fresh corn in summer cooking. To use only the kernels, take an ear of corn and stand it on one end securely on a plate. Hold the other end with your hand. Take a knife and slice down the ear on all sides to cut off the corn kernels.

1. Prepare the zucchini by chopping off each end and splitting it in half lengthwise. Turn it flat side down on the cutting board and cut half moon shapes about ¼ inch thick. Remove the seeds and veins of the bell pepper and dice.

2. Heat a skillet on medium-high heat and add the olive oil. Add the zucchini, bell pepper, and corn. Cook for about 7 minutes or until the vegetables begin to brown and soften.

3. Stir in the salt and pepper. Sprinkle with rosemary just before serving.

PER SERVING Calories: 118 | Fat: 7g | Sodium: 600mg | Carbohydrates: 13g | Fiber: 3g | Protein: 3g

Spinach Pesto and Corn Pasta

Making pesto with spinach results in a creamy sauce for pasta. Fresh corn gives this dish a sweet flavor and adds bright color, making the dish both delicious and appealing to the eye.

INGREDIENTS | SERVES 4

4 quarts water

½ teaspoon salt

1 pound pasta

2 cups fresh spinach

2 cloves garlic

2 tablespoons walnut pieces

2 tablespoons grated Parmesan cheese

¼ cup plus 1 tablespoon olive oil

1 teaspoon salt

¼ teaspoon black pepper

1 cup corn kernels

Salt and pepper, to taste

Choosing a Pasta

Any type of pasta will work for this dish, but rigatoni or other varieties with deep grooves are ideal for holding the pesto sauce. You can choose white or whole-wheat pasta, or consider some of the new alternative pastas made with quinoa or brown rice.

1. Bring 4 quarts of water to a boil; add ½ teaspoon of salt and then the pasta. Cook until tender but still firm. Drain in a colander and set aside.

2. In a food processor, combine the spinach, garlic, walnuts, and cheese. Put on the lid and pulse 5 to 7 times or until the ingredients begin to blend into a paste. Pour in ¼ cup olive oil, salt, and pepper and pulse again until combined. Set aside.

3. Heat a skillet on medium-high heat and add 1 tablespoon of olive oil. Add the corn and cook 3 to 5 minutes or until the corn is heated through and slightly browned. Add salt and pepper if desired.

4. In a large bowl, combine the pasta, pesto, and corn. Toss to coat the pasta and mix the ingredients. Divide into 4 portions and serve warm.

PER SERVING Calories: 646 | Fat: 22g | Sodium: 645mg | Carbohydrates: 94g | Fiber: 5g | Protein: 5g

Whole-Grain Pancakes with Berries

These hearty whole-grain pancakes contain almonds and wheat germ for vitamin E and a fresh berry topping rich in vitamin C. They are a great way to start a relaxing weekend morning.

INGREDIENTS | SERVES 3

1 egg, beaten

1 cup milk

½ cup whole-wheat flour

½ cup white whole-wheat flour

2 tablespoons wheat germ

1 tablespoon muscovado sugar

3 teaspoons baking powder

¼ teaspoon salt

1 teaspoon ground cinnamon

2 tablespoons butter, melted

⅓ cup sliced almonds

1 cup fresh blueberries

1 cup fresh raspberries

1. Place the egg in a mixing bowl and whisk in the milk. In a separate bowl, sift together the flours, wheat germ, sugar, baking powder, salt, and cinnamon.

2. Mix the dry ingredients into the egg and milk. Stir in the melted butter and almonds.

3. Heat a nonstick griddle and ladle ¼ cup of batter onto the griddle for each pancake. Allow to cook until it begins to bubble, about 1½ minutes, then flip and cook the same amount on the other side.

4. Place 2 pancakes on each plate and top with ⅓ cup of each of the berries. Serve warm.

PER SERVING Calories: 420 | Fat: 19g | Sodium: 785mg | Carbohydrates: 56g | Fiber: 11g | Protein: 14g

CHAPTER 10

Celiac Disease

If you don't know much about celiac disease, you may be surprised to learn that, according to the National Institutes of Health, the condition affects over 2 million people in the United States. Symptoms are triggered by specific foods and can be controlled or eliminated by regulating dietary intake.

What Is Celiac Disease?

Celiac disease is a digestive disease that results in malabsorption, or the inability of the small intestines to absorb necessary nutrients from food. Individuals with the disease have an abnormal immune system response to gluten, which is a protein found in wheat, barley, and rye. This reaction damages the villi that line the inside of the small intestine and interferes with the ability to absorb nutrients during digestion. When gluten is consumed, symptoms including bloating, abdominal pain, diarrhea, vomiting, and constipation can occur.

FACT

Because of its symptoms, celiac disease it is often incorrectly diagnosed or not diagnosed at all. If you notice your pain worsen after eating and you have a progressive weight loss, it is important to contact your doctor. Individuals who have celiac disease and continue to eat gluten increase their chances of gastrointestinal cancer by 40 to 100 times that of the normal population.

Nutrients That Increase the Symptoms of Celiac Disease

For those suffering with celiac disease, there is less focus on identifying nutrients that alleviate symptoms and more focus on eliminating the one component that worsens them, gluten. A gluten-free diet relieves uncomfortable symptoms, corrects the damage done to the small intestine, and maximizes nutrient absorption. While celiac disease cannot be cured, it can be controlled through eating only gluten-free foods.

Foods That Contain These Nutrients

If you have celiac disease, it is important to closely monitor your diet to ensure that you consume no wheat, rye, or barley. There are plenty of foods, even grains, that are gluten-free and can easily be substituted. However, gluten hides in many packaged and processed products. Wheat is used in a surprisingly large number of items, and many products are made in the same factories as gluten-containing foods. Therefore, it is important to check labels carefully to ensure that there is no gluten in the products you are buying.

ALERT

Surprising foods that contain gluten include soy sauce, brown rice syrup, seasoned tortilla chips, packaged rice mixes, meal kits, canned soup, bouillon cubes, chips, and frozen vegetables in sauces. Versions of these foods can be made gluten-free, and will state this on the label. Stick to eating fresh, naturally gluten-free foods as often as possible.

Meats, fish, fruits, and vegetables can all be consumed safely when purchased fresh and cooked at home. Most individuals can safely consume gluten-free or low-gluten grains, which include amaranth, buckwheat, tapioca or cassava, corn, flax, millet, rice, quinoa, and teff. Nuts and seeds are also gluten free.

Tips for Avoiding These Foods

Aim to consume fewer processed foods, which will reduce the chances that your meals contain hidden gluten. Buy fresh foods and cook them yourself as often as possible. This may seem overwhelming at first, but tools such as a slow cooker and practices such as cooking large quantities and freezing them can make daily cooking an achievable goal.

QUESTION

Can I eat oatmeal if I have celiac disease?
Oats were once considered a food to avoid, but a small amount can be tolerated by some people. If you enjoy oats, gradually add a small amount to your diet to learn if you can tolerate the grain. Some oats are processed in factories with other grains, leading to gluten contamination, so check the labels and experiment with different sources.

If you are diagnosed with celiac disease, you will likely need to change your baking techniques, since wheat flours are the most commonly used in cakes, muffins, and cookies. Fortunately, many companies are developing gluten-free flour blends for baking, or you can create your own using the flours of such foods as amaranth, quinoa, potato, cassava, and brown rice.

Baked Sweet Potatoes

Sweet potatoes make a delicious, gluten-free side dish that is also a source of antioxidants. This recipe uses sweet and crunchy toppings, but savory toppings such as broccoli and a little cheese work well too.

INGREDIENTS | SERVES 4

4 sweet potatoes

2 tablespoons butter

4 tablespoons muscovado sugar

2 teaspoons cinnamon

4 tablespoons pecans, chopped

Microwave Potatoes

Microwave ovens come in handy for quick-cooking baked potatoes. Check your settings closely. Many newer models have buttons with preset cooking temperatures and times for potatoes. If yours does, all you have to do is put the potatoes in and push a few buttons, and they will be cooked to perfection.

1. Scrub the potatoes under running water to remove any dirt. Pierce the flesh of each potato in several places with a fork. Microwave on high for 12 to 16 minutes. Cooking times vary depending on the size of your potatoes. Remove and allow to cool for 5 minutes.

2. Cut a slit in each potato and open to expose the flesh. Top the flesh of each potato with ½ tablespoon of butter, 1 tablespoon of sugar, ½ teaspoon of cinnamon, and 1 tablespoon of chopped pecans. Serve hot.

PER SERVING Calories: 263 | Fat: 11g | Sodium: 116mg | Carbohydrates: 41g | Fiber: 5g | Protein: 3g

Simple Green Salad

A healthy salad is the way to go when you need a gluten-free side dish. This simple version uses flavored vinegar for the dressing, which adds a tang that goes well with green bell peppers and parsley.

INGREDIENTS | SERVES 4

1 head romaine lettuce
4 cups spinach leaves
1 green bell pepper
¼ cup parsley, chopped
½ teaspoon salt
3 tablespoons olive oil
2 tablespoons flavored vinegar

Flavored Vinegars

In this recipe you can use a standard salad vinegar or balsamic vinegar. However, consider trying a flavored vinegar for something different. Flavored vinegars using herbs or fruits such as orange or raspberry can be found at many gourmet and health food stores. Be sure to check the labels for any hidden gluten.

1. Prepare the vegetables by washing them and then chop the head of romaine. Slice the bell pepper into rings.

2. Toss the romaine and spinach in a bowl and lay the pepper rings on top, followed by the parsley.

3. Sprinkle with the salt, and then drizzle with the olive oil and vinegar. Toss ingredients and serve immediately.

PER SERVING Calories: 127 | Fat: 11g | Sodium: 307mg | Carbohydrates: 7g | Fiber: 4g | Protein: 2g

Potato Chive Pancakes

These savory pancakes provide a great use for leftover mashed potatoes. Served with eggs at breakfast or a chicken breast at dinner, they make a delicious new side dish for your next gluten-free meal.

INGREDIENTS | SERVES 6

1½ cups mashed potatoes

¼ cup fresh chives, chopped

2 cloves garlic, minced

3 tablespoons milk

2 tablespoons potato flour

1 egg, beaten

¼ teaspoon black pepper

2 tablespoons butter

Easy on the Seasonings

When using leftovers to create new dishes, remember that the original dish has already been seasoned. For example, with this recipe you likely added salt and pepper to the mashed potatoes the first time you had them. This means you can cut back, or eliminate, the amount added in the new recipe.

1. In a large bowl, mix together the mashed potatoes, chives, garlic, milk, potato flour, and egg. Stir in the pepper. Form the mixture into 6 patties.

2. Heat a skillet on medium-high heat and melt the butter. Add the potato pancakes and cook for 2 to 3 minutes or until the bottom edge begins to crisp and brown. Flip and repeat the cooking time on the other side. Serve hot.

PER SERVING Calories: 123 | Fat: 7g | Sodium: 210mg | Carbohydrates: 12g | Fiber: 1g | Protein: 3g

Herbed Black Rice

Black rice is sometimes called "forbidden rice" and can be found in most health food stores. It has a beautiful dark purple color when cooked and a delicious nutty flavor that is unique among rice varieties.

INGREDIENTS | SERVES 4

1 tablespoon olive oil
1 cup black rice
1 teaspoon fresh thyme, chopped
1 teaspoon fresh parsley, chopped
1 teaspoon fresh chives, chopped
½ teaspoon salt

Substituting Dried Herbs

You can substitute dried for fresh herbs, but dried herbs have a more concentrated flavor. Use ¼ to ⅓ the amount of dried herbs when substituting for fresh. For example, if the recipe calls for 1 tablespoon of fresh, use 1 teaspoon dried. If it calls for 1 teaspoon of fresh, you can use ¼ teaspoon dried.

1. Heat the olive oil in a deep soup pot. Add rice and cook, stirring often, for 3 minutes.

2. Pour in 2 cups of water; bring the rice to a boil and reduce heat to simmer. Simmer, covered, stirring occasionally, for about 25 minutes or until rice is tender.

3. Stir in the herbs and salt. Serve warm or at room temperature.

PER SERVING Calories: 190 | Fat: 5g | Sodium: 293mg | Carbohydrates: 34g | Fiber: 2g | Protein: 5g

Quinoa and Summer Squash

Quinoa is a seed that is classified as a grain for culinary purposes. It is gluten-free and cooks up in 15 minutes with a fluffy, crunchy texture and a nutty flavor. It pairs nicely with a variety of herbs and vegetables, including the yellow summer squash used here.

INGREDIENTS | SERVES 4

1 cup quinoa, rinsed and drained

2 tablespoons olive oil

2 cloves garlic, minced

½ yellow onion, chopped

3 yellow squash, sliced

1 tablespoon fresh rosemary, chopped

1 teaspoon salt

¼ teaspoon black pepper

Rinse Well

Rinsing removes saponins from the surface of the quinoa. Saponins are natural plant chemicals that protect quinoa from insects that could destroy the plant; however, they can cause a bitter flavor in your final dish. Place the quinoa in a strainer and rinse well with running water before cooking.

1. Place the quinoa in a saucepan and add 2 cups of water. Bring to a boil; reduce heat, cover, and simmer until the liquid is absorbed and the quinoa is fluffy, about 15 minutes. Set aside.

2. Heat a skillet on medium-high heat and add the olive oil. Add the garlic, onion, and squash. Cook 5 to 7 minutes or until the vegetables are tender and begin to brown. Add the rosemary, salt, and pepper.

3. Stir the vegetables into the quinoa and serve warm.

PER SERVING Calories: 232 | Fat: 9g | Sodium: 585mg | Carbohydrates: 31g | Fiber: 4g | Protein: 7g

CHAPTER 11

Chronic Fatigue Syndrome

Chronic fatigue syndrome (CFS) is a condition that greatly impacts daily life and the ability to perform day-to-day activities and meet family and professional responsibilities. Though it is difficult to diagnose and its cause is unknown, research continues to show that correcting nutrient deficiencies may play a role in reducing symptoms of CFS.

What Is Chronic Fatigue Syndrome?

CFS is diagnosed when a person has four or more specific symptoms for six months or longer. The symptoms of CFS go beyond general fatigue, and there is a dramatic decline in the ability to be and stay active. Other symptoms used for diagnosis include decreased memory and concentration, sore throat, joint and muscle pain, a change in headache type or severity, and sleep that does not restore energy.

While the cause of CFS is still unknown, some researchers believe that it could be a result of a viral infection, or possibly due to trauma, stress, or toxins. One theory is that there is a dysfunction of the immune system. White blood cells called B cells and T cells work to fight off infection in a healthy immune system, and these cells may be impaired in those with CFS.

There are several correctable nutrient deficiencies associated with CFS patients, as well as vitamins and minerals that can promote healthy function of the immune system. Changing the diet may influence some symptoms of CFS.

Nutrients That Alleviate CFS

A deficiency of vitamins, minerals, and fatty acids is related to CFS. By increasing your intake of foods that contain these nutrients you can nourish the body, improve immunity, and increase energy levels.

Beta carotene gives a yellowish-orange color to many fruits and vegetables. Mangoes, papayas, carrots, yams, sweet potatoes, squash, apricots, and pumpkin are all high in beta carotene. Spinach, kale, and other green leafy vegetables are also good sources.

B Vitamins

Stress can increase the symptoms of CFS, and B vitamins are nutrients that influence the effect of stress on the body. These vitamins are necessary for the function of nerve and brain cells. Therefore, adequate intake can aid the body in dealing with stress, including physical manifestations such as tight muscles and elevated blood pressure.

Antioxidants and Minerals

Antioxidants protect cells and strengthen the immune system. Beta carotene and vitamin C are two antioxidants that may help combat the nutrient deficiencies that weaken the immune system in individuals with CFS.

Research has shown that magnesium and zinc levels can also be low in people with CFS. Magnesium is a mineral that promotes a healthy immune system and may help reduce fatigue because of its role in energy metabolism. Zinc also supports immune function and is involved in cellular metabolism.

Essential Fatty Acids

A deficiency in omega-3 fatty acids and high intake of omega-6 fatty acids has also been associated with CFS and its symptoms. Both omega-3 fatty acids and omega-6 fatty acids are essential, meaning that these nutrients must be consumed through food. However, for many Americans, the ratio of omega-6 intake to omega-3 intake is out of balance because omega-6 fatty acids are plentiful in foods regularly consumed, notably processed oils, margarines, snack foods, and fried foods.

Foods That Contain These Nutrients

It's clear that many foods can influence the immune system and fatigue, and this is great news for your dietary intake. With so many delicious and nutrient-rich foods to choose from, it is easy to follow a diet that can relieve the symptoms of CFS.

Foods with Vitamins

Multiple B vitamins are found in vegetables—and when in doubt, choose green. Spinach, broccoli, turnip and mustard greens, and asparagus are all rich in B vitamins that will help the body cope with the effects of stress. Double up on your antioxidant intake by eating fruits and vegetables that contain both vitamin C and beta carotene. Watermelon, cantaloupe, and carrots are good choices. If you need more variety, increase your intake of red bell peppers for vitamin C and pumpkin for beta carotene. Use parsley in your cooking and you will boost both your vitamin B and vitamin C intake.

Foods with Zinc and Magnesium

Oysters top the list as sources for zinc; however, you probably don't cook or eat them often unless you live in an area where they are easy to find. Red meat, poultry, and some beans, including chickpeas, or garbanzo beans, are also rich in zinc. Cashews and almonds contain zinc and magnesium, as do whole grains.

ALERT

Both animal and plant foods contain zinc; however, phytates in grains and legumes can inhibit your ability to absorb zinc during digestion by binding to the mineral. Plants can provide some zinc, but zinc from animal products is more available for use in the body.

Some herbs and spices, including dill weed, coriander, and basil, contain magnesium. You will also get a good dose of magnesium from the greens you eat to increase your B vitamin intake. And, of course, the best has been saved for last. Chocolate and cocoa powder contain magnesium, so don't be afraid to fulfill that chocolate craving!

Foods with Omega-3 Fatty Acids

One of the best sources for omega-3 fatty acids is oily cold-water fish. Wild Alaskan salmon has always been the popular choice, but more types of fish are entering the spotlight. Trout is another good choice along with halibut; however, halibut is higher in mercury, so limit your intake to only one serving a week. Walnuts and flaxseed are also rich in omega-3s.

Tips for Incorporating These Foods

Make vegetable trays a regular dish not just for parties, but for lunch and snacks as well. The most common items—carrots, broccoli, and red bell pepper strips—are also some of the best choices to improve symptoms of

CFS. Top a spinach salad with almonds or cashews and then sprinkle on some chopped parsley for a meal in which all three ingredients are active in prevention.

ESSENTIAL

Fat is essential for the absorption of fat-soluble vitamins and antioxidants, so eat your vegetables with some healthy fats. Drizzle your salads with cold-pressed walnut or avocado oil, or sprinkle on almonds or chopped avocado. Sauté your dark leafy greens or Brussels sprouts in olive oil.

Improve your omega-3 fatty acid to omega-6 fatty acid ratio. You can do this by decreasing your intake of processed, packaged, and fried foods and increasing the amount of fish you eat each week. Incorporate walnuts into your daily snacks and sprinkle ground flaxseed on your oatmeal or yogurt.

Melon Salad with Mint

Mixed melon salads are light and refreshing, and this one is full of nutrients for a healthy immune system. A little salt sprinkled on melon gives a wonderful contrast to the sweetness; however, this recipe is still delicious if you choose to leave it out.

INGREDIENTS | SERVES 6

3 cups watermelon, cubed

3 cups cantaloupe, cubed

1 teaspoon sea salt

¼ cup fresh mint leaves

1. Combine the melon cubes in a large bowl and sprinkle with the salt.

2. Finely chop the mint into small pieces and add to the bowl of fruit. Mix well to incorporate the salt and mint. Serve immediately.

PER SERVING Calories: 53 | Fat: 0g | Sodium: 403mg | Carbohydrates: 13g | Fiber: 2g | Protein: 1g

Ripe Melons

Choosing a ripe melon can feel like a guessing game, but these tips will help. For cantaloupe, choose melons that are brown, not green, under the rough netting on the skin. The end should press in gently and should emit a sweet fragrance. For watermelons, choose those with a cream or yellow bottom, not one that is white or green.

Quick Homemade Hot Cocoa

Don't turn to a packaged mix full of additives when you need a quick cup of hot cocoa. This recipe is made from scratch, but takes only minutes. Use a milk frother to make the finished cup even creamier.

INGREDIENTS | SERVES 1

1½ tablespoons cocoa powder

1 cup milk

1 teaspoon demerara sugar

Spice It Up!

The flavors of hot cocoa blend wonderfully with savory spices. Experiment with adding ¼ teaspoon of cinnamon, nutmeg, curry, or even cayenne pepper to the milk before heating. Add the milk to the cocoa and mix well. Don't be afraid to combine spices for even more complex flavors.

1. Place the cocoa in a mug and add 2 tablespoons of the milk and the sugar. Use a milk frother, small whisk, or spoon to rapidly whip the cocoa into the liquid. This will form a chocolate paste.

2. Pour the remaining milk in a microwave-safe mug and heat on high for 45 to 60 seconds, careful not to let it boil.

3. Gradually pour the milk into the mug with the chocolate as you whisk or stir. Continue stirring until the chocolate, sugar, and milk are fully combined. Drink immediately.

PER SERVING Calories: 176 | Fat: 9g | Sodium: 100mg | Carbohydrates: 20g | Fiber: 3g | Protein: 9g

Grilled Asparagus

Asparagus holds up well to a hot grill and results in a crisp spear with a smoky flavor. If you don't have a grill, place the asparagus on a baking sheet and roast in the oven at 400°F for about 7 to 10 minutes.

INGREDIENTS | SERVES 4

1 pound asparagus

2 tablespoons olive oil

1 teaspoon sea salt

½ teaspoon black pepper

½ teaspoon garlic powder

½ teaspoon dried basil

½ teaspoon dried thyme

½ teaspoon dried parsley

½ teaspoon ground mustard seed

1. Trim the ends of your asparagus. Wash under running water and pat dry. Place on a baking sheet in a single layer.

2. Drizzle the asparagus with the olive oil and sprinkle with all of the herbs and spices. Turn the asparagus to coat it evenly.

3. Using tongs, carefully place each shoot crosswise on a hot grill, careful not to move them too much to prevent losing them between the slots in the grill rack. Close the grill and cook for about 5 minutes.

4. Remove from the grill and serve immediately.

PER SERVING Calories: 57 | Fat: 4g | Sodium: 584mg | Carbohydrates: 5g | Fiber: 3g | Protein: 3g

Roasted Pumpkin Smoked Cheddar Risotto

Risotto is made from arborio rice and the cooking process takes about 20 to 30 minutes. However, the result is completely worth the time. The starch from the rice becomes so creamy and rich that you will think you slipped in some cream without knowing it.

INGREDIENTS | SERVES 4

1 tablespoon olive oil

1 tablespoon unsalted butter

¼ cup onion, chopped

2 cloves garlic, minced

1 cup arborio rice

4 cups chicken stock, warm

1 cup roasted pumpkin, puréed

½ cup smoked Cheddar cheese, shredded

¼ teaspoon salt

¼ teaspoon pepper

¼ cup parsley, chopped

Roasting Pumpkin

For roasted pumpkin, choose a smaller variety such as a pie pumpkin. Cut it in half and remove the seeds. Coat the surface with olive oil and pierce the flesh with a fork. Place cut side down on a baking sheet and bake at 400°F for about 1 hour. Scoop out the flesh and purée in a blender.

1. Heat the olive oil and butter over medium heat in a large soup pot. Add the onion and garlic and cook about 3 minutes or until the onion becomes tender. Add the rice and cook 2 minutes more.

2. Add ¼ cup of the chicken stock and slowly stir the rice until the liquid has been completely absorbed. You may need to reduce the heat if the liquid wants to boil. Repeat this process, adding ¼ cup of stock at a time, until you have used all of the stock and the rice has become creamy and tender.

3. Stir in the pumpkin, cheese, salt, and pepper. Stir and heat through, then remove the pot from the heat. Divide into 4 servings and garnish each with chopped parsley. Serve hot.

PER SERVING Calories: 371 | Fat: 11g | Sodium: 753mg | Carbohydrates: 55g | Fiber: 1g | Protein: 13g

Cashew Chicken Stir-Fry

Cashews contain magnesium and zinc, and this recipe provides a delicious way to add them to your diet. Serve this Asian-inspired dish over ⅓ cup of cooked brown rice to complete your meal.

INGREDIENTS | SERVES 4

2 tablespoons olive oil

3 cloves garlic, minced

1 cup onion, diced

½ cup celery, sliced

1 cup carrots, diced

½ cup red bell pepper, diced

2 cups cooked chicken, shredded

2 tablespoons water

2 tablespoons tamari

1 tablespoon cornstarch

½ cup unsalted cashew halves

1. Heat the olive oil in a large, deep skillet or a wok over medium-high heat. Add the garlic and onion and cook for 2 to 3 minutes.

2. Add in the celery, carrots, and bell pepper. Cook for an additional 5 to 7 minutes or until the vegetables are tender. Add the chicken and heat through.

3. In a small bowl, whisk together the 2 tablespoons of water, the tamari, and the cornstarch. Pour this over the chicken and vegetables. Stir and allow it to bubble and thicken.

4. Stir in the cashews and remove the pan from heat. Serve hot over rice.

PER SERVING (WITHOUT BROWN RICE) Calories: 327 | Fat: 19g | Sodium: 593mg | Carbohydrates: 17g | Fiber: 3g | Protein: 23g

CHAPTER 12

Cold and Flu

Unfortunately, everyone is familiar with cold and flu. The sniffling, coughing, and aching are symptoms you have likely experienced more than a few times. However, you can prevent becoming victim to the next circulating bug by boosting your immune system with healthy foods.

Symptoms and Causes of Cold and Flu

A cold and the flu are similar in that they are caused by viruses and classified as respiratory illnesses. They are caused by two different viruses, however, and while the symptoms are similar, the severity is what distinguishes the two. With the flu you are more likely to experience fever, body aching, and fatigue. Colds bring about coughing, a runny nose, and congestion. The flu can also develop into more serious conditions, including pneumonia, if proper care is not taken to rest and recover.

ESSENTIAL

There were several influenza pandemics in the twentieth century, including the Asian Flu (H2N2) in 1957 and the Hong Kong Flu (H3N2) in 1968. The most recent occurred in 2009. This flu strain, called H1N1, was dubbed the "swine flu" and is thought to be the mutation of four known flu strains: one human, one bird, and two pig. To date, 14,286 people have died from H1N1.

Nutrients That Prevent or Alleviate Cold and Flu

Cold and flu prevention requires maintaining a healthy immune system to ward off infection. Beta carotene plays a role in the function of skin and mucus membranes that line the nose and lungs. This is your body's first defense against invading germs that could cause a cold or the flu. Beta carotene increases the presence of T cells, which attack invaders that can cause you to get sick. In addition, vitamin E, selenium, and zinc all play a role in a healthy immune system.

Vitamin C has long been associated with prevention and treatment of the common cold, but unfortunately there is not much science to support the claim. However, while vitamin C does not have antiviral properties, there is evidence that it has anti-inflammatory properties. This means that it can have an effect similar to over-the-counter pain medication, providing relief once cold and flu symptoms occur. Vitamin C also has plenty of other health benefits, such as being an antioxidant, so keep eating foods that contain it—just don't expect it to be a miracle cure.

FACT

The major source for selenium in your diet is through fruits and vegetables. However, the amount of selenium in the produce depends on the richness of selenium in the soil the food was grown in. Crops grown in areas where the soil has been depleted of selenium will be selenium-deficient.

Foods That Contain These Nutrients

Orange vegetables and dark leafy greens supply you with a bounty of immunity-boosting beta carotene. Carrots, pumpkin, sweet potatoes, spinach, collard greens, and kale top the list. Cashews, almonds, and sunflower seeds provide selenium, zinc, and vitamin E. Mushrooms are also rich in selenium.

Once a cold or the flu has set in, consider incorporating some hot peppers into your diet if your appetite can tolerate it. The capsaicin in chilies can clear your stuffed-up nose by thinning mucus, and cayenne peppers are an excellent source of vitamin A, which is the same vitamin formed from beta carotene.

Believe it or not, chicken soup stays on the list for foods to eat when you have a cold or the flu. Researchers have found that the soup actually does have an anti-inflammatory effect, which means that it can ease common symptoms such as a sore throat. Get even more benefit by adding plenty of fresh garlic. Garlic's sulfur-containing compounds are antibacterial and antiviral, which fights off infecting viruses and could reduce sickness.

Tips for Incorporating These Foods

If you like mushrooms, add them to your meals more often. Even the less-expensive white button variety contains active nutrients for the immune system. Top salads and pizzas with fresh mushrooms, add them to soups and stir-fries, and stir some into casseroles before baking.

ESSENTIAL

In addition to selenium for a healthy immune system, mushrooms contain a substance called beta glucan, which is considered antimicrobial with the ability to fight off infection. Mushrooms complement meat and poultry entrées, but can also be used as a filling and satisfying substitute for meat in cooking.

Leafy greens can be sautéed and added to omelets and soups. Pumpkin adds a holiday flavor to your morning oatmeal when combined with a sprinkle of cinnamon.

Vegetable Couscous

Couscous looks like a grain, but it is actually a small pasta. Most of the couscous you can find in your supermarket is previously steamed, which makes it a quick-cooking side dish for a busy weeknight.

INGREDIENTS | SERVES 4

2¾ cups chicken stock

1½ cups couscous

12 button mushrooms

1 large carrot

½ yellow onion

1 tablespoon olive oil

1 cup spinach, chopped

½ teaspoon garlic powder

½ teaspoon salt

¼ teaspoon pepper

Types of Couscous

Couscous comes in several varieties. The small presteamed granule that is found in most supermarkets is Moroccan couscous. Israeli and Lebanese couscous have larger, almost pea-size pieces. You can also find whole-wheat couscous. Any type can be substituted in this recipe, but cooking times may vary, so check the package.

1. Bring the chicken stock to a boil in a saucepan. Add the couscous, stir, cover with a lid, and remove from the heat. The couscous will absorb the water after about 5 minutes and become light and fluffy.

2. Gently wipe the mushrooms with a damp cloth. Peel the carrot and the onion. Cut each into a small dice.

3. In a skillet, heat the olive oil over medium-high heat. Add the mushrooms, carrot, and onion. Cook 5 to 7 minutes or until the vegetables begin to brown and are tender. Add the spinach and cook until it wilts. Stir in the garlic powder, salt, and pepper.

4. Pour the cooked vegetables into the couscous and stir to combine. Serve warm.

PER SERVING Calories: 318 | Fat: 4g | Sodium: 670mg | Carbohydrates: 57g | Fiber: 5g | Protein: 13g

Mashed Sweet Potatoes

These smooth and creamy mashed sweet potatoes have a mild citrus flavor. They are way too delicious to eat only at the holidays. For a special meal, top them with chopped candied pecans.

INGREDIENTS | SERVES 4

4 sweet potatoes
2 tablespoons butter
¼ cup fresh orange juice
1 tablespoon orange zest, grated
½ teaspoon salt

Spiked Sweet Potatoes

A splash of spirits can add a kick of flavor to sweet potato dishes. This is an especially nice touch around the holidays. Reduce the orange juice by 1 tablespoon and substitute 1 tablespoon of spiced rum or orange liqueur. Feel free to experiment with the flavors available. Hazelnut, pecan, and fruit-flavored liqueurs may result in a brand-new side dish!

1. Scrub the potatoes under running water and pierce the flesh in several places with a fork. Microwave on high for 12 to 16 minutes or until the flesh is tender. Allow to cool enough to handle.

2. Scoop the potato flesh into a large saucepan. Add the butter, juice, zest, and salt. Use a potato masher or electric mixer to mash and cream the sweet potatoes.

3. Turn the heat to medium-high and heat the potatoes through, stirring often. Serve hot.

PER SERVING Calories: 172 | Fat: 6g | Sodium: 372mg | Carbohydrates: 28g | Fiber: 4g | Protein: 2g

Sautéed Kale with Sunflower Seeds

Kale is a dark leafy green that tops the list for nutrient-rich vegetables. It is easy to cook and maintains a firmer texture than spinach and many other greens. When you combine it with sunflower seeds, you get a nutty crunch with even more antioxidants to fight the cold and flu.

INGREDIENTS | SERVES 4

1 tablespoon olive oil

2 cloves garlic, minced

½ yellow onion, finely chopped

1 pound kale, chopped

¼ cup salted sunflower seeds

¼ teaspoon black pepper

Types of Kale

There are several different varieties of kale. Curly kale is recognizable due to its curly leaves, thick rigid stalk, and dark green color. Ornamental kale can have leaves that are green, white, or purple. Dinosaur kale has dark blue-green leaves. Each has a slightly different flavor, and any variety can be used in this recipe.

1. Heat a skillet over medium-high heat and add the olive oil, garlic, and onion. Cook for about 3 minutes, or until onion becomes tender.

2. Add the kale and turn to coat it in the oil. Add ¼ cup of water, cover the skillet with a lid, and reduce the heat to medium. Cook for about 10 minutes, or until the kale becomes wilted and tender. Remove the lid and continue cooking until any remaining liquid evaporates.

3. Stir in the sunflower seeds and black pepper. Remove from heat and serve warm.

PER SERVING Calories: 141 | Fat: 8g | Sodium: 82mg | Carbohydrates: 15g | Fiber: 3g | Protein: 6g

Grilled Veggie and Mushroom Burger

This recipe not only serves up immune-boosting mushrooms, but it is topped with healthy grilled vegetables, too! Feel free to substitute your favorite veggies or add a strong cheese, such as Gorgonzola or goat cheese, to finish off the burger.

INGREDIENTS | SERVES 4

1 medium zucchini
1 yellow onion
4 portobello mushroom caps
¼ cup olive oil
1 teaspoon sea salt
1 teaspoon black pepper
4 whole-grain burger buns

Washing Mushrooms

Mushrooms absorb water, so it is not ideal to wash them under running water to remove dirt and residue. Instead, wet a clean rag or strong paper towel. Gently rub the rag over the flesh of the mushroom to wipe away any dirt, and then pat the mushroom dry with a towel.

1. Cut the ends off of the zucchini and slice lengthwise into 4 to 8 thin slices depending on the size of the vegetable. Slice the onion, keeping the rings intact for grilling.

2. Lay the zucchini, onion, and mushrooms on a flat tray and brush with 2 tablespoons of olive oil. Sprinkle with ½ teaspoon each of salt and pepper.

3. Carefully place the vegetables on a hot grill, oiled and seasoned side down. Brush the remaining olive oil on the top and sprinkle with the remaining salt and pepper. Close the grill lid and cook for 3 to 4 minutes.

4. Flip the vegetables and cook for 3 to 4 minutes more. Remove the zucchini and onion and cook the mushroom 2 to 3 minutes more if necessary until it is tender.

5. Cut the zucchini slices in half. Place a mushroom cap on the bottom of each bun. Stack on the grilled onion and zucchini slices. Finish with the tops of the buns and serve hot.

PER SERVING Calories: 352 | Fat: 17g | Sodium: 900mg | Carbohydrates: 42g | Fiber: 6g | Protein: 11g

Ultimate Chicken Soup

This chicken soup packs in all of the beneficial ingredients that will help you fight off cold and flu. If you'd like something heartier, you can add a grain such as wild rice or noodles to the broth for a filling meal that will boost your immune system.

INGREDIENTS | SERVES 4

1 tablespoon olive oil

2 cloves garlic, minced

½ cup onion, chopped

½ cup celery, diced

1 cup carrots, diced

1 cup mushrooms, sliced

1 teaspoon poultry seasoning

¼ teaspoon ground cayenne pepper (optional)

4 cups chicken stock

1 cup kale, chopped

1 cup cooked chicken, shredded

1. In a large soup pot on medium-high heat, add the olive oil, garlic, and onion. Cook for 1 to 2 minutes and add the celery, carrots, and mushrooms. Cook for 5 to 7 minutes or until the vegetables start to brown and become tender. Add the poultry seasoning, and cayenne pepper if using, and cook 1 minute longer.

2. Pour in the chicken stock and add the kale. Bring to a boil, add the chicken, and reduce to a simmer. Cover and simmer for about 15 minutes. Serve hot with a side of jalapeños or hot sauce if desired. Add salt and black pepper if desired.

PER SERVING Calories: 146 | Fat: 6g | Sodium: 578mg | Carbohydrates: 9g | Fiber: 2g | Protein: 15g

CHAPTER 13

Cold Sores

If you've had a cold sore before you are probably familiar with that slight tingling sensation on your lip, which is
followed by a red blister a few days later. Cold sores can
be frustrating and embarrassing. They tend to strike when
your stress levels are high, but research indicates that eating the right foods may help prevent an outbreak.

What Is a Cold Sore?

Cold sores are also sometimes called fever blisters. They are contagious lesions filled with fluid that most often form around the mouth, but may also appear in your nostrils, on your chin, or on your fingers. A cold sore is caused by herpes simplex virus type 1. It usually begins with a prodrome, a pain or tingling sensation. The prodrome typically occurs one to two days before the cold sore appears. The lesion will eventually dry up, but cold sores can last from ten to fourteen days and can be recurring.

FACT

Although both are lesions that occur near the mouth, cold sores are different from canker sores. Cold sores are viral and occur around the mouth; canker sores develop on the soft tissue inside the mouth and are considered ulcers. Canker sores are not caused by the herpes simplex virus.

Once you have been infected with the herpes simplex virus type 1 and an outbreak occurs, the virus can then go dormant for extended periods of time. Later it can return as an active infection near the original outbreak site. Breakouts most often occur when you are overly tired or stressed, but fever, menstruation, and sun exposure can also cause the active infection to resurface.

Nutrients That Prevent or Alleviate Cold Sores

The amino acids arginine and lysine play a role in the development of cold sores. Arginine is necessary for the creation of a new herpes virus that will lead to a lesion. However, lysine is stored by way of the same receptors used to store arginine. Simply put, the lysine takes the place of arginine and the cell is unable to produce a new virus and cold sore. Increasing your intake of lysine may help prevent a new breakout.

Foods That Contain These Nutrients

Lysine is found in a variety of animal protein sources including dairy products, beef, pork, and chicken. Cod and some other fish provide lysine. If you are looking for a plant source, try legumes such as lentils and beans.

ESSENTIAL

Vitamin C and zinc are beneficial not just for fighting existing cold sores but for helping to bolster your immune system to prevent future outbreaks. Calcium is also good at keeping your body free from cold-sore eruptions.

Tips for Incorporating These Foods

According to the United States Department of Agriculture, most Americans consume an adequate amount of protein in the form of meat and other animal products, thus adequate lysine. If you already consume these foods, it may not be necessary to consume more. However, you can further prevent cold sores and increase the lysine in your meals by also incorporating legumes.

Lentils can be simmered in chicken or vegetable stock for a flavorful side dish, and you can also add them to soups and stews. Black beans and other beans can be served warm in tacos or with rice, or cold in vegetable salads. When cooked and blended with citrus juices, herbs, and oils, beans make delicious dips.

Easy Bean Dip

This dip whips up quickly in a small food processor or blender. It can be used as a dip for carrots or bell pepper strips and it makes a flavorful, protein-rich filling for quesadillas.

INGREDIENTS | MAKES 1½ CUPS

1 cup black beans, cooked or canned

1 clove garlic

1 jalapeño pepper

3 tablespoons fresh lime juice

¼ cup fresh cilantro

1 teaspoon salt

½ teaspoon black pepper

¼ to ⅓ cup olive oil

1. Place the beans and garlic in a small food processor. Remove the stem and cut open the jalapeño. Remove the seeds and veins if you prefer less heat. Add it to the food processor.

2. Pulse the processor until the garlic and jalapeño are chopped and the beans form a paste. Add the lime juice and cilantro and process on high for 20 seconds.

3. Add the salt and pepper along with ¼ cup olive oil. Process until smooth. Check the consistency and add more olive oil if desired. Serve immediately or refrigerate.

PER ¼ CUP SERVING Calories: 122 | Fat: 9g | Sodium: 457mg | Carbohydrates: 8g | Fiber: 3g | Protein: 3g

Quick Yogurt Parfait

For a breakfast that supplies lysine, try a yogurt parfait. A great way to reduce fillers and artificial sweeteners in your parfait is to use plain yogurt with fresh fruit and sweeten it to taste with honey.

INGREDIENTS | SERVES 2

12 ounces plain Greek yogurt
1 apple, diced
2 tablespoons honey
1 banana, diced
6 strawberries, diced

Granola and Cold Sores

Crunchy granola can make a nice addition to a yogurt parfait; however, it is best to skip the grains, nuts, and seeds on your breakfast during times of high stress or fatigue. All contain arginine, which could contribute to the development of a cold sore.

1. Divide the yogurt into 6 equal portions for layering.

2. Divide the apples into 2 portions and place each in a bowl or parfait dish. Top with 1 portion of the yogurt and then drizzle with 1 teaspoon of honey.

3. Add a layer of banana to each dish and top it with another portion of yogurt. Drizzle with 1 teaspoon of honey.

4. Layer the strawberries and remaining yogurt. Drizzle with honey. Serve immediately.

PER SERVING Calories: 287 | Fat: 6g | Sodium: 87mg | Carbohydrates: 55g | Fiber: 4g | Protein: 8g

Parmesan Crusted Cod Fillets

This dish comes together quickly, and both cod and Parmesan cheese are sources of lysine.
Serve this fish with your favorite steamed vegetables for a balanced, healthy meal.

INGREDIENTS | SERVES 4

4 cod fillets
2 tablespoons olive oil
½ cup bread crumbs
1 teaspoon salt
½ teaspoon black pepper
1 teaspoon garlic powder
1 teaspoon dried parsley
¼ cup Parmesan cheese, grated

1. Preheat the oven to 400°F and grease or spray a baking dish.

2. Place the cod fillets on a plate and coat with the olive oil. Set aside.

3. In a flat dish, combine the bread crumbs, salt, pepper, garlic powder, parsley, and cheese. One at a time, place the cod fillets in the bread crumbs and coat one side, pressing gently to get the bread crumbs to stick.

4. Place the fillets, bread crumb side up, in a baking dish. Bake for 15 to 20 minutes, or until fish is white and flaky. Serve warm.

PER SERVING Calories: 303 | Fat: 8g | Sodium: 901mg | Carbohydrates: 11g | Fiber: 1g | Protein: 46g

Beef Chili with Lentils

Chili is one food that is made differently across the United States. This version uses ground beef and lentils for plenty of lysine to prevent cold sores. If you like a kick, add some chopped pickled jalapeños or more crushed red pepper.

INGREDIENTS | SERVES 8

1 pound ground beef

1 yellow onion, chopped

1 green bell pepper, chopped

2 cloves garlic, minced

1 (28-ounce) can diced canned tomatoes

1 (14-ounce) can tomato sauce

3 tablespoons chili powder

2 teaspoons cumin

1 teaspoon salt

½ teaspoon black pepper

½ teaspoon crushed red pepper

1½ cups dried lentils

BPA in Canned Tomatoes

Bisphenol A (BPA) is a chemical present in the lining of many food cans, and reacts with the acid in tomato products. BPA mimics estrogen and can also impact brain health of young children. Companies are working to develop BPA-free cans, but for now concerned consumers can buy tomato products in glass jars and Tetra Paks.

1. In a soup pot, brown the ground beef over medium-high heat. Add the onion, bell pepper, and garlic and cook 2 to 3 more minutes. Drain if there is excess fat present.

2. Pour in the tomatoes and tomato sauce. Add the chili powder, cumin, salt, pepper, and red pepper. Bring to a slight boil and add the lentils.

3. Reduce heat, cover, and simmer for about 15 minutes, stirring occasionally. Cook until the lentils are tender. Serve with jalapeños, shredded cheese, or a dollop of sour cream if desired.

PER SERVING Calories: 358 | Fat: 18g | Sodium: 760mg | Carbohydrates: 33g | Fiber: 9g | Protein: 19g

Black Bean Chicken Salad

This recipe gives a Southwest twist to traditional chicken salad. It is a mayonnaise-free salad that is best served with slices of ripe tomato or on a salad of greens.

INGREDIENTS | SERVES 4

1 cup black beans, cooked or canned

1 cup cooked chicken, cubed

½ cup corn kernels

½ cup red bell pepper, diced

¼ cup red onion, chopped

3 tablespoons fresh lime juice

2 tablespoons olive oil

1 teaspoon cumin

2 tablespoons cilantro, chopped

1 teaspoon salt

½ teaspoon black pepper

1. In a bowl, combine the drained black beans, chicken, corn, bell pepper, and red onion.

2. In a separate small bowl, whisk together the lime juice, olive oil, cumin, cilantro, salt, and pepper.

3. Pour the dressing over the chicken and beans and toss to coat. Refrigerate for at least 30 minutes before serving to allow flavors to mix.

PER SERVING Calories: 207 | Fat: 10g | Sodium: 715mg | Carbohydrates: 17g | Fiber: 5g | Protein: 14g

Cilantro Substitutions

Cilantro is an herb with flat green leaves and a strong, fragrant flavor. While loved by many, others don't like the taste. If you don't like cilantro, simply replace it with the same amount of chopped flat leaf parsley. If you don't like either, you can leave the fresh herbs out altogether.

CHAPTER 14

Constipation

Constipation is most often linked to a poor diet. For those who suffer from the condition, this is good news because it means minor changes in your eating habits can relieve constipation and the associated discomfort.

What Is Constipation?

Constipation is defined as having a bowel movement less than three times per week. There may be difficult passage, pain, and dry stool. When determining if you are constipated, remember that everyone is different. Many people think that if they don't go each day, they suffer from constipation. However, the truth is, some individuals may go three times per day and some three times per week.

Constipation is caused when the colon absorbs too much water from the waste passing through it. In addition, the muscle contractions moving the waste can be slow or sluggish. In many cases, constipation is temporary, and can be relieved and prevented.

Nutrients That Alleviate Constipation

Fiber, the portion of plant foods that you can't digest in the gut, is the key nutrient that influences constipation. If you eat too little fiber you can trigger constipation, but you can also alleviate constipation by increasing your fiber intake. There are two types of fiber, soluble and insoluble.

ESSENTIAL

Hydration plays an important role in constipation. When increasing your fiber intake, you should also drink water regularly. Staying hydrated will allow the insoluble fiber to create bulk and soften stool. Drink a glass of water with each meal, and sip on water throughout your day. Try adding a squeeze of lime or lemon juice to add flavor.

It is important to eat both types of fiber for a healthy digestive system, but insoluble fiber is more closely associated with regularity and relieving constipation. Insoluble fiber speeds up the passage of waste through the colon. It binds to water, which creates bulk and also softens stool.

Foods That Contain These Nutrients

Plant foods contain both soluble and insoluble fiber, so by increasing your intake of fruits, vegetables, and grains you will promote a healthy digestive system. According to the Harvard School of Public Health, the fiber from grains such as wheat bran and oat bran is more effective for relieving constipation when compared to the fibers from fruits and vegetables. To relieve constipation, concentrate on increasing foods that contain more insoluble fiber. Wheat bran (including whole-wheat bread), cabbage, Brussels sprouts, turnips, and cauliflower are good choices.

FACT

According to the Harvard School of Public Health, women should eat more than 20 grams of fiber a day and men should aim to eat more than 30 grams per day. Increase the amount of fiber gradually, eating a little more each week to decrease the gas and discomfort possible when you have a rapid increase in fiber intake.

Tips for Incorporating These Foods

Add a tablespoon of unprocessed wheat bran to your muffins and breads when baking. It can also be used as a topping to sprinkle over yogurt or other cereals for breakfast. Cauliflower can be eaten raw as a snack, added to stir-fries and soups, and steamed and mashed similar to mashed potatoes. Turnips may not be your idea of a treat, but if you didn't like them once or as a child, give them another chance. They can be delicious when roasted with other root vegetables.

Easy Coleslaw

Coleslaw is a favorite summer side dish when served with grilled burgers or pulled pork barbecue. This recipe uses spicy brown mustard for flavor and plenty of cabbage for fiber.

INGREDIENTS | SERVES 8

1 head cabbage, shredded

2 carrots, shredded

2 tablespoons onion, grated

½ cup mayonnaise

3 tablespoons spicy brown mustard

1 teaspoon muscovado sugar

½ teaspoon salt

¼ teaspoon black pepper

1. In a large bowl, combine the shredded cabbage and carrot and grated onion.

2. In a small bowl, whisk together the mayonnaise, mustard, sugar, salt, and pepper. Pour over the vegetables and toss to coat evenly.

3. Refrigerate for at least 30 minutes before serving.

PER SERVING Calories: 99 | Fat: 5g | Sodium: 323mg | Carbohydrates: 13g | Fiber: 4g | Protein: 2g

Cauliflower and Toasted Walnuts

Cauliflower is a versatile cruciferous vegetable that is full of fiber. Use this dish as a side for grilled chicken or toss it with whole-wheat pasta or couscous for a quick meal.

INGREDIENTS | SERVES 6

1 head cauliflower

1 tablespoon olive oil

2 cloves garlic, minced

⅓ cup walnuts, chopped

1 teaspoon salt

½ teaspoon black pepper

1. Remove the stem and leaves from the head of cauliflower and chop into small florets that are about bite-size pieces. Rinse well under running water and pat dry. Set aside.

2. In a deep skillet, heat the olive oil over medium-high heat and add the garlic. Next, add the cauliflower. Cook for 3 to 5 minutes, or until the edges of the cauliflower are browned.

3. Pour in ¼ cup of water, reduce the heat to simmer, and cover with a lid. Allow the cauliflower to cook about 7 minutes or until it is tender. Remove the lid, return the heat to medium, and allow any liquid to evaporate.

4. Add the walnuts and stir to toast evenly. Finish by adding the salt and pepper. Serve hot.

PER SERVING Calories: 101 | Fat: 7g | Sodium: 430mg | Carbohydrates: 9g | Fiber: 4g | Protein: 4g

Homemade Muesli with Wheat Bran

Muesli is a Swiss cereal that combines whole grains, nuts, seeds, and dried fruits for a hearty and healthy breakfast. This recipe adds wheat bran to boost the insoluble fiber for a healthy digestion.

INGREDIENTS | SERVES 2

⅔ cup rolled oats

2 tablespoons wheat bran

2 tablespoons raisins

2 tablespoons dried cranberries

2 tablespoons pecans, chopped

2 tablespoons sunflower seeds

2 teaspoons muscovado sugar

1. In each of 2 bowls, combine ⅓ cup oats and 1 tablespoon each of wheat bran, raisins, cranberries, pecans, and sunflower seeds.

2. Sprinkle each with 1 teaspoon of the sugar. Add milk or yogurt and serve immediately or refrigerate overnight.

PER SERVING Calories: 278 | Fat: 11g | Sodium: 5mg | Carbohydrates: 42g | Fiber: 6g | Protein: 7g

Enjoy It Three Different Ways

Muesli is often combined with milk or yogurt and refrigerated overnight to soften and sweeten the cereal. You can enjoy it this way, or use it as a dry cereal and pour over the milk just before eating. It can also be used as a topping for yogurt.

Raspberry Bran Muffins

A great way to increase your soluble fiber intake is through bran muffins.
They make a delicious breakfast when served with fresh fruit or alongside a vegetable omelet.
This recipe uses raspberries, but any berry or raisins would work well.

INGREDIENTS | SERVES 12

½ cup butter, melted
½ cup demerara sugar
¾ cup yogurt
1 egg, beaten
½ teaspoon vanilla
½ cup white whole-wheat flour
¼ cup wheat bran
½ teaspoon salt
1 teaspoon baking soda
1 teaspoon baking powder
1 teaspoon cinnamon
1½ cups defrosted raspberries

Use Greek Yogurt

Greek yogurt is different from other varieties of yogurt because all of the excess liquids have been removed. This leaves a product that is very thick and creamy. Greek yogurt creates moist baked goods, and if you use a naturally flavored variety such as vanilla or honey, it will also add sweetness.

1. Preheat the oven to 350°F and grease a 12-muffin tin.

2. In a mixing bowl, whisk together the melted, cooled butter, sugar, and yogurt. Whisk in the egg and vanilla and set aside.

3. Sift together the flour, wheat bran, salt, baking soda, baking powder, and cinnamon. Gradually add the dry ingredients to the wet ingredients, stirring just until combined.

4. Gently stir in the raspberries and evenly distribute the batter into the muffin cups.

5. Bake for 20 to 25 minutes or until a toothpick inserted into the center comes out clean. Cool for about 5 minutes; remove muffins and place on a cooling rack. Eat warm or at room temperature.

PER SERVING Calories: 147 | Fat: 9g | Sodium: 310mg | Carbohydrates: 16g | Fiber: 2g | Protein: 2g

Roasted Root Vegetables

Root vegetables provide a comforting and hearty side dish for the cold winter months. If there is a specific one you don't care for, such as parsnip or turnip, you might be surprised at how a combination of a few along with fresh herbs can harmonize the flavors.

INGREDIENTS | SERVES 4

2 white potatoes

2 sweet potatoes

2 parsnips

2 turnips

2 large carrots

3 cloves garlic, chopped

⅛ cup olive oil

1 teaspoon salt

½ teaspoon black pepper

1 tablespoon fresh rosemary, chopped

Winter Squash

If you can't find some of the root vegetables listed in this recipe, try substituting some winter squash. Cubed pumpkin or butternut squash adds a sweetness that goes well with root vegetables. Just be sure to roast it only until it is tender and not mushy.

1. Preheat the oven to 400°F. Scrub the potatoes under running water and peel if desired. Scrub the parsnips, turnips, and carrots under water, peel off the skin, and remove any stems. Chop all vegetables into similar bite-size pieces.

2. Spread the vegetables and garlic evenly on 1 large baking sheet or 2 smaller baking sheets. Drizzle with olive oil and turn to coat each piece. Sprinkle with salt, pepper, and fresh rosemary.

3. Bake for 45 to 60 minutes, stirring every 15 minutes. The vegetables are done when they have browned and are tender when pierced with a fork. Serve warm.

PER SERVING Calories: 296 | Fat: 7g | Sodium: 693mg | Carbohydrates: 57g | Fiber: 10g | Protein: 5g

CHAPTER 15

Depression

Carbohydrates, fats, proteins, and vitamins play a role in brain health and mood. Replenishing deficiencies in some nutrients can reduce symptoms of depression and enable antidepressant medications to work more effectively.

What Is Depression?

The term "depressed" is used loosely to refer to feeling down or sad. How-ever, the depressive disorder known as "depression" is a much more seri-ous condition that lasts for extended periods of time, not just a day or two every now and then. It results in feelings of sadness and anxiety and can cause a loss of appetite and a loss of interest in doing things the sufferer once enjoyed. Inability to sleep, as well as excessive sleep, is a symptom, in addition to lack of concentration.

FACT

Depression is a condition that can occur at any point in life. It may de-velop out of a major life change or a stressful situation that is out of the sufferer's control, such as loss of a loved one or diagnosis of a dis-ease. Physical and social changes associated with aging and meno-pause (Chapter 25) can also lead to depression.

The cause of depression is not known, but its presence is associated with substances called neurotransmitters. Neurotransmitters are chemical messengers in the brain, and those most often linked to depression include serotonin, dopamine, norepinephrine and y-aminobutyric acid. A deficiency or imbalance in these chemicals may lead to depression. Some nutrients from the foods you eat promote production and action of these neurotrans-mitters; therefore, nutrient deficiencies can affect proper function and risk for depression.

Nutrients That Prevent or Alleviate Depression

A variety of chemicals in the brain (for example, serotonin, dopamine, and norepinephrine) influence your mood. Some amino acids consumed through protein in foods are precursors for the brain chemicals, meaning that they are converted to the chemicals once digested or absorbed. Trypto-phan and tyrosine are two such amino acids.

Research shows that individuals suffering from depression often have low levels of folate, and this vitamin can help medications for depression to work more effectively. Omega-3 fatty acids have been found to have antidepressant effects and can ease the symptoms of depression.

ALERT

Carbohydrates come from a variety of sources, but simple carbohydrates such as sugars and sweet snacks lead to a spike in insulin. This can be followed by a crash that depresses the mood. Stick with whole grains, beans, vegetables, and other complex carbohydrates. They take longer to digest, resulting in longer-lasting energy and less of a crash in mood.

Carbohydrates, especially whole-grain sources, can improve mood. The spike in insulin that occurs after eating carbohydrates delivers sugar to the cells for energy production, which sends tryptophan to the brain. This influences those neurotransmitters that can improve mood.

Foods That Contain These Nutrients

Meat, fish, poultry, eggs, and milk are complete proteins, meaning that they supply all nine essential amino acids, some of which are important for mental health and improved mood. If you are a vegetarian, currently there are two plant sources considered to be complete proteins: soybeans and quinoa.

To increase your folate intake, try Great Northern beans, spinach, asparagus, pinto beans, lentils, and oranges. Wild salmon, flaxseed, and walnuts are almost always recommended for increasing omega-3 fatty acid intake, but don't overlook shrimp, scallops, albacore tuna, and lake trout. These foods also provide amino acids through the protein they supply.

Tips for Incorporating These Foods

According to the National Institutes of Health, two to three servings of protein-rich foods, such as 3 ounces of cooked meat or half a cup of cooked beans, supply adequate protein and amino acids. Increase your intake of meals that include beans and whole grains for folate and complex carbohydrates in addition to protein.

You can create complete proteins in your meals by combining different protein-rich plant foods, such as beans and nuts with grains. For example, try entrées with brown rice and beans, or soups with corn and beans. Added whole grains will also give you plenty of mood-boosting complex carbohydrates.

Increase your intake of fish and shellfish as a source of omega-3 fatty acids. You can take advantage of such sources as canned tuna, which is often less expensive than fresh fish.

White Bean Tuna Salad

This salad contains tuna and walnuts for protein and omega-3 fatty acids, and white beans for folate. If you are feeling adventurous, make it a hearty grain salad by stirring in cooked brown rice or wheat berries.

INGREDIENTS | SERVES 4

1½ cups Great Northern beans, canned or cooked

2 (6-ounce) cans albacore tuna, drained

¼ cup walnuts, chopped

2 green onions, sliced

1 tablespoon fresh parsley, chopped

3 tablespoons fresh lime juice

1 tablespoon olive oil

½ teaspoon garlic powder

½ teaspoon salt

¼ teaspoon ground black pepper

1. Combine the beans, tuna, walnuts, and onion in a bowl.

2. In a separate small bowl, whisk together the parsley, lime juice, olive oil, garlic powder, salt, and pepper. Pour dressing over the salad and toss to coat.

3. Refrigerate for 15 to 30 minutes to allow flavors to blend. Serve cold or at room temperature.

PER SERVING Calories: 334 | Fat: 15g | Sodium: 497mg | Carbohydrates: 20g | Fiber: 5g | Protein: 30g

Canned Tuna

Both light and albacore canned tuna contain omega-3 fatty acids; however, higher-quality albacore has been shown to contain a little more. Considering this and its appealing chunked texture and mild flavor, it is often worth the few cents more per can. Whichever you choose, pick the variety packed in water, not oil, for the healthier option.

Herbed Quinoa Pilaf

Quinoa is an excellent choice for quick side dish. It cooks for 15 minutes and you can work on the rest of your meal during that time. It makes an attractive pilaf, which you can top with a grilled salmon fillet or baked chicken breast.

INGREDIENTS | SERVES 4

1 cup quinoa

2 cups chicken or vegetable stock

1 teaspoon garlic powder

1 teaspoon dried parsley

1 teaspoon dried basil

½ teaspoon dried thyme

½ teaspoon salt

¼ teaspoon ground black pepper

1. Rinse the quinoa well under running water and drain with a strainer.

2. Place the chicken or vegetable stock in a saucepan and bring to a bowl. Stir in the quinoa, reduce the heat, and simmer covered for about 15 minutes or until the liquid has been absorbed and the quinoa is softened.

3. Add all of the herbs and spices and toss to mix. Serve warm.

PER SERVING Calories: 203 | Fat: 4g | Sodium: 465mg | Carbohydrates: 32g | Fiber: 3g | Protein: 9g

Savory Barley Salad

This salad combines a mood-boosting whole grain with flavors of basil pesto. It is best cold and can be served over fresh spinach for folate or with grilled salmon for omega-3 fatty acids.

INGREDIENTS | SERVES 4

1½ cups cooked barley
½ cup button mushrooms, chopped
1 cup fresh basil leaves
1 clove garlic
2 tablespoons walnuts, chopped
2 tablespoons grated Parmesan cheese
3 tablespoons olive oil
1 teaspoon salt
½ teaspoon black pepper

1. In a large bowl, combine the barley with the mushrooms. Set aside.

2. In a food processor, combine the basil, garlic, walnuts, Parmesan cheese, olive oil, salt, and pepper. Pulse until all ingredients are chopped and blended. If pesto is too thick, add more olive oil.

3. Pour the pesto over the barley and mushrooms. Stir to mix all ingredients. Refrigerate about 30 minutes before serving.

PER SERVING Calories: 202 | Fat: 14g | Sodium: 623mg | Carbohydrates: 18g | Fiber: 3g | Protein: 3g

Asparagus Shrimp Pasta

This recipe cooks the asparagus quickly to help preserve as much of the folate as possible during the process. The nutritious vegetable is then mixed with garlic, lemon zest, and shrimp for a wonderful pasta meal.

INGREDIENTS | SERVES 4

1 pound fresh asparagus

1 cup ice

1 pound whole-wheat spaghetti

2 tablespoons olive oil

3 cloves garlic, minced

1 pound shrimp, cleaned

1 tablespoon lemon zest

1 teaspoon salt

½ teaspoon ground black pepper

4 lemon wedges, for garnish

Blanching Vegetables

Blanching is a technique that cooks vegetables quickly in boiling water just until they become tender. Then they are submerged in an ice bath to discontinue the cooking process. This results in a bright green, crisp vegetable and is a great method to use with asparagus, broccoli, or green beans.

1. Wash the asparagus and trim about 1 inch from the bottom edge of each shoot. Chop the asparagus into 1-inch pieces. In a large soup pot, bring 4 quarts of water to a boil; in a separate pan, bring 2 quarts of water to a boil. Prepare a large bowl with 1 cup of ice and fill about halfway with water.

2. Once the 2 quarts of water begins to boil, drop in the asparagus and cook for 3 minutes. Remove with a slotted spoon and immediately place in the ice bath. Remove from the ice bath and place in a separate bowl. Set aside.

3. Once the 4 quarts of water begins to boil, toss in the pasta and stir gently. Cook until the pasta is tender, but still slightly firm. Drain in a colander and set aside.

4. In a large, deep skillet, heat the olive oil over medium-high heat and add the garlic. Stir in the shrimp and cook until opaque. Add the lemon zest, salt, and pepper. Reduce heat.

5. Add the pasta and asparagus to the skillet and toss with the shrimp and oil. Remove from heat and serve warm. Garnish with lemon wedges.

PER SERVING Calories: 602 | Fat: 10g | Sodium: 759mg | Carbohydrates: 92g | Fiber: 2g | Protein: 42g

Whole-Grain Orange Flax Muffins

These hearty muffins can be used as a base for a variety of ingredients. Add some of your favorites to the batter just before dividing it into muffin cups for baking—for example, ½ cup raisins, ¼ cup shredded coconut, or chopped pecans.

INGREDIENTS | SERVES 12

½ cup butter, melted

½ cup demerara sugar

2 eggs

¼ cup plain Greek yogurt

½ cup fresh orange juice

1 teaspoon vanilla

1 tablespoon orange zest

2 cups white whole-wheat flour

¼ cup ground flaxseed

1 tablespoon baking powder

1 teaspoon salt

Ground Versus Whole Flaxseed

Choose ground flaxseed for your baking. Whole flaxseed can be difficult to digest, which decreases the amount of nutrients your body can absorb from it. Eating the ground version is like helping your gut with the digestion process. Store ground flaxseed in an airtight container in the refrigerator and use within a month.

1. Preheat oven to 400°F and grease a 12-muffin tin.

2. In a bowl, mix together the butter and sugar, then mix in the eggs. Stir in the yogurt, orange juice, vanilla, and zest.

3. Sift together the flour, flaxseed, baking powder, and salt. Gradually incorporate the dry ingredients into the wet ingredients, stirring just until combined. For tender muffins, avoid overmixing.

4. Divide the batter evenly between the 12 muffin cups. Bake for 17 to 20 minutes or until a toothpick inserted in the center comes out clean. Remove from oven and cool for 3 minutes. Enjoy warm or at room temperature.

PER SERVING Calories: 190 | Fat: 10g | Sodium: 384mg | Carbohydrates: 23g | Fiber: 3g | Protein: 5g

CHAPTER 16

Diabetes

Diabetes is a disease that affects your body's ability to use the sugar you eat in food. According to the American Diabetes Association, 23.6 million Americans suffer from type 2 diabetes, the most common form.

What Is Diabetes?

Diabetes is a disease that involves insulin. When you eat, the carbohydrates in the food are converted to glucose; insulin is necessary to help transport that glucose into the cells to be used for energy. In diabetes, there are problems with insulin function and production.

For those with type 1 diabetes, the body does not produce the insulin. For those with type 2 diabetes, the production of insulin is decreased or the cells don't respond to insulin. A third form of diabetes, gestational diabetes, occurs during pregnancy but often corrects itself soon after birth. Type 2 diabetes is both controllable and preventable. It is linked to obesity, lack of exercise, high blood cholesterol, and high blood pressure.

Nutrients That Control or Prevent Diabetes

Fiber is one nutrient that helps the body stabilize blood sugar levels and control diabetes. Zinc plays a role in the formation and action of insulin and assists the action of antioxidants. Decreased zinc has been associated with reduced production and secretion of insulin. Reduced production and secretion of insulin is a contributing factor for development of diabetes.

ALERT

Diabetes requires that you maintain balanced blood sugar levels. Spikes in blood sugar that occur after a meal or rapid drops in blood sugar that can occur when you don't eat regularly are dangerous and can be life threatening if you have diabetes.

Anthocyanins in dark reddish-purple fruits and vegetables are linked to a decrease in the inflammation associated with heart disease and diabetes. This phytochemical and flavonoid may also increase insulin activity and decrease blood sugar levels.

Foods That Contain These Nutrients

Irish steel-cut oats, almonds, and lentils contain fiber and zinc for preventing and controlling diabetes. Raspberries, pears, and apples are some of the fruits with the highest fiber content. Tart cherries have been found to benefit diabetes because of their anthocyanin content. Vinegar has been shown to increase insulin sensitivity after a meal in those with type 2 diabetes. Insulin sensitivity is a term used to indicate the function of insulin in the body, or how well insulin is doing its job. When insulin does not function properly to reduce blood sugar to healthy levels after a meal, this is often referred to as insulin resistance, or reduced insulin sensitivity. Foods that help to increase insulin sensitivity improve the function of insulin and its ability to reduce blood sugar.

ESSENTIAL

If fresh tart cherries are out of season or you can't find them in your area, try tart cherry juice, dried tart cherries, or even frozen cherries. All varieties appear to produce the same results. However, make sure that the form you choose doesn't have added processed sugars.

Tips for Incorporating These Foods

Enjoy oatmeal for breakfast several times a week. Instead of sweetening it with sugar, use fresh fruits such as cherries or dark-colored berries. Boost the fiber content of your meals by including a green salad or a steamed vegetable, and snack on whole fruits with the skin. Vinegar can be used in a variety of homemade salad dressings.

Cherry Feta Grain Salad

This delicious cold grain salad is full of fiber. The dried cherries add a slight tart, yet sweet, flavor that goes well with the strong feta cheese.

INGREDIENTS | SERVES 4

2 cups wheat berries, cooked
¼ cup dried tart cherries
¼ cup feta cheese, crumbled
2 tablespoons fresh lemon juice
1 tablespoon olive oil
1 teaspoon fresh parsley, chopped
½ teaspoon sea salt
¼ teaspoon black pepper

1. In a large bowl, combine cooled wheat berries, cherries, and feta cheese.

2. Top with the lemon juice, olive oil, parsley, salt, and pepper. Toss to coat the salad evenly.

3. Refrigerate about 20 to 30 minutes and serve cold.

PER SERVING Calories: 249 | Fat: 6g | Sodium: 398mg | Carbohydrates: 43g | Fiber: 8g | Protein: 8g

Cherry Lime Mocktail

This drink has all the flavor of a fresh cocktail without the alcohol. It combines fresh cherries and lime with cherry juice for an antioxidant-rich beverage. You can pour it over ice with pieces of the fruit included, or shake it with ice in a cocktail shaker and strain before serving.

INGREDIENTS | SERVES 1

3 tart or sweet cherries, pitted

¼ of a fresh lime

4 ounces tart cherry juice

Smart Combinations

Fresh and 100 percent fruit juices can be a healthy choice, but they do contain natural sugars from the fruit. Pair a sweet drink such as the one described here with a protein and fiber-rich snack to help control your blood sugar and prevent a spike and a rapid drop.

1. In a glass or cocktail shaker, mull together the lime and fresh cherries. Break up the fruits until the juice is extracted.

2. Add the cherry juice and stir or shake the drink. Pour and serve cold.

PER SERVING Calories: 63 | Fat: 0g | Sodium: 5mg | Carbohydrates: 15g | Fiber: 0g | Protein: 0g

Cherry Vinaigrette

This dressing is delicious over a salad of greens topped with almonds.
It combines the benefits of vinegar and tart cherries for the control and prevention of diabetes.

INGREDIENTS | SERVES 6

2 cloves garlic, minced
3 tablespoons vinegar
3 tablespoons tart cherry juice
⅓ cup olive oil
½ teaspoon salt
¼ teaspoon pepper

1. In a small dish, whisk together the garlic, vinegar, and cherry juice. Slowly whisk in the olive oil.

2. Stir in the salt and pepper. Add more to taste if desired. Pour over a fresh green salad, toss to coat, and serve immediately.

PER SERVING Calories: 112 | Fat: 12g | Sodium: 195mg | Carbohydrates: 1g | Fiber: 0g | Protein: 0g

Autumn Oatmeal

Irish steel-cut oats provide a hearty breakfast that is full of fiber.
They take a little longer to cook than rolled oats, but the flavor and texture are worth the wait.

INGREDIENTS | SERVES 4

1 cup steel-cut oats
1 apple, diced
1 pear, diced
½ cup slivered almonds
1 teaspoon cinnamon

Sweeten It Without Sugar

When you stir in some of the fruit with the oatmeal just before it is done cooking, you will add more sweetness without adding sugar. The fruit, whether it is apples, pears, berries, or cherries, will cook down and soften slightly, adding even more flavor, and sometimes color, to your breakfast.

1. In a saucepan, combine 4 cups of water with the oats. Cook on medium-high heat, stirring often, until the oats begin to simmer and thicken. It will take about 30 to 40 minutes for the oats to cook completely.

2. At about 25 minutes of cooking time, stir half of the diced apple and half of the diced pear into the oatmeal. Continue to stir and cook for 5 more minutes if you prefer firmer oats, 7 to 10 more minutes if you prefer softer oats.

3. Remove the oatmeal from the heat and stir in the remaining fruit and the almonds. Divide into 4 bowls and sprinkle with cinnamon.

PER SERVING Calories: 284 | Fat: 10g | Sodium: 1mg | Carbohydrates: 45g | Fiber: 9g | Protein: 8g

Lentils and Brown Rice

In this recipe, lentils are cooked with flavorful seasonings and brown rice. It is a delicious meatless meal that is full of fiber. If you prefer a little extra spice, try topping it with hot sauce before serving!

INGREDIENTS | SERVES 4

1⅓ cups dried green lentils

2 to 3 cups chicken stock

1 teaspoon cumin

1 teaspoon chili powder

¾ cup brown rice

1 teaspoon salt

½ teaspoon black pepper

1. In a large saucepan, combine the lentils, 2 cups chicken stock, cumin, and chili powder. Bring the pot to a boil, then reduce heat and simmer for about 10 minutes.

2. Stir in the brown rice and add enough additional chicken stock to cover the lentils and rice. Cover the pan with a lid and simmer for about 20 to 30 minutes longer, until the lentils and rice are tender and the liquid has all been absorbed.

3. Remove the pan from the heat and stir in the salt and pepper. Serve hot.

PER SERVING Calories: 343 | Fat: 3g | Sodium: 853mg | Carbohydrates: 64g | Fiber: 11g | Protein: 18g

CHAPTER 17

Diarrhea

Diarrhea is uncomfortable and embarrassing, and if not corrected it can cause serious dehydration and health complications. Eating may be the last thing you think about when suffering from the condition, but some common foods have been associated with relieving the symptoms of diarrhea.

What Causes Diarrhea?

Diarrhea that lasts only one to two days can be caused by an infection from bacteria, a virus, or a parasite. It may occur because of a flu bug you have contracted or because you ate contaminated food or water. Food intolerances, such as lactose intolerance, and reactions to medications can also cause diarrhea. Long-lasting cases of diarrhea can be due to conditions that affect intestinal health, such as irritable bowel syndrome (Chapter 24).

FACT

Diarrhea occurs when food passes too quickly through your colon. Normally your colon absorbs liquid from the food you eat, resulting in semihard stool; if food passes through too quickly, this absorption does not have time to occur and the results are loose or watery bowel movements.

Nutrients That Prevent or Alleviate Diarrhea

Eating a low-fiber diet is important when you have diarrhea because these foods are easy to digest. Probiotics are live, active microorganisms that help to maintain gastrointestinal health and can prevent the occurrence of diarrhea. Since probiotics are found in dairy products and dairy products can aggravate diarrhea, they are more effective for prevention than for when you already have the condition.

Foods That Contain These Nutrients

Many experts still recommend the BRAT diet for diarrhea—bananas, rice, applesauce, and toast. Bananas help to bind stool, and the low-fiber white rice, cooked applesauce, and white toast are easy to digest. Clear broths and porridge can also help. In addition, garlic is considered an antimicrobial and may help to fight the infections that cause diarrhea, and ginger has been found to ease discomfort in the gastrointestinal tract.

Tips for Incorporating These Foods

Begin slowly with incorporating foods, but continue to drink fluids as often as possible to prevent dehydration. Cook broths with garlic or sip on ginger tea for added benefit. Add sliced banana to a rice pudding. Eat toast dry or with applesauce, and avoid adding butter or other fat to toast until your stomach begins to feel better.

QUESTION

Are there foods I should avoid if I have diarrhea?
Yes, the National Institutes of Health recommends avoiding caffeine, milk and milk products, greasy or sugary foods, and high-fiber foods. These can all irritate the condition, so it is important to eliminate them until you have recovered.

Garlic Broth Soup

Warm broths are one of the best foods for a stomach in distress.
This soup combines chicken stock with the benefits of garlic.

INGREDIENTS | SERVES 4

4½ cups chicken stock

4 cloves garlic, finely minced

½ teaspoon dried rosemary

½ teaspoon dried thyme

Salt and pepper, to taste

Ready for More?

If you feel your stomach is up to a hearty meal, try adding 1 cup of long-grain white rice to the broth and simmer the soup until the rice is cooked. Or you can add 1 cup egg noodles and cook for about 5 to 7 minutes or until tender.

1. In a soup pot, combine the chicken stock, garlic, rosemary, and thyme. Bring to a boil. Reduce heat and simmer for about 10 minutes.

2. Taste the soup and add more salt and pepper if necessary. Often the chicken stock provides enough salty flavor.

3. Divide into mugs and sip to ease your stomach.

PER SERVING Calories: 28 | Fat: 0g | Sodium: 574mg | Carbohydrates: 2g | Fiber: 0g | Protein: 5g

Buttered Noodles

A plain white spaghetti or egg noodle can be a good meal to start with as your stomach begins to feel better. The butter is added only for flavor, so go easy on it. Too much greasy fat can aggravate diarrhea.

INGREDIENTS | SERVES 2

2 ounces egg noodles
1 tablespoon butter
1 clove garlic, minced
¼ teaspoon salt

1. In a large saucepan, bring 3 cups of water to a boil. Add in the egg noodles and cook until tender. Drain and set aside.

2. In a deep skillet, melt the butter over medium heat and add the garlic immediately after it has melted. Stir and cook for about 30 seconds.

3. Turn off the heat and add the noodles to the skillet. Toss to coat with the butter and garlic. Sprinkle with salt and serve warm.

PER SERVING Calories: 160 | Fat: 7g | Sodium: 337mg | Carbohydrates: 20g | Fiber: 1g | Protein: 4g

Ginger Tea

Ginger tea is a simple drink that sends a warming, comforting sensation through your body. The ginger can ease an upset stomach and have you on your way to recovery.

INGREDIENTS | SERVES 4

1 (2-inch) piece fresh ginger
5 cups water

1. Carefully peel the skin off the ginger using a sharp knife and slice it into thin pieces.

2. Pour the water into a large pot and add the ginger. Bring to a boil, reduce heat and simmer for 10 to 15 minutes.

3. Ladle the tea into mugs, leaving the ginger in the bottom of the pot. Serve hot.

PER SERVING Calories: 1 | Fat: 0g | Sodium: 0mg | Carbohydrates: 0g | Fiber: 0g | Protein: 0g

Ginger Applesauce

Applesauce provides a bland, easy-to-digest food. This homemade version uses ginger, which eases an upset stomach. Making it yourself allows you to spice it up with cinnamon or add a little brown sugar if you desire.

INGREDIENTS | SERVES 4

4 apples
1 tablespoon fresh ginger, grated

The Right Apple

Different apples are good for different things. Some are better for eating fresh while others cook up wonderfully when added to recipes. For a great applesauce, try McIntosh, Crispin, or Empire apples if they are available in your area.

1. Wash the apples under running water, and then peel and core them using a sharp knife. Cut the apples into medium-size chunks.

2. Place the apples and ginger in a medium saucepan and cover with ¾ cup of water. Cook on medium-high heat, covered, until apples are tender, about 20 minutes.

3. Remove from the heat and mash with a potato masher or fork until a slightly chunky sauce results. Serve warm or refrigerate for 2 hours and serve cold.

PER SERVING Calories: 78 | Fat: 0g | Sodium: 0mg | Carbohydrates: 21g | Fiber: 2g | Protein: 0g

Banana Rice

Plain white rice with bananas is a simple dish that is easy to digest. In this recipe, the bananas are slightly sautéed until warm, and then added to the rice for a mildly sweet side dish or a simple meal to help you get well soon!

INGREDIENTS | SERVES 4

1 tablespoon butter
1 cup long-grain white rice
1 banana

1. In a large pot, melt ½ tablespoon of butter. Add the rice and cook, stirring, for 1 to 2 minutes. Add 2 cups of water, cover, and simmer for 15 to 18 minutes until tender.

2. Meanwhile, chop the banana into small pieces. In a skillet, melt the other ½ tablespoon of butter. Add the banana and cook until browned and softened.

3. Add the banana to the rice and toss together. Serve warm or at room temperature.

PER SERVING Calories: 220 | Fat: 3g | Sodium: 23mg | Carbohydrates: 44g | Fiber: 1g | Protein: 4g

CHAPTER 18

Fibromyalgia

The pain and fatigue that result from fibromyalgia can make it difficult to accomplish daily tasks. The condition affects an estimated 10 million Americans and is more common in women than men.

What Is Fibromyalgia?

Fibromyalgia is a chronic pain disorder, and because there is no known cause, it is referred to as a syndrome rather than a disease. Individuals with the syndrome experience widespread pain throughout the body. Tender points that are painful when pressure is applied are present in different areas of the body—for example, the back of the head, tops of the shoulders, and sides of the hips. In addition, fatigue and sleep disturbances are common symptoms.

ESSENTIAL

Other theories for the causes of fibromyalgia include stress and stress-related syndromes, such as post-traumatic stress syndrome; a dysfunction in the body's ability to produce dopamine; an abnormal serotonin metabolism (the neurotransmitter responsible for sleep, concentration, and pain); deficient growth hormones; and psychological issues.

The exact cause is unknown, but many researchers believe the pain results from increased sensitivity to pain signals in the brain. This changes the chemicals of the brain and causes an overreaction to pain signals in the body. Fibromyalgia may coexist with other conditions, such as chronic fatigue syndrome (Chapter 11), depression (Chapter 15), and irritable bowel syndrome (Chapter 24).

Nutrients That Prevent or Alleviate Fibromyalgia

Anthocyanins give plants a deep red or purple color and can inhibit substances called cyclooxygenase-1 and -2 (COX-1 and COX-2), which are pro-inflammatory. This means that anthocyanins can act like over-the-counter pain medications such as ibuprofen and may help reduce the pain associated with fibromyalgia. Curcumin is a food substance associated with decreased inflammation, which may also benefit the symptoms of fibromyalgia.

Foods That Contain These Nutrients

Eat dark-colored fruits for plenty of anthocyanins. Try tart cherries, black-berries, blueberries, red grapes, and red plums. Cherries and berries make flavorful and healthy smoothies, and can easily be used to top cereals or salads. Enjoy plums and grapes as a snack, or chop and mix them into your summer drinks such as sangria or a nonalcoholic version made with juices.

FACT

In 2007 several studies described the positive effects of anthocyanins. In one study, black raspberries, which contain the highest amounts of anthocyanins, inhibited cancer in rat esophaguses by 30 to 60 percent and colon cancer by 80 percent. It was discovered that the black rasp-berries not only stalled the growth of cancer cells but also accelerated the cell turnover, causing the cancer cells to die faster.

Curcumin is found in the spice turmeric. Turmeric is used in yellow mustard and curry powders. Use yellow mustard as a condiment for sandwiches or in homemade dips and salad dressings. Add turmeric or curry to your spice rubs for beef, chicken, or fish.

Ricotta Stuffed Plums

This sweet treat combines a slightly sweetened ricotta cheese with nutrient-rich dark-colored plums. It is ideal for a midday snack or as a healthy dessert to end a meal.

INGREDIENTS | SERVES 4

4 red or purple plums

1 cup ricotta cheese

4 teaspoons muscovado sugar

1 teaspoon ground cinnamon

Mint leaves (optional)

Decorative Display

When cutting your plums, use a knife to cut a zigzag design along the edge. You can also put the ricotta cheese in a large cake decorating bag with a star tube for filling the plums. This makes for a much more elegant presentation if you decide to turn this healthy recipe into a course for your next dinner party.

1. Wash plums and cut in half. Remove the pit. Gently remove some of the flesh to create a small cup for the ricotta.

2. In a bowl, combine the ricotta cheese, sugar, and cinnamon. Stir well to blend the sugar.

3. Scoop an equal amount of ricotta cheese into each plum. Garnish with some mint leaves if you have them, and serve immediately.

PER SERVING Calories: 128 | Fat: 5g | Sodium: 78mg | Carbohydrates: 14g | Fiber: 1g | Protein: 7g

Curry Chicken with Pineapple

This quick dish combines spicy curry with sweet pineapple. It can be made into a vegetarian dish by simply omitting the chicken. Serve it on a bed of brown rice.

INGREDIENTS | SERVES 4

2 tablespoons olive oil

3 cloves garlic, minced

1 onion, chopped

3 cups chicken, cubed

2 cups broccoli florets

⅓ cup pineapple juice

1 tablespoon curry powder

1 tablespoon cornstarch

1 cup pineapple chunks

1. In a deep skillet, heat the olive oil. Add the garlic and onion and cook for about 1 minute. Add the chicken.

2. When the chicken begins to brown, add the broccoli and cook until the chicken is cooked through and no pieces are pink in the middle.

3. In a small bowl, combine the pineapple juice, curry powder, and cornstarch. Pour over the chicken and cook on medium-high to allow the sauce to thicken.

4. Add in the pineapple chunks and continue to cook until the sauce has thickened and coats the meat and vegetables. Serve hot.

PER SERVING Calories: 307 | Fat: 14g | Sodium: 97mg | Carbohydrates: 17g | Fiber: 2g | Protein: 29g

Apple Grape Salad

This recipe uses red grapes, which contain anthocyanins that may reduce pain and inflammation common with fibromyalgia. Make it even more delicious by mixing the salad with 1 cup of cold brown or wild rice.

INGREDIENTS | SERVES 4

2 Granny Smith apples, chopped

1 cup seedless red grapes, halved

¼ cup celery, sliced

⅓ cup walnuts, chopped

1 tablespoon mayonnaise

2 tablespoons Greek yogurt

2 teaspoons muscovado sugar

½ teaspoon cinnamon

1. In a bowl, combine the apples, grapes, celery, and walnuts.

2. Add the mayonnaise, Greek yogurt, sugar, and cinnamon. Stir well to coat the fruit, and serve.

PER SERVING Calories: 142 | Fat: 8g | Sodium: 35mg | Carbohydrates: 19g | Fiber: 3g | Protein: 2g

Soggy Salad

Salads that have either a mayonnaise or yogurt base should be served soon after making. Thirty minutes to a couple of hours in the fridge allows flavors to blend, but by the next day your ingredients could be soggy, and separated water could be in the bottom of the bowl. Serve them the same day you make them for best results.

Cherry French Toast

This special breakfast uses both tart cherry juice and tart cherries.
Blueberries make the perfect substitute or addition if you have them on hand.

INGREDIENTS | SERVES 4

½ cup tart cherries, pitted and chopped
1 tablespoon demerara sugar
1 egg, beaten
½ teaspoon vanilla
2 tablespoons tart cherry juice
4 slices whole-grain bread
1 tablespoon butter
4 tablespoons pecans, chopped

1. In a small saucepan, combine the cherries, sugar, and 1 tablespoon of water. Simmer on medium-high heat 5 to 7 minutes, until the cherries break down and the juice thickens. Set aside.

2. Combine the egg, vanilla, and cherry juice in a shallow baking dish. Arrange each slice of bread in the dish. Flip to coat evenly and allow to sit for 2 to 3 minutes.

3. Melt the butter in a skillet. Cook the bread slices for about 3 minutes on each side or until nicely browned.

4. Put each slice on a plate; top with ¼ of the cherry syrup and pecans. Serve warm.

PER SERVING Calories: 183 | Fat: 10g | Sodium: 149mg | Carbohydrates: 18g | Fiber: 3g | Protein: 6g

Cherry Berry Juice Cocktail

This recipe combines fresh fruit and fruit juices for a nonalcoholic drink that is similar to sangria.
Serve it over ice and garnish with a leaf of mint. Be sure to eat the delicious fruit when your drink is gone!

INGREDIENTS | SERVES 8

1 cup red seedless grapes, halved
½ cup fresh blackberries
½ cup fresh blueberries
1 red plum, sliced
2 cups tart cherry juice
2 cups 100% cranberry juice
1 liter club soda

1. In a large pitcher or punch bowl, combine all of the fruit.

2. Pour in the cherry juice, cranberry juice, and club soda. Stir well and ladle both juice and fruit into each glass over ice. Serve cold.

PER SERVING Calories: 89 | Fat: 0g | Sodium: 33mg | Carbohydrates: 23g | Fiber: 1g | Protein: 1g

Make It Sangria

You can turn this recipe into a sangria using wine if you like. One option is to replace the club soda with a bottle of sweet red or rosé wine. If you prefer more of a sangria spritzer, use 1 bottle of the wine, half the club soda, and 1 cup of each of the juices.

CHAPTER 19

Headaches

Headaches are caused by a variety of factors, including stress or even sleeping in an awkward position. Some headaches, such as migraines, can be severe and debilitating. Food and nutrition have been linked to both the causes and the prevention and treatment of headaches.

Types of Head Pain

A headache is classified as any pain in the head, scalp area, or neck. The most common types are those associated with tension that results from stress, anxiety, or depression. Headaches can also occur due to overexertion or improper alignment when sitting at a desk or while sleeping, and sinus headaches often accompany a sinus infection or cold. Migraine headaches are much more severe; they include nausea and can affect vision, such as causing light flashes during the "aura" period preceding or during the headache.

FACT

The pain of a headache does not actually come from your brain. The brain tissue does not contain pain receptors and so is impervious to pain. The pain actually comes from the pain-sensitive areas around the brain, including several areas in the head and neck.

Nutrients That Alleviate Head Pain

Low levels of the mineral magnesium have been linked to headaches. Magnesium has many functions in the body, including reducing pain and calming the central nervous system, and thus reduces stress levels. It is involved in the regulation and production of the brain chemical serotonin, and it helps to regulate blood sugar levels. Current research suggests that rapid drops in blood sugar may be one trigger for migraine sufferers. Some studies have also found a link between increased riboflavin, a B vitamin, and decreased migraine headaches.

Foods That Contain These Nutrients

Pumpkin seeds, Swiss chard, peanuts, and peanut butter all contain magnesium. Cremini mushrooms, spinach, and eggs supply riboflavin. Choose spinach, almonds, and almond butter and you will get both magnesium and riboflavin.

Tips for Incorporating These Foods

Pumpkin seeds and nuts make great toppings for a leafy green salad that also includes plenty of spinach. You can top toast with peanut butter or almond butter or add a tablespoon to your morning smoothie. Try sautéing Swiss chard in olive oil with salt and pepper, and add it to scrambled eggs.

ALERT

Tyramine is an amino acid that has been found to cause migraines in some people. It can be found in fermented and aged foods, including aged cheese, processed meats, and soy sauce. If you are trying to identify foods that trigger your headaches, pay attention to your tyramine intake and experiment with reducing the foods you eat that contain it.

Nutty Fruit Toast

This quick breakfast provides both magnesium and riboflavin. Use high-fiber, whole-grain toast and you will better stabilize your blood sugar and prevent a rapid drop that is sometimes associated with headaches.

INGREDIENTS | SERVES 1

1 slice whole-grain bread
1 tablespoon almond butter
1 tablespoon slivered almonds
½ tablespoon pumpkin seeds, shelled
2 fresh strawberries, diced

1. Adjust your toaster to the desired setting and add the bread. Once toasted, spread the almond butter over the slice of bread.

2. Sprinkle the almonds and pumpkin seeds over the almond butter. Add the strawberries and eat right away while the almond butter is still gooey and warm.

PER SERVING Calories: 252 | Fat: 17g | Sodium: 135mg | Carbohydrates: 19g | Fiber: 4g | Protein: 9g

Egg Panini with Spinach

A simple egg sandwich makes a delicious breakfast or lunch. Turning it into a hot, grilled panini only makes it better! This recipe includes fresh spinach for even more riboflavin and other healthy nutrients.

INGREDIENTS | SERVES 1

½ tablespoon unsalted butter

1 egg

¼ teaspoon salt

¼ teaspoon black pepper

¼ teaspoon garlic powder

3-inch piece of whole-grain baguette

½ cup spinach leaves

No Panini Press?

You don't need a panini press to make this sandwich. Simply place the constructed sandwich in a standard skillet or in a grill pan. Place a small piece of foil over the top and then place another, heavy skillet on top of the sandwich. Press down slightly to sear and heat the sandwich through.

1. In a skillet, melt ½ tablespoon of butter. Crack the egg into the skillet. Discard the shell and sprinkle the egg with the salt, pepper, and garlic powder. Cook 1 to 2 minutes and flip. Cook until desired doneness.

2. Split the baguette in half and place the spinach inside. Put the egg on top of the spinach, close the sandwich and place it on a panini press. Close the press and cook for 2 to 3 minutes. Remove and serve warm.

PER SERVING Calories: 302 | Fat: 14g | Sodium: 975mg | Carbohydrates: 35g | Fiber: 5g | Protein: 13g

Easy Trail Mix

A quick snack between meals is the best way to keep your blood sugar from dropping, which has been found to cause headaches in some people. This trail mix is easy to toss together and provides carbohydrates along with protein and healthy fat.

INGREDIENTS | SERVES 4

½ cup raw almonds

½ cup unsalted, dry-roasted peanuts

2 tablespoons hulled pumpkin seeds

½ cup dried cranberries

¼ cup old-fashioned rolled oats

Combine all ingredients in a bowl and mix well. Divide into transportable containers to carry with you when you need a snack.

PER SERVING Calories: 307 | Fat: 21g | Sodium: 4mg | Carbohydrates: 25g | Fiber: 5g | Protein: 10g

Mushroom, Garlic, and Spinach Pizza

This pizza is so flavorful that you will never miss the cheese. Choose your favorite whole-grain pizza dough and roll it thin. Coat the bottom with a little cornmeal before placing it on the baking sheet for a crispy crust.

INGREDIENTS | SERVES 4

1 head of garlic
1½ tablespoons olive oil
½ cup cremini mushrooms, sliced
½ cup white button mushrooms, sliced
1 tablespoon fresh rosemary, chopped
½ teaspoon salt
¼ teaspoon black pepper
1 (14-inch) pizza crust
1 cup fresh spinach leaves

1. Preheat the oven to 400°F. Carefully slice the top quarter off the head of garlic to expose the cloves. Place the head of garlic on a sheet of aluminum foil and drizzle with ½ tablespoon of olive oil. Wrap the garlic and bake for 45 minutes.

2. In a skillet, heat the remaining 1 tablespoon of olive oil on medium-high heat. Add the mushrooms. Cook 3 to 5 minutes or until browned and softened. Add the rosemary, salt, and pepper. Cook 1 minute more and turn off the heat.

3. Remove the garlic from the foil and squeeze the flesh into a bowl, careful to remove any skins that may have fallen in. Using a spoon, spread the roasted garlic over the pizza crust.

4. Top the garlic with the mushrooms and then the fresh spinach leaves. Bake for 15 minutes, or until the crust is browned and cooked through and the spinach has slightly wilted. Slice and serve warm.

PER SERVING Calories: 372 | Fat: 10g | Sodium: 842mg | Carbohydrates: 58g | Fiber: 3g | Protein: 12g

Cremini and Chard Frittata

A frittata is a simple egg dish that is great for any meal of the day. Eat it for breakfast or pair it with soup or a green salad for lunch or dinner. A frittata is cooked on the stovetop and then baked, so be sure to use an oven-safe skillet.

INGREDIENTS | SERVES 6

1 tablespoon olive oil

2 cloves garlic, minced

1 cup Swiss chard, chopped

¾ cup cremini mushrooms, sliced

5 eggs

⅓ cup milk

½ teaspoon salt

¼ teaspoon black pepper

½ teaspoon smoked paprika

½ teaspoon dried rosemary

Frittata Substitutions

The frittata is another versatile dish that can be altered to meet your preferences. Experiment with different vegetables, such as green and red bell peppers and thinly sliced potatoes. If you have determined that aged cheese has no influence on your migraines, you can also add grated Parmesan cheese.

1. Preheat oven to 400°F. In a deep skillet, heat the olive oil over medium-high heat. Add the garlic, chard, and mushrooms. Cover with a lid and cook for 3 to 5 minutes or until the vegetables are tender.

2. In a separate bowl, whisk together the eggs, milk, salt, pepper, paprika, and rosemary. Pour the egg mixture over the vegetables in the skillet. Bake for about 7 minutes, or until the center is set.

3. Allow the frittata to cool for about 5 minutes, then cut into slices and serve warm.

PER SERVING Calories: 93 | Fat: 7g | Sodium: 77mg | Carbohydrates: 2g | Fiber: 0g | Protein: 6g

CHAPTER 20

Heartburn

Heartburn can be caused by foods that are acidic or greasy. For those who suffer from the condition, changing dietary habits along with incorporating foods that alleviate heartburn make relief and prevention possible.

What Is Heartburn?

Heartburn results from acid in the esophagus. The esophagus is a tube that carries food from your mouth to your stomach. When acid from the stomach backs up into the esophagus, it causes heartburn. It is characterized by a burning sensation in your chest that is often painful and uncomfortable, and intensifies when you lie down.

Food is a major cause of heartburn, but it may also be caused by pregnancy, alcohol, and medication. In addition, some individuals have a condition where the muscles of the esophagus do not close tightly enough, resulting in a backup of acid. This is called gastroesophageal reflux disease, or GERD.

Nutrients That Alleviate Heartburn

Specific anti-inflammatory compounds in some foods help to relieve gastrointestinal distress, including heartburn. The digestive enzymes papain and bromelain may also help to relieve heartburn.

ESSENTIAL

Other things you can do to avoid heartburn include waiting two to three hours after eating to lie down, avoid wearing tight or restrictive clothing around your waist, elevating your head a few inches while you sleep, eating smaller and more frequent meals, and relaxing to reduce your stress levels.

Foods That Contain These Nutrients

Ginger contains gingerols, which are the anti-inflammatory compound related to reducing heartburn. Fennel seed has been found to counteract muscle spasms of the gastrointestinal tract, which can also relieve heartburn. Papaya contains the digestive enzyme papain and fresh pineapple contains bromelain.

Other nutritional tips to help alleviate heartburn include eating fiber from vegetables and whole grains, and drinking plenty of fluids to keep your digestive system working properly. You should also try to avoid using fats in cooking and incorporate exercise into your lifestyle.

ALERT

While there are a few foods that relieve heartburn, there are many more that cause it. If heartburn is a problem for you, incorporate the foods mentioned in the chapter, but also reduce your intake of high-fat and spicy foods, tomatoes, citrus, garlic, onion, milk, coffee, tea, chocolate, and mints.

Tips for Incorporating These Foods

Fresh ginger can be added to stir-fry vegetables and soups. Along with fennel seed, it can also be used to make a hot tea. Eat papaya and pineapple with your breakfast or cut it into chunks and transport it to work for lunch in a resealable container.

Grilled Pineapple

When you have the grill heated for your outdoor cooking, why not end the meal with some delicious grilled pineapple? If you've never had grilled pineapple before, be prepared to discover a new favorite dessert!

INGREDIENTS | SERVES 8

1 fresh pineapple
Olive oil
1 teaspoon cinnamon

1. Peel and core the pineapple with a sharp knife. Slice the pineapple into 8 equal slices. If you cut the pineapple in half lengthwise to core it, create 8 slices with each half for a total of 16 half slices.

2. Brush the grill with olive oil and place each slice of pineapple on the hot grill. Close the lid and cook for about 5 minutes or until grill marks begin to show on the underside.

3. Flip the pineapple and cook the same amount on the other side. Sprinkle each slice with the cinnamon. Remove from the grill and serve warm.

PER SERVING Calories: 57 | Fat: 0g | Sodium: 1mg | Carbohydrates: 15g | Fiber: 0g | Protein: 1g

Ginger Pineapple Papaya Juice

Fresh homemade juice is a delicious way to start your day, and this recipe combines all the heartburn-fighting power of ginger, papaya, and pineapple. You will need a juicer for this recipe.

INGREDIENTS | SERVES 1

2 cups fresh pineapple chunks

1 cup fresh papaya chunks

1-inch piece fresh ginger, peeled

No Juicer?

If you don't own a juicer, you can re-create this same flavor combination as a smoothie. Try freezing your pineapple before making the drink and combine the pineapple, papaya, and a grated ½-inch piece of ginger in the blender. Pulse until all ingredients are puréed. Add ½ cup milk or yogurt if desired.

1. Using the plunger, press the pineapple, papaya, and ginger through the juicer. Once the juice has been extracted and is in the cup, stir well to mix the flavors.

2. Add ice and drink immediately.

PER SERVING Calories: 205 | Fat: 1g | Sodium: 8mg | Carbohydrates: 53g | Fiber: 0g | Protein: 3g

Tropical Oatmeal

This breakfast is the perfect choice when you need a hearty, comforting meal to warm you up, but want a summery, tropical twist. It combines fruits that contain the digestive enzymes that help relieve heartburn.

INGREDIENTS | SERVES 1

½ cup old-fashioned oats

¼ cup fresh pineapple, diced

¼ cup fresh papaya, diced

1 tablespoon unsweetened, shredded coconut

1 tablespoon raw cashews, chopped

1 tablespoon muscovado sugar (optional)

1. Bring 1 cup water to boil in a saucepan. Add the oats and cook, stirring, for about 5 minutes or until thick and tender.

2. Transfer the oats to a bowl and top with the pineapple, papaya, and coconut. Stir to incorporate. Sprinkle on the cashews and sugar if using and serve hot.

PER SERVING Calories: 275 | Fat: 11g | Sodium: 7mg | Carbohydrates: 41g | Fiber: 6g | Protein: 8g

Pineapple Chicken with Ginger

This sweet and tangy main course is delicious when served over rice.
You can also make a flavorful salad by serving it over a bed of mixed greens.

INGREDIENTS | SERVES 4

1 tablespoon olive oil

3 cups raw chicken, cubed

1 red bell pepper, sliced

1 cup fresh pea pods

1-inch piece ginger, peeled and grated

½ cup pineapple juice

1 cup fresh pineapple, cubed

1 teaspoon cornstarch

1 teaspoon salt

½ teaspoon black pepper

¼ teaspoon crushed red pepper

1. Heat the oil in a skillet over medium-high heat. Add the chicken and cook until slightly browned, but not completely cooked through, for about 5 minutes.

2. Add the bell pepper and pea pods and continue cooking until the chicken is cooked through and the vegetables become tender, about 5 to 7 minutes more. Add the ginger and turn the heat to low.

3. In a small dish, dissolve the cornstarch in the pineapple juice. Pour the juice over the chicken. Return the heat to medium and continue to cook until the sauce thickens.

4. Add the fresh pineapple, salt, black pepper, and red pepper. Stir to coat with the sauce. Remove the pan from the heat; divide the food into 4 portions and serve warm.

PER SERVING Calories: 246 | Fat: 11g | Sodium: 672mg | Carbohydrates: 12g | Fiber: 1g | Protein: 25g

Cherry Fennel Scones

Fennel seed adds a slight licorice flavor to foods and it goes well with sweet baked goods. These scones are made with white whole-wheat flour for a healthy, hearty breakfast.

INGREDIENTS | SERVES 8

1¾ cups white whole-wheat flour

2¼ teaspoons baking powder

2 tablespoons muscovado sugar

½ teaspoon salt

¼ cup unsalted butter, cold

½ cup dried tart cherries, chopped

1 tablespoon fennel seed

1 teaspoon vanilla

½ to ¾ cup milk or heavy cream

2 tablespoons raw or demerara sugar

Liquid for Baked Goods

You have likely seen recipes for baked goods that list a range for the amount of liquid needed. This is because such factors as elevation and humidity affect how dry a batter or dough may be and the final baking results. Begin with the minimum amount listed and gradually add more by the tablespoon until the described consistency is reached.

1. Preheat the oven to 400°F. Grease a baking sheet and set aside.

2. In a large bowl, stir together the flour, baking powder, muscovado sugar, and salt. Cut the butter into small cubes and add to the bowl. Use 2 knives or a pastry blender to mix and cut the dough until the butter is blended into pea-size pieces.

3. Add the cherries, fennel seed, and vanilla. Gradually pour in the milk or cream and stir until the dough comes together. It should be just moist enough to form a ball and be rolled out, not sticky. Remove from the bowl and place on a floured surface.

4. Gently knead the dough for about 30 seconds and form into a ball. Flatten or roll out the circle until it reaches ½-inch thickness. Cut into 8 triangular pieces.

5. Place the scones on the baking sheet and sprinkle each with the raw sugar, gently pressing it into the top. Bake for about 15 minutes or until the edges are slightly browned. Allow the scones to rest on a cooling rack and serve warm or at room temperature.

PER SERVING Calories: 174 | Fat: 7g | Sodium: 290mg | Carbohydrates: 26g | Fiber: 4g | Protein: 4g

CHAPTER 21

High Blood Pressure

High blood pressure is a risk factor for several medical conditions and diseases. There is a strong relationship between food and blood pressure. By incorporating some foods with specific nutrients into your diet, you can control your high blood pressure.

What Is High Blood Pressure?

Blood pressure is a measure of the amount of pressure the blood exerts on the artery walls when it is being pumped through the body by the heart. Too much pressure can result in damage and health issues.

Blood pressure is measured in millimeters of mercury and is reported using two numbers. The top number, or the systolic blood pressure, measures the pressure during the beat of the heart. The bottom number, the diastolic blood pressure, measures the pressure between beats when the heart is at rest.

ESSENTIAL

Blood pressure is usually measured on your upper arm. It is measured on the inside of the elbow at the brachial artery. The brachial artery is the major artery of the arm and carries the blood away from the heart.

A blood pressure that is greater than 140 over 90 is classified as high blood pressure, or hypertension. With high blood pressure your heart has to work harder to pump blood, which can lead to a heart attack, stroke, and kidney failure. This makes it very important to incorporate foods into your diet that help control it.

Nutrients That Prevent or Reduce High Blood Pressure

Potassium and magnesium help to keep blood pressure within normal levels by creating a better ratio with sodium intake and balancing its effects on blood pressure. Low calcium intake may lead to increased risk for high blood pressure. According to Health Publications from Harvard Medical School, the exact reason is still unclear, but it may be because low calcium causes the body to retain sodium and the sodium could increase blood pressure.

A food compound called phthalide has the potential to dilate arteries by relaxing the muscles that surround them. This allows for more blood flow and can result in reduced blood pressure.

Foods That Contain These Nutrients

Celery has been linked to reduced blood pressure because it contains phthalides and potassium, as well as some magnesium and calcium. Yogurt contains calcium, magnesium, and potassium.

Excess sodium is linked to high blood pressure and celery contains about 100 milligrams per 1 cup chopped. More research is needed, but celery is widely used to treat high blood pressure in Chinese medicine. Thus far, the small amount of sodium doesn't seem to outweigh the other beneficial nutrients it contains when it comes to high blood pressure.

Eat potatoes with the skin and bananas for potassium and magnesium. If you like nuts, go for almonds, which provide calcium and magnesium. Try dried apricots and avocados for even more potassium.

Tips for Incorporating These Foods

Baked potatoes make a delicious side dish for any meal, or you can turn them into a meal themselves by adding beans, broccoli, or other healthy toppings. Bananas make a great on-the-go snack, or try making your own trail mix with dried apricots and almonds. Eat fresh celery and fill it with almond butter for more blood-pressure-lowering power.

Almond Stuffed Celery

Celery makes an ideal base for all kinds of tasty ingredients. This recipe takes advantage of using almonds to add a little calcium and magnesium for combating high blood pressure.

INGREDIENTS | SERVES 4

8 (3-inch) pieces celery
½ cup almond butter
¼ cup raw almonds, chopped

Choosing Almond Butter

With nut butters increasing in popularity, there are a variety of almond butters available on the market. Choose the most natural option by selecting those made only with ground roasted or raw almonds. Check the ingredient labels carefully for added sugars and salt.

1. Fill each piece of celery with 1 tablespoon of almond butter. Sprinkle with chopped almonds and gently press the almonds into the almond butter.

2. Refrigerate the stuffed celery for at least 30 minutes to keep the almond butter from being too soft and running out of the celery. Serve cold.

PER SERVING Calories: 237 | Fat: 21g | Sodium: 35mg | Carbohydrates: 9g | Fiber: 2g | Protein: 6g

Easy Guacamole

Guacamole at home is a lot easier than you might think. Use this as a dip, with your homemade tacos, or as a topping for your baked potato!

INGREDIENTS | SERVES 4

1 ripe avocado
1 tomato, chopped
2 green onions, sliced, greens reserved
1 clove garlic, minced
2 tablespoons fresh lime juice
4 pickled jalapeño slices, minced
1 teaspoon salt

Mild or Hot

If you prefer a mild guacamole, simply leave out the pickled jalapeños. If you are looking for more ways to spice it up, consider adding crushed red pepper or hot sauce. You can sprinkle in ½ teaspoon of the sauce from a can of chipotles in adobo sauce, or chop up a chipotle and add it to the guacamole before mixing.

1. Halve the avocado and remove the pit. Scrape the pulp out of the shell with a spoon and place in a medium-size mixing bowl. Add the chopped tomato and onion. Slice the onion greens and set aside for garnish.

2. Add the garlic clove, lime juice, and jalapeños. Stir together, gently mashing the avocado to create a creamy yet chunky dip. Add the salt. Refrigerate for at least 30 minutes.

3. Transfer to a serving bowl and garnish with the reserved sliced onion greens.

PER SERVING Calories: 91 | Fat: 7g | Sodium: 662mg | Carbohydrates: 7g | Fiber: 4g | Protein: 1g

Apricot and Celery Salad

*This light and flavorful salad makes a great addition to any breakfast or lunch.
It combines dried apricots, celery, almonds, and yogurt, providing many nutrients associated
with reducing and preventing high blood pressure.*

INGREDIENTS | SERVES 4

1½ cups celery, sliced

½ cup dried apricots, chopped

2 tablespoons plain Greek yogurt

1 tablespoon fresh lemon juice

2 teaspoons honey

2 tablespoons slivered almonds

1. In a medium-size mixing bowl, toss together the celery and dried apricots. In a small bowl, whisk together the yogurt, lemon juice, and honey.

2. Pour the yogurt sauce over the celery and apricots. Toss to coat evenly and then top with slivered almonds. Serve immediately, or refrigerate for 30 minutes to 1 hour before serving.

PER SERVING Calories: 81 | Fat: 2g | Sodium: 36mg | Carbohydrates: 16g | Fiber: 2g | Protein: 2g

Mustard Potato Salad

This potato salad uses less mayonnaise and incorporates spicy brown mustard for flavor. It makes an ideal side dish for grilled summer meats and vegetables!

INGREDIENTS | SERVES 4

5 medium red potatoes
½ cup celery, diced
½ cup red bell pepper, diced
2 tablespoons onion, grated
3 tablespoons mayonnaise
1 tablespoon spicy brown mustard
1 teaspoon hot sauce
1 teaspoon garlic powder
1 teaspoon salt
½ teaspoon black pepper

1. Scrub the potatoes under running water to remove any dirt and place them in a large saucepan. Cover the potatoes with water. Place a lid on the potatoes and bring to a boil over medium-high heat.

2. Allow the potatoes to boil 1 to 2 minutes and turn off the heat. Let them sit in the hot water, covered, for 45 to 60 minutes. Drain the potatoes; allow them to cool to the touch. Remove the skins if desired and chop into bite-size cubes.

3. Place the potatoes in a large bowl and add the celery, bell pepper, onion, mayonnaise, mustard, and hot sauce. Stir until everything is combined.

4. Stir in the garlic powder, salt, and pepper. Add more to taste. Refrigerate for 3 to 4 hours and serve cold.

PER SERVING Calories: 243 | Fat: 4g | Sodium: 752mg | Carbohydrates: 48g | Fiber: 5g | Protein: 6g

Tex-Mex Breakfast Baked Potato

Who says that baked potatoes can't be served at breakfast? This recipe combines all the flavors of a hearty morning meal and spices them up with salad and chopped avocado!

INGREDIENTS | SERVES 4

4 baking potatoes
1½ tablespoons olive oil
1 small onion, diced
1 green bell pepper, diced
4 eggs
½ teaspoon black pepper
1 cup prepared salsa
½ avocado, diced

1. Preheat the oven to 400°F. Scrub each potato under running water and dry. Divide ½ tablespoon of the olive oil over the potatoes and rub over the skins. Pierce each potato multiple times with a fork. Place on a baking sheet or directly on the oven rack and bake for about 45 minutes, or until potatoes are tender.

2. About 10 minutes before the potatoes are done, heat 1 tablespoon of olive oil in a skillet and add onion and bell pepper. Cook about 2 minutes or until they begin to brown and become tender.

3. Whisk the eggs slightly in a separate bowl and add the eggs to the onions and peppers. Cook over medium heat, scrambling the eggs. Once eggs reach your desired consistency, sprinkle with pepper.

4. Allow the potatoes to cool for about 5 minutes, then cut a slit in each, being careful of steam burns. Top each potato with ¼ of the scrambled eggs, ¼ cup salsa, and ¼ of the avocado. Serve warm.

PER SERVING Calories: 341 | Fat: 14g | Sodium: 211mg | Carbohydrates: 44g | Fiber: 7g | Protein: 12g

CHAPTER 22

High Cholesterol

Cholesterol is a fat-like substance that plays an important role in normal body function. However, when too much cholesterol is present, it can build up on the walls of arteries and increase your risk for a heart attack.

What Is High Cholesterol?

Cholesterol has several different components, and determining if you have high cholesterol requires that you get a blood test called a lipoprotein profile. Total cholesterol is a measure that combines all of the components of blood cholesterol. If your total cholesterol is 240 milligrams per deciliter or higher, you are considered high risk.

FACT

The American Heart Association and the National Institutes of Health not only identify high levels of blood cholesterol, but also borderline high levels. If you are in the borderline high category, you are at risk for high cholesterol and it is time to take action to improve your lipoprotein profile. A total cholesterol reading of 200 to 239 mg/dL is borderline high.

Low-density lipoprotein, or LDL, cholesterol is often referred to as "bad cholesterol." It can increase the risk of a heart attack. If your LDL is greater than 160 milligrams per deciliter, it is considered high. High-density lipoprotein, or HDL, cholesterol is termed "good cholesterol." This is because it removes excess cholesterol from your arteries and brings it to your liver for disposal, which can protect you from a heart attack. Women should aim for an HDL level of at least 50 milligrams per deciliter and men for a level of at least 40 milligrams per deciliter. Triglycerides are fats in the blood that contribute to high cholesterol. If your triglycerides are higher than 200 milligrams per deciliter, this is considered high.

Nutrients That Prevent or Control High Cholesterol

Monounsaturated fatty acids are a type of fat associated with lowering high cholesterol. Soluble fiber binds to substances for excretion, which improves gut health while lowering cholesterol. Phytochemicals from plant foods, such as flavonoids and anthocyanins, and vitamin E act as antioxidants and protect against high cholesterol.

Foods That Contain These Nutrients

Almonds have monounsaturated fatty acids, vitamin E, and flavonoids in both the meat of the nut and the skin for fighting high cholesterol. Avocados contain monounsaturated fatty acids that are especially effective at lowering LDL cholesterol and in some cases raising HDL cholesterol (the good cholesterol). Barley and oat bran are high in soluble fiber, and according to the U.S. Department of Agriculture, blueberries contain a special antioxidant called pterostilbene associated with lower LDL cholesterol.

ESSENTIAL

Omega-3 fatty acids are also good for lowering cholesterol. Omega-3s stop triglycerides from converting excess calories into fat by reducing the number of triglycerides. You can find omega-3 fatty acids in salmon, tuna, trout, flaxseeds, walnuts, beans, and olive oil. Be careful how you prepare these foods, though, because frying often damages the omega-3s and reduces their benefits.

Tips for Incorporating These Foods

Almonds and blueberries make one of the best snacks around. They are easy to transport and packed with nutrition. They also make great toppers for cereals and salads. Barley and oat bran are two grains delicious as a hot breakfast cereal, and barley is a good base for cold grain salads. Avocados can be added to smoothies, sandwiches, and salads to boost nutrition and create a creamy texture and buttery flavor.

Grilled Blueberry Almond Butter Sandwich

If you like a good PB & J, you will love this variation on the traditional sandwich. Use a high fiber, whole-grain bread and natural almond butter, and you'll get all the health benefits without a lot of excess sugar.

INGREDIENTS | SERVES 1

1½ tablespoons almond butter
2 slices whole-grain bread
½ tablespoon almonds, finely chopped
10 to 15 fresh blueberries

1. Divide the almond butter and spread half on each slice of bread. Top the almond butter on one side with the chopped almonds and blueberries. Place the other slice of bread on top, almond butter side down.

2. Heat a nonstick skillet, grill pan, or panini press. Place the sandwich in the pan and cook until the bread browns and the filling begins to melt. If using a skillet or grill pan, flip the sandwich and cook the same amount of time on the other side. Serve warm.

PER SERVING Calories: 318 | Fat: 18g | Sodium: 221mg | Carbohydrates: 31g | Fiber: 6g | Protein: 11g

Almond Crusted Salmon

Fish coated with a nutty crust is a weeknight meal you can put together in minutes.
If you are using frozen fish, which is often the most affordable, be sure to place it in the fridge in the
morning and it will be thawed by dinnertime.

INGREDIENTS | SERVES 4

1½ tablespoons olive oil
½ cup bread crumbs
½ cup almonds, finely chopped
1 teaspoon garlic powder
1 teaspoon dried parsley
1 teaspoon salt
½ teaspoon black pepper
4 (3-ounce) salmon fillets

1. Preheat the oven to 400°F. Coat a baking sheet or dish with ½ tablespoon of olive oil. On a plate or in a flat dish, combine the bread crumbs, almonds, garlic powder, parsley, salt, and pepper.

2. Pour 1 tablespoon of olive oil over the thawed fillets and rub to coat each evenly. Place each fillet, one at a time, in the bread crumb mixture. Press gently to adhere the coating to the fish. Only one side of the fish will get the coating.

3. Place the fillets, coated side up, on the baking sheet. Bake for 10 to 12 minutes or until fish flakes with a fork. Serve warm.

PER SERVING Calories: 268 | Fat: 15g | Sodium: 738mg | Carbohydrates: 13g | Fiber: 2g | Protein: 21g

Avocado Blueberry Salsa

The sweetness of fruit is an excellent addition to any salsa because it balances the salty, spicy flavors. This salsa combines two ingredients associated with lower blood cholesterol—avocado and blueberry.

INGREDIENTS | SERVES 6

1 avocado, diced
1 small onion, minced
1 fresh jalapeño, minced
1 clove garlic, minced
2 Roma tomatoes, diced
3 tablespoons fresh lemon juice
½ cup fresh blueberries
1 tablespoon olive oil
2 tablespoons fresh cilantro, chopped
Salt and pepper, to taste

1. In a medium bowl, combine the avocado, onion, jalapeño, garlic, and tomatoes. Pour in the lemon juice and toss well. You can slightly break up the avocado if desired.

2. Add the blueberries, drizzle in the olive oil, and add the cilantro. Stir to combine all ingredients. Add salt and pepper to taste.

PER SERVING Calories: 92 | Fat: 7g | Sodium: 4mg | Carbohydrates: 8g | Fiber: 3g | Protein: 1g

Serving This Salsa

Fresh avocado can be difficult to work with because it browns easily once exposed to the air. Be sure to stir the salsa well to ensure that the avocado is covered in lemon juice, which will reduce browning. For the best presentation, serve immediately. This salsa is delicious on grilled fish or as a topping for a spicy taco salad.

Barley Blueberry Almond Salad

Cold grain salads can really add some excitement to your side dishes.
They go especially well with sandwiches and salads.
This recipe uses fresh blueberries, but dried would work well too.

INGREDIENTS | SERVES 4

1 cup hulled barley
¾ cup fresh blueberries
½ cup raw almonds
1 tablespoon honey
2 tablespoons fresh lemon juice
½ teaspoon ground cinnamon

Types of Barley

Hulled barely is more nutritious than pearled barley because it still contains the high-fiber bran. Hulled barley does take longer to cook—30 to 45 minutes instead of 15. To turn your hulled barley into a quick meal, soak it overnight before cooking or make extra and store it in the refrigerator for use later in the week.

1. In a medium saucepan, bring 3 cups of water to a boil. Add the barley and cook for 30 to 45 minutes or until the grain is tender. Drain any excess liquid and rinse in cold water to cool.

2. In a large bowl, toss together the barley, blueberries, and almonds. In a small dish, whisk together the honey, lemon juice, and cinnamon. Pour the dressing over the barley salad and toss to coat.

3. Refrigerate for at least 30 minutes before serving.

PER SERVING Calories: 300 | Fat: 10g | Sodium: 6mg | Carbohydrates: 47g | Fiber: 11g | Protein: 10g

Carrot Cake Oat Bran

Oat bran makes a delicious, high-fiber breakfast that can reduce cholesterol. This recipe will help you make it into a special treat that mimics a favorite dessert.

INGREDIENTS | SERVES 2

¼ teaspoon salt

2 teaspoons virgin coconut oil

¼ cup carrot, shredded

1 teaspoon cinnamon

2 tablespoons golden raisins

1 tablespoon muscovado sugar

⅔ cup oat bran

2 tablespoons raw almonds, chopped

Virgin Coconut Oil

Coconut oil contains lauric acid, which has antibacterial properties and medium-chain fatty acids. Some studies in animals show that coconut oil may reduce cholesterol. More research is needed, but if it doesn't improve blood cholesterol, many researchers also feel that it won't hurt it. Just be sure to buy the cold-pressed virgin oil, as processed varieties contain unhealthy hydrogenated fats.

1. Bring 2 cups of water and the salt to a boil in a medium-size saucepan.

2. Meanwhile, melt the coconut oil in a skillet over medium-high heat. Add the carrots and cook 3 to 5 minutes, just until the carrots become tender. Stir in the cinnamon, raisins, and sugar. Set aside.

3. Once the water is boiling, stir in the oat bran. Cook for about 2 minutes. Stir the carrot mixture into the oats. Remove from heat and divide into 2 serving bowls. Sprinkle with almonds and serve hot.

PER SERVING Calories: 206 | Fat: 10g | Sodium: 304mg | Carbohydrates: 37g | Fiber: 7g | Protein: 7g

CHAPTER 23

Insomnia

According to the Mayo Clinic, insomnia is one of the most common medical complaints. Fortunately, there are many foods that can have calming effects to improve your ability to sleep well and wake feeling rested.

What Is Insomnia?

Insomnia is a disorder that results in problems with sleep. If you have insomnia, you may have trouble falling asleep or you may fall asleep easily but then wake too early and be unable to return to sleep. Some people experience both. If you have had insomnia, you know it can influence your mood, alertness, and productivity. Difficulty focusing and tension headaches are also results of insomnia.

Insomnia can be caused by a variety of factors. Stress and anxiety may trigger it, or it may result from a separate medical condition or current medication. Caffeine and alcohol can cause insomnia, as can eating late at night.

Nutrients That Alleviate Insomnia

According to the National Sleep Foundation, the amino acid tryptophan can cause sleepiness. Through a series of chemical reactions, tryptophan raises levels of serotonin, which helps regulate sleep patterns, in the brain. Carbohydrates can help to make you sleepy because they make the tryptophan more available to the brain for use.

ESSENTIAL

Other food remedies for insomnia include lettuce, honey, and foods containing vitamin B. Lettuce contains lectucarium, which induces sleep. Vitamin B has been proved to enhance relaxation, which can lead to better sleep; you can find vitamin B in cereals and nuts. Honey, a common home remedy for sleep, can be stirred into a cup of hot water before bedtime.

Foods That Contain These Nutrients

Tryptophan is found in foods that contain protein. Shrimp, scallops, cod, chicken, and turkey are ideal protein sources. When choosing your carbohydrate source, consider oats, buckwheat, Bulgur, barley, and brown rice, or try bananas and baked potatoes. Sunflower seeds and sesame seeds also contain tryptophan.

Tips for Incorporating These Foods

Heavy, savory foods may not be your idea of a good bedtime snack, but eating a small portion may help to improve your sleep patterns. Mix a few leftover shrimp with brown rice or make a cold salad with barley. Sprinkle sunflower seeds on your oatmeal.

ALERT

Many foods can disrupt sleep and are linked to insomnia. If you suffer from insomnia, eat foods that can improve sleep, but also eliminate high-fat and spicy foods, caffeine, and alcohol. These foods can keep you from falling asleep, or cause you to wake up before you are fully rested.

For a better night's sleep, a snack about four hours before bedtime should be one that combines carbohydrates and protein. The best choices are proteins with the highest amount of tryptophan combined with some of the few carbohydrate sources that also contain the amino acid.

Peanut Butter Banana Smoothie

This simple smoothie is both comforting and delicious. When bananas are ripe, chop them into large pieces and freeze them in a freezer-safe bag or container. They will create a creamy, frosty smoothie.

INGREDIENTS | SERVES 1

1 banana, frozen

1 cup milk

1 tablespoon natural peanut butter

Place all ingredients in a blender. Process on low until ingredients are puréed and drink is smooth. Add more milk if you desire a thinner smoothie. Serve cold.

PER SERVING Calories: 351 | Fat: 16g | Sodium: 151mg | Carbohydrates: 43g | Fiber: 4g | Protein: 13g

Turkey Salad with Bulgur Wheat

This recipe takes a few of the flavors of the Thanksgiving holiday season and turns them into a light salad that is perfect any time of year. It is a great recipe for leftovers and contains all the ingredients to promote restful sleep.

INGREDIENTS | SERVES 6

½ cup Bulgur wheat

2½ cups cooked turkey, shredded

⅓ cup celery, finely chopped

3 green onions, chopped

½ cup dried cranberries

3 tablespoons fresh lemon juice

3 tablespoons olive oil

1 teaspoon poultry seasoning

½ teaspoon salt

¼ teaspoon black pepper

Cooking with Bulgur Wheat

Bulgur wheat is a whole grain that can be used in all types of salads or as a breakfast. Try substituting it for rice in some recipes to add new texture and nutty flavor. When cooking Bulgur, remember that you will need 2 cups of water for every cup of Bulgur wheat.

1. In a saucepan, bring 1 cup of water to a boil. Add the Bulgur wheat and bring back to a boil. Cover and cook about 15 minutes, or until the liquid has been absorbed and the grain is tender. Rinse with cold water and set aside to cool.

2. In a large bowl, combine the turkey, celery, onions, and cranberries. Stir in the Bulgur wheat.

3. In a small bowl, whisk together the lemon juice, olive oil, poultry seasoning, salt, and pepper. Pour over the turkey salad and toss to coat. Refrigerate 30 minutes before serving.

PER SERVING Calories: 235 | Fat: 10g | Sodium: 10g | Carbohydrates: 19g | Fiber: 3g | Protein: 19g

Banana Bread Oatmeal

This breakfast is like banana bread in a bowl! It is a warm and comforting recipe that can be a relaxing evening snack, or give you plenty of nutritious energy to fuel your day.

INGREDIENTS | SERVES 2

⅛ teaspoon salt

1 cup old-fashioned rolled oats

1 banana

2 tablespoons milk

½ teaspoon ground cinnamon

¼ teaspoon ground nutmeg

¼ teaspoon ground cloves

¼ cup walnuts, chopped

Creamier Oats

In this recipe, the banana helps to make the oats rich and creamy. However, if you want creamy oats without adding banana, try making them with milk. You can substitute milk for all or just half of the water the recipe calls for. Bring the milk only to a simmer before adding the oats, and stir often to prevent the milk from burning.

1. In a saucepan, bring 1¾ cups of water and the ⅛ teaspoon of salt to a boil. Add the oatmeal and cook, stirring, for about 5 minutes. Remove from heat and set aside.

2. In a small bowl, mash together the banana and milk. Stir in the cinnamon, nutmeg, and cloves. Stir the mashed banana into the oatmeal.

3. Divide into 2 bowls and top each with chopped walnuts. Serve warm.

PER SERVING Calories: 312 | Fat: 13g | Sodium: 155mg | Carbohydrates: 45g | Fiber: 7g | Protein: 9g

Orange Sesame Shrimp and Vegetables

Hearty brown rice makes a great side for this light and flavorful dish.
Start preparations early, because the shrimp will need to marinate for at least 30 minutes.

INGREDIENTS | SERVES 4

1 pound shrimp, peeled and deveined
½ cup tamari
½ cup fresh orange juice
3 cloves garlic, minced
1 tablespoon olive oil
1 small onion, sliced
¼ cup celery, sliced
¾ cup white button mushrooms, sliced
1 red bell pepper, sliced
1 tablespoon orange zest
1 tablespoon cornstarch
2 tablespoons sesame seeds

1. In a sealable container, combine the shrimp, ¼ cup tamari, ¼ cup orange juice, and 2 cloves of garlic. Coat the shrimp evenly, seal with the lid, and place in the refrigerator for about 30 minutes.

2. In a deep skillet, heat the olive oil over medium-high heat and add 1 clove of the garlic, onion, celery, mushrooms, and bell pepper. Cook for 3 minutes; reduce the heat to medium and add the orange zest and shrimp. Cook until the shrimp are cooked through and turn white in color.

3. In a small dish, dissolve the cornstarch in the remaining ¼ cup of tamari and ¼ cup of orange juice. Pour over the shrimp and vegetables and cook on medium-high heat until slightly thickened.

4. Sprinkle with the sesame seeds and serve hot over rice.

PER SERVING Calories: 179 | Fat: 3g | Sodium: 1180mg | Carbohydrates: 11g | Fiber: 2g | Protein: 26g

Scallops with Broccoli and Soba Noodles

Soba noodles are made of buckwheat flour and make a great substitution for standard pasta. Soba has a slightly nutty flavor that pairs nicely with the sweet, tender scallops and the vibrant flavor and crunch of broccoli.

INGREDIENTS | SERVES 4

1 pound soba noodles

1 head broccoli

3 tablespoons olive oil

2 cloves garlic, minced

Salt and pepper, to taste

12 to 16 sea scallops

1 tablespoon butter

Cooking Scallops

Scallops are very delicate and can be over-cooked easily. Be sure the scallops are dry before cooking and use a very hot pan. Cook them only about 1 minute on each side until they are no longer translucent. By adding a little butter during the cooking process, you can add to the caramelizing and flavor.

1. Bring 4 quarts of water to a boil in a large pot. Add the soba noodles and reduce the heat to a simmer. Cook for about 7 minutes, or until the noodles are slightly tender but not mushy. Drain, rinse, and set aside.

2. Chop the broccoli into small florets. Heat 2 tablespoons of the olive oil in a deep skillet and add the garlic. Cook 1 minute and add the broccoli. Cook 3 to 5 minutes, just until the broccoli is bright green and slightly tender. Stir in the soba noodles and coat with the oil. Salt and pepper to taste and set aside.

3. In a large skillet, heat 1 tablespoon of olive oil over medium-high heat. Use a clean kitchen towel to dry each scallop. Sprinkle the scallops with salt and pepper as desired. Place the scallops, seasoned side down, in the hot skillet.

4. Cook for 1 minute, flip, and add the butter to the pan. As the butter melts, spoon it over the cooking scallops. After 1 minute, remove the scallops from heat.

5. Divide the noodles and broccoli onto 4 plates and top each with 3 to 4 scallops. Serve hot.

PER SERVING Calories: 526 | Fat: 14g | Sodium: 956mg | Carbohydrates: 87g | Fiber: 1g | Protein: 21g

CHAPTER 24

Irritable Bowel Syndrome

Irritable bowel syndrome (IBS) is an uncomfortable and often painful condition that affects the gastrointestinal system. According to the National Institutes of Health, about one in five Americans suffer from symptoms of IBS. Unfortunately, most people with IBS do not seek help, and an amazing 70 percent of people with IBS are not receiving medical care.

What Is Irritable Bowel Syndrome?

IBS is a disorder with a combination of symptoms. Most often, abdominal pain and bloating are present. Some individuals experience constipation (Chapter 14), some have diarrhea (Chapter 17), and some have alternating bouts with both. While the symptoms of IBS are troublesome, the good news is that the condition does not cause long-term damage to the digestive system.

Additional factors that can worsen your IBS symptoms include eating large meals, stress or emotional upsets, medicines, the hormones occurring during menstruation, depression, anxiety, drinks with caffeine, and some grains, including wheat, barley, and rye.

IBS does not have one specific cause, but there are many theories. One is that those with IBS have a large intestine that is highly sensitive to specific foods and stress. The immune system is thought to be involved, as well as possibly decreased serotonin receptor activity in the colon that causes increased pain sensitivity. Serotonin is a "feel good" chemical in the brain that is also present in the gastrointestinal tract.

Nutrients That Alleviate IBS

Fiber is the one nutrient that appears to help those with IBS. It may not alleviate all symptoms, but according the National Institutes of Health, it may help prevent muscle spasms of the colon. It can also help to ease the constipation associated with IBS.

Foods that can trigger IBS symptoms and should be avoided include dairy foods, red meat, spicy foods, caffeine, alcohol, artificial sweeteners, caffeinated beverages, and overconsumption of high-fiber foods such as broccoli, cauliflower, and beans.

Foods That Contain These Nutrients

Some foods high in fiber include black beans, kidney beans, green peas, sweet potatoes, pumpkin, raspberries, and pears. Intake of fiber should be gradually increased by only two to three grams per day. Drinking plenty of fluids, especially water, will also aid your digestive system when increasing fiber intake.

QUESTION

Can I get fiber from juice?
Juice is not a good source of dietary fiber. Fresh fruit and vegetable juices provide plenty of vitamins and minerals, but the fiber is in the pulp and skin of the fruit or vegetable. Eating these parts of the produce provides the natural fiber, but it has been reduced or eliminated in the juice.

Tips for Incorporating These Foods

High-fiber foods can be used to make delicious side dishes for meals. When added to green salads, cold beans create a more filling meal, and peas can be added to pasta dishes.

Try mashing sweet potatoes and add them to oatmeal with a sprinkle of cinnamon. This also works well with puréed pumpkin.

Kidney Bean Salad

This salad comes together quickly and makes an ideal lunch or side dish for your next potluck. Serve it cold as you would a potato or macaroni salad.

INGREDIENTS | SERVES 6

2 (15-ounce) cans kidney beans
¼ cup red onion, diced
¼ cup cucumber, diced
¼ cup celery, diced
¼ cup green bell pepper, diced
2 cloves garlic, minced
3 tablespoons mayonnaise
1 teaspoon fresh lemon juice
1 teaspoon demerara sugar
½ teaspoon salt
¼ teaspoon black pepper

1. Rinse and drain the kidney beans. In a large bowl, combine the beans, onion, cucumber, celery, bell pepper, and garlic.

2. In a small dish, combine the mayonnaise, lemon juice, sugar, salt, and pepper. Add more salt and pepper to taste if desired.

3. Pour the dressing over the beans and vegetables and stir to coat well. Refrigerate for at least 30 minutes before serving.

PER SERVING Calories: 155 | Fat: 3g | Sodium: 664mg | Carbohydrates: 26g | Fiber: 8g | Protein: 8g

Mashed Peas

Mashed peas make an excellent alternative to mashed potatoes. Add similar flavorings and spices and mash them well, and you will end up with a dish similar in texture to mashed potatoes, but with a whole new exciting flavor!

INGREDIENTS | SERVES 4

1 tablespoon olive oil

¼ cup onion, diced

2 cloves garlic, minced

¼ cup chicken stock

10 ounces peas, thawed if frozen

1 teaspoon salt

½ teaspoon black pepper

Mashing Peas

A potato masher will work well if you like your peas with a little texture. If you would like a creamier consistency, consider using an immersion blender or standard blender to combine all of the ingredients after cooking. Adding a few tablespoons of milk can also make the mashed peas creamier.

1. Heat the oil in a large skillet over medium-high heat. Add the onion and garlic and cook for 2 minutes.

2. Add the chicken stock and peas to the skillet and cook until the peas are tender, about 5 minutes. Remove from the heat.

3. Using a potato masher or blender, mash the peas until they reach your desired consistency. Stir in the salt and pepper, and add more to taste if desired. Serve hot.

PER SERVING Calories: 92 | Fat: 4g | Sodium: 690mg | Carbohydrates: 11g | Fiber: 3g | Protein: 4g

Pear, Raspberry, and Walnut Salad

This recipe is a twist on the traditional Waldorf salad. The raspberries are added at the end as more of a garnish, to prevent them being broken during preparation.

INGREDIENTS | SERVES 4

3 pears, chopped

½ cup celery, sliced

½ cup walnuts, chopped

⅓ cup plain Greek yogurt

1 teaspoon fresh lemon juice

2 teaspoons honey

½ teaspoon ground cinnamon

¼ teaspoon black pepper

1 cup fresh raspberries

1. In a bowl, combine the pears, celery, and walnuts. In a small dish, stir together the yogurt, lemon juice, honey, cinnamon, and black pepper.

2. Pour the dressing over the fruit and nuts and stir well to coat. Divide into 4 servings and top each with ¼ cup raspberries. Serve immediately or refrigerate for up to 1 day.

PER SERVING Calories: 215 | Fat: 11g | Sodium: 22mg | Carbohydrates: 31g | Fiber: 7g | Protein: 4g

Fresh Pesto Pea Salad

In this recipe, a fresh basil pesto is combined with cooked peas for a delicious cold salad that provides plenty of fiber. Enjoy it by itself or toss it with a whole-grain pasta or brown rice.

INGREDIENTS | SERVES 4

10 ounces peas, thawed if frozen

1½ cups fresh basil leaves

2 cloves garlic

¼ cup walnuts, chopped

2 tablespoons Parmesan cheese, grated

1 teaspoon salt

½ teaspoon black pepper

¼ cup olive oil

Pesto

Pesto is an Italian sauce that is made with basil and pine nuts. You can substitute a variety of ingredients in standard pesto to create a new sauce. Here walnuts are used for the pine nuts. You can also use spinach or arugula instead of basil. Add less olive oil for a dip or more for a thin salad dressing.

1. Place peas in a saucepan and cover with water. Bring to a boil over medium-high heat and cook until tender, about 5 to 7 minutes. Drain and set aside.

2. In a food processor, combine the basil, garlic, walnuts, Parmesan cheese, salt, and pepper. Pulse until all ingredients are chopped. Turn on low and pour in the olive oil. Process until a thick paste is formed.

3. In a bowl, mix together the pesto and the warm peas. Stir until the peas are coated evenly. Serve immediately or refrigerate for up to 2 days and serve cold.

PER SERVING Calories: 189 | Fat: 15g | Sodium: 696mg | Carbohydrates: 11g | Fiber: 3g | Protein: 5g

Pumpkin Bean Chili

Pumpkin is not a typical ingredient in a hearty chili, but it makes a surprisingly delicious addition. The thick texture and slight sweetness goes well with this spicy, comforting soup.

INGREDIENTS | SERVES 6

2 tablespoons olive oil

1 large onion, diced

3 cloves garlic, minced

1 green bell pepper, diced

1 (28-ounce) can diced tomatoes

1 (14-ounce) can tomato sauce

1 tablespoon hot sauce

3 teaspoons chili powder

2 teaspoons ground cumin

1 teaspoon salt

½ teaspoon black pepper

2 cups pumpkin purée

2 cups black beans, canned or cooked

2 cups red kidney beans, canned or cooked

1. In a large soup pot, heat the olive oil over medium-high heat. Add the onion and the garlic and cook for 2 to 3 minutes. Add the green pepper and cook 1 minute more.

2. Stir in the tomatoes, tomato sauce, and hot sauce. Next, add the chili powder, cumin, salt, and pepper. Stir well.

3. Add the pumpkin purée and stir in the beans. Bring to a simmer with the pot partially covered to prevent splashing. Simmer, stirring occasionally, for 10 to 15 minutes. Serve warm.

PER SERVING Calories: 276 | Fat: 6g | Sodium: 1384mg | Carbohydrates: 48g | Fiber: 15g | Protein: 13g

No Salt Added

When shopping for canned products such as tomatoes, select the "No Salt Added" varieties. Most canned goods, even simple diced tomatoes, have unnecessary added sodium. Choosing the unsalted varieties allows you to add your own seasonings to taste and can reduce your sodium intake overall.

CHAPTER 25

Menopause

Menopause is a natural process of life, not a medical illness, but along with it come physical and mental symptoms. Some foods naturally alleviate these symptoms, reducing the need for drug therapy.

What Is Menopause?

Menopause is a stage of life, not an illness or ailment. It is defined as the end of menstruating and fertility, and begins twelve months after your last menstrual period. Hormonal changes occur during menopause that cause many of the common physical symptoms. Hot flashes, irregular sleep, and mood swings are all symptoms of menopause.

FACT

Menopause usually occurs in women between the ages of forty-five and fifty-five, although some woman go through menopause earlier in life. A hysterectomy (the surgical removal of the uterus) can also send a woman into early menopause.

The mental and emotional responses to this major life event as well as the hormonal changes can affect mood. Often stress and anxiety can result when dealing with the changes of the body and the physical symptoms.

Nutrients That Alleviate Symptoms of Menopause

Plant substances called isoflavins that act like estrogen in the body are most closely associated with reducing the main symptoms of menopause—hot flashes, vaginal dryness, and mood swings. These substances are often called phytoestrogens.

The mineral boron, found in vegetables and fruit, is also helpful in alleviating the symptoms of menopause. Boron increases the body's ability to hold on to estrogen and also helps keeps bones strong by decreasing the amount of calcium lost by the body.

The top sources of boron and phytoestrogens are:

- Apples
- Grapefruit
- Plums and prunes
- Strawberries

- Red raspberries
- Asparagus
- Broccoli
- Cauliflower
- Carrots
- Soybeans
- Sweet potatoes

Foods That Contain These Nutrients

Soy has long been associated with relieving menopause symptoms, and research still suggests that consuming soy may help. Choose natural minimally processed soy foods such as tofu, and steer clear of packaged burgers and similar meat substitutes that contain unnecessary additives. Flaxseed also contains isoflavins. Sage is an herb that is associated with reduced symptoms because of its estrogen-like activity.

ESSENTIAL

Soy is a common remedy for hot flashes, though there is no conclusive proof that it works. Soy does, however, lower bad cholesterol and may reduce the risk of some cancers. Some ways to add soy to your diet include drinking soy milk, stir-frying tofu with vegetables, baking tofu and adding it to salads, or adding soy beans to soups.

Tips for Incorporating These Foods

If you have never had tofu, try different cooking methods before you determine whether or not you like it. Chopped tofu can be added to soups, or grilled with a barbecue sauce, or sautéed with vegetables and soy sauce to serve with rice or noodles. Use fresh sage to season your vegetables, sauces, and soups.

Sweet Soy Grilled Tofu

Grilled tofu makes a quick meal for any busy weeknight. It only needs to marinate for about 10 minutes, and once on the grill it is ready in 5. Serve this with Spicy Sautéed Greens (Chapter 3) or Herbed Quinoa Pilaf (Chapter 15).

INGREDIENTS | SERVES 6

6 slices firm or extra-firm tofu, pressed
½ cup tamari
1 teaspoon sesame oil
2 tablespoons honey
2 cloves garlic, minced
3 green onions, sliced

Pressing Tofu

It is important that tofu be pressed and dried before grilling. To do this, cut the tofu block into 6 slices. Place the tofu slices on a clean kitchen towel or paper towel. Lay another towel on top and then place a baking sheet on top for 2 minutes. Replace the towels with dry ones and repeat 2 more times.

1. Place the tofu slices in a shallow baking dish. In a bowl, combine the tamari, sesame oil, honey, and garlic. Whisk until smooth and add the green onions. Pour the marinade over the tofu.

2. Allow the tofu to marinate for 10 minutes, turning it every 2 to 3 minutes.

3. Heat a well-oiled grill pan on medium-high heat. Place the tofu on the pan and cook 2 to 3 minutes on each side or until the grill marks appear. Serve hot.

PER SERVING Calories: 51 | Fat: 2g | Sodium: 187mg | Carbohydrates: 2g | Fiber: 0g | Protein: 6g

Pumpkin Flax Pancakes

These pumpkin pancakes are made with healthy whole-grain flour and flaxseed.
Top them with warm, pure maple syrup for an autumn-inspired breakfast.

INGREDIENTS | SERVES 3

1 egg
¾ cup Milk
⅓ cup puréed pumpkin
2 tablespoons melted butter
1 cup white whole-wheat flour
¼ cup ground flaxseed
3 teaspoons baking powder
¼ teaspoon salt
½ teaspoon cinnamon
½ teaspoon pumpkin pie spice

1. Break the egg into a medium-size bowl and beat lightly. Add the milk, pumpkin, and cooled, melted butter.

2. In a separate bowl, mix together the flour, flaxseed, baking powder, salt, cinnamon, and pumpkin pie spice. Gradually add the dry ingredients into the wet ingredients. Consistency will vary based on the thickness of your pumpkin purée, so add more milk, 1 tablespoon at a time, if necessary.

3. Drop batter by ¼-cup portions onto a nonstick griddle. Cook about 90 seconds or until bubbles begin to form; flip and cook for the same amount of time on the other side. Serve warm.

PER SERVING Calories: 359 | Fat: 18g | Sodium: 776mg | Carbohydrates: 42g | Fiber: 11g | Protein: 14g

Tofu Vegetable Stir-Fry

This stir-fry is full of healthy vegetables and can be tailored to your taste.
Add an extra bell pepper, or substitute cauliflower for the broccoli.
Serve it over rice noodles or brown rice. You can make it any way you like it!

INGREDIENTS | SERVES 4

2 tablespoons olive oil

2 cloves garlic, minced

1 small onion, diced

½ cup celery, sliced

1 carrot, sliced

½ cup white button mushrooms, sliced

1 cup broccoli florets

2 cups bok choy, sliced

1 block firm tofu, drained and cubed

¼ cup olive oil

⅛ cup vinegar

¼ cup demerara sugar

2 tablespoons soy sauce

1. Heat the oil in a deep skillet over medium-high heat and add the garlic, onion, celery, and carrot. Cook for 2 minutes.

2. Add the mushrooms, broccoli, and bok choy. Cook for 1 more minute. Stir in the tofu and continue to cook until the tofu is browned.

3. In a small saucepan, combine the oil, vinegar, sugar, and soy sauce over medium-high heat. Bring to a boil and boil for 1 minute. Remove from heat. Pour over the vegetables and tofu, and stir to coat. Serve hot.

PER SERVING Calories: 304 | Fat: 23g | Sodium: 537mg | Carbohydrates: 18g | Fiber: 2g | Protein: 8g

Meat Eaters and Vegetarians

If you are serving diners who don't like tofu, there are several options. First, you can simply leave out the tofu. Otherwise, once the vegetables are almost cooked, divide them into 2 skillets and add cubed cooked chicken to one and tofu to the other. Divide the sauce between the two dishes.

Carrot Flaxseed Bread

One of the best ways to incorporate flaxseed into your diet is through healthy, whole-grain baked goods. This bread combines the sweetness of carrots and the spice of cinnamon for a breakfast you can feel good about.

INGREDIENTS | SERVES 8

1 teaspoon virgin coconut oil
1½ cups carrots, shredded
1 teaspoon ground cinnamon
1¼ cups whole-wheat flour
2 tablespoons ground flaxseed
1 teaspoon baking soda
1 teaspoon baking powder
½ teaspoon salt
¾ cup demerara or raw sugar
2 eggs
½ cup virgin coconut oil, melted
½ teaspoon vanilla

1. Preheat the oven to 350°F. Grease an 8.5" x 4.5" loaf pan and set aside. In a nonstick skillet, melt the 1 teaspoon of coconut oil over medium-high heat. Add the carrots and the cinnamon. Cook for 3 minutes or until carrots become slightly tender.

2. In a medium-size bowl, mix together the flour, flaxseed, baking soda, baking powder, and salt. In a larger bowl, whisk together the sugar and eggs. Add the coconut oil and vanilla.

3. Gradually add the dry ingredients to the wet, stirring just until combined. Add the carrots and gently mix them in the batter.

4. Pour the batter into the prepared loaf pan and bake for 25 minutes or until a toothpick inserted in the center comes out clean. Cool in the pan for 10 minutes, then remove bread and cool on a wire rack. Serve warm or at room temperature.

PER SERVING Calories: 283 | Fat: 18g | Sodium: 336mg | Carbohydrates: 30g | Fiber: 4g | Protein: 5g

Lemon and Sage Grilled Chicken

The marinade in this recipe goes wonderfully with chicken. You can also use it to marinate vegetables—for example, portobello mushroom caps and sliced eggplant and zucchini are also delicious on the grill.

INGREDIENTS | SERVES 4

½ cup fresh lemon juice

4 slices of fresh lemon

½ cup olive oil

2 cloves garlic, minced

6 leaves fresh sage, chopped

½ teaspoon salt

¼ teaspoon black pepper

4 (4-ounce) chicken breasts

1. In a zip-top bag or a deep dish with a lid, combine the lemon juice, lemon, oil, garlic, sage, salt, and pepper. Stir or whisk to mix well.

2. Add the chicken breasts and turn to coat evenly with the marinade. Seal the bag or lid and marinate for 30 minutes in the refrigerator.

3. Place chicken on a hot grill and cook for about 4 to 5 minutes on each side or until the internal temperature reaches 165°F.

PER SERVING Calories: 98 | Fat: 2g | Sodium: 113mg | Carbohydrates: 0g | Fiber: 0g | Protein: 19g

Cooking Temperatures

A meat thermometer is a helpful tool for grilling. It is important that all meats are cooked to a temperature that ensures food safety and reduces the risk of contracting a foodborne pathogen that can cause food poisoning. The U.S. Department of Agriculture urges that chicken breasts be cooked to at least 165°F.

As you ... uscles. When

a musc ... spasm. When

the sp ... can't relax, it

becom ... dening of the

muscl ... st often occur

in the ... le and painful.

Fortu ... educe the oc-

curren ...

Types and Causes of Muscle Cramps

A muscle cramp can last anywhere from a few minutes to an entire day. Cramps can involve just an isolated muscle or can comprise a group of related muscles. Most often, cramps are caused by a nerve malfunction, and many occur after physical activity or during the night. Dehydration and reduced mineral intake are two dietary causes of this malfunction that result in a cramp.

Other causes of cramps include:

- Heavy exercising (or exercising too long)
- Hormonal imbalances
- Being overweight
- Medications
- Electrolyte imbalances
- Dehydration
- Muscle fatigue
- Lack of calcium or potassium

A cramp of the calf muscle, also commonly referred to as a "charley horse," is one of the most common types of cramps. These cramps can last anywhere from a minute to several hours and can be very painful. Leg cramps occur when the muscles suddenly and forcefully contract, and muscles that cross two joints (as the calf muscle crosses the ankle and the knee) are especially likely to contract in this way.

There are two main types of muscle cramps that occur in the body. Heat cramps often result from intense exercise in a hot environment. These cramps last longer and are often more intense than a nighttime cramp, and can occur in the calf, arm, stomach, or back. It is important to stop exercise, rest, rehydrate, and practice gentle stretching when a heat cramp occurs. It is recommended to avoid strenuous activity for several hours after the heat cramp goes away.

Night cramps most often occur in the calves, legs, and feet. Most occur due to no specific reason and are harmless. However, some can be related to medical conditions such as peripheral artery disease or diabetes. In addition, aging increases risk of night cramps as does pregnancy. Cramps related to these conditions are usually harmless and go away quickly, but if you experience severe cramping that is recurring or regularly disrupts your sleep patterns you should seek medical care.

Nutrients That Prevent or Alleviate Muscle Cramping

Electrolytes are minerals in body fluids that influence hydration, blood acidity, and muscle action. Adequate intake of the electrolytes potassium, sodium, magnesium, and calcium can reduce the risk of cramps due to the role these minerals play in hydration and muscle action. Potassium and sodium work together in cell membranes to regulate muscular contractions, and too little potassium can result in muscle weakness and cramping. In a similar way, calcium also plays a role in the contraction of muscles. Magnesium is necessary because it facilitates the transport of the calcium and potassium across cell membranes. Maintaining a healthy balance of these minerals in the body reduces the risk of muscle cramps.

ESSENTIAL

If you do get a muscle cramp, try to avoid following the old myth that you need to forcefully stretch the muscle to get rid of the cramp. Hard stretching of a cramped muscle can actually lead to tearing of the muscle. Instead, gently massage or slowly stretch the muscle, try a warm bath, or place a warm compress on the muscle.

Foods That Contain These Nutrients

Some of the best sources for potassium include potatoes with the skin, prunes, and raisins. Lima beans and bananas are good sources as well. If you eat spinach and almonds, you will be getting a little bit of all three nutrients—potassium, magnesium, and calcium.

FACT

Cooking can greatly reduce potassium levels. In a study conducted by the U.S. Department of Agriculture's Agricultural Research Service, cubing or shredding potatoes before boiling reduced potassium by as much as 75 percent. Boil whole potatoes with the skin on and include raw vegetables in your diet to increase potassium intake.

Tips for Incorporating These Foods

A spinach salad topped with raisins and almonds provides valuable potassium as well as other nutrients to reduce muscle cramps. If you aren't a fan of prunes because of the texture, try tossing one in your next smoothie just to add sweetness. Lima beans, also a good source of potassium, are a great addition to vegetable soups.

Easy Banana Almond Muffins

Banana is a classic muffin flavor and the favorite of many.
With this easy recipe, you will have a piping hot muffin on the breakfast table in no time.

INGREDIENTS | MAKES 12 MUFFINS

1½ cups white whole-wheat flour

1 teaspoon baking soda

1 teaspoon baking powder

1 teaspoon cinnamon

½ teaspoon salt

¾ cup demerara sugar

2 eggs

½ cup butter, melted

½ teaspoon vanilla

2 very ripe bananas, mashed

½ cup slivered almonds

White Whole-Wheat Flour

White whole-wheat flour is milled from hard white spring wheat. It has a lighter texture and milder flavor than whole-wheat flour milled from red wheat. An excellent choice for whole-grain baking, this flour results in a product that is much closer in texture to items using refined white flour, but with the nutrients of whole wheat.

1. Preheat the oven to 350°F and grease a 12-muffin tin. In a medium-size bowl, sift together the flour, baking soda, baking powder, cinnamon, and salt. Set aside.

2. In a separate bowl, whisk together the sugar, eggs, butter, and vanilla. Stir in the banana and the almonds. Gradually incorporate the dry ingredients into the wet ingredients, stirring just until everything is blended.

3. Scoop the batter into the muffin tin, dividing it evenly among the 12 muffin cups. Bake for about 20 minutes or until a toothpick inserted into the center of the muffins comes out clean.

4. Remove from the oven. Allow to cool for about 5 minutes, then remove muffins from tin and transfer to a cooling rack. Serve warm or at room temperature.

PER SERVING Calories: 210 | Fat: 11g | Sodium: 309mg | Carbohydrates: 26g | Fiber: 3g | Protein: 4g

Breakfast Potatoes with Spinach

*A hearty weekend breakfast always calls for potatoes to go with your eggs.
Try this easy recipe that also adds a dose of dark leafy greens to the mix. Top the final dish with hot
sauce or add some crushed red pepper while cooking if you prefer your breakfast spicy!*

INGREDIENTS | SERVES 4

4 medium potatoes

2 tablespoons olive oil

½ cup onion, diced

2 cloves garlic, minced

2 cups fresh spinach leaves

1 teaspoon salt

½ teaspoon black pepper

1. Scrub the potatoes, prick with a fork, and microwave for about 5 minutes. You want the potatoes slightly cooked, but not completely cooked through. Remove and allow to cool slightly. Dice into bite-size pieces, keeping the skins on.

2. In a skillet, heat the olive oil over medium-high heat and add the onion and garlic. Cook for 2 minutes, then add the potatoes. Cook for 5 to 7 minutes or until the potatoes become slightly browned.

3. Add the spinach and cook just until wilted. Season with the salt and pepper and serve warm.

PER SERVING Calories: 221 | Fat: 7g | Sodium: 607mg | Carbohydrates: 39g | Fiber: 6g | Protein: 4g

Blue Cheese Almond Stuffed Prunes with Honey

This recipe may sound fancy and difficult to make, but it is a quick and easy appetizer that combines the sweet and salty flavors of fruit and cheese. You will also get plenty of the minerals you need to prevent muscle cramps.

INGREDIENTS | MAKES 20 PIECES

2 ounces blue cheese

¼ cup almonds, finely chopped

1 teaspoon honey

10 large prunes, halved

Honey, for drizzling

Appetizer Options

This same blue cheese filling is delicious with dates or figs as well. You can also place the cheese, almonds, honey, and prunes in a small food processor and combine them into a spread. Serve with mini toasts or crackers and a side of honey for drizzling.

1. In a small bowl, combine the blue cheese, almonds, and honey. Use a fork to mash all of the ingredients into a paste.

2. Gently open each prune half and arrange on a plate. Using a ½-teaspoon scoop or larger, depending on the size of your prunes, fill each half with the blue cheese. Drizzle the prunes with honey and serve.

PER 1 PIECE Calories: 29 | Fat: 1g | Sodium: 39mg | Carbohydrates: 4g | Fiber: 0g | Protein: 1g

Spinach Salad with Almond Butter Dressing

This salad pairs nutritious spinach with an Asian-inspired dressing.
The almonds sprinkled on top add a nice crunch and extra magnesium.

INGREDIENTS | SERVES 4

4 cups spinach, chopped

1 cup bok choy, chopped

1 medium carrot, shredded

¼ cup chopped almonds

¼ cup almond butter

1 tablespoon fresh lime juice

2 tablespoons soy sauce

¼ teaspoon garlic powder

1 teaspoon muscovado sugar

¼ teaspoon crushed red pepper

2 tablespoons fresh cilantro, chopped

1. Toss the vegetables in a large bowl. Sprinkle the almonds on top.

2. In a small bowl, whisk together the almond butter, lime juice, soy sauce, garlic powder, sugar, and red pepper. If the dressing is too thick, add a teaspoon of olive oil until it reaches desired consistency. Stir in the cilantro.

3. Pour the dressing over the salad and toss to coat evenly. Divide into 4 bowls and serve.

PER SERVING Calories: 157 | Fat: 12g | Sodium: 499mg | Carbohydrates: 9g | Fiber: 3g | Protein: 5g

Garlic Mashed Potatoes with Lima Beans

*Mashed starchy vegetables make a great addition to potatoes.
Here, potatoes are combined with lima beans and plenty of savory flavor for a new and improved mashed side dish perfect with grilled chicken.*

INGREDIENTS | SERVES 4

1 head garlic
½ tablespoon olive oil
3 medium potatoes, baked
1 cup lima beans, cooked
⅓ cup plain Greek yogurt
2 tablespoons fresh chives, chopped
1 teaspoon salt
½ teaspoon black pepper

Baking Potatoes for Mashing

Cook potatoes whole to preserve mineral content. Bake for 45 minutes in a 400°F oven, cool, and scoop out the flesh. You can also put them in a pot, cover with water and a lid, and boil for 5 minutes. Allow them to sit in the hot water until they are cool enough to handle. Peel and mash.

1. Preheat the oven to 400°F. Chop off the top ¼ of the garlic head to expose the cloves. Place on a piece of foil. Drizzle with the olive oil, wrap, and place in the oven for 45 minutes.

2. Meanwhile, combine the flesh of the potatoes and the lima beans in a large pan or bowl. Using a hand masher or a mixer, blend the two until the desired consistency is reached. You can leave them chunky or mix them until smooth.

3. Stir in the yogurt. Once the garlic is cool enough to touch, squeeze the flesh into the potatoes, being careful not to drop in any of the skin. Add the chives, salt, and pepper, and mix well. Serve hot.

PER SERVING Calories: 202 | Fat: 3g | Sodium: 706mg | Carbohydrates: 39g | Fiber: 4g | Protein: 6g

CHAPTER 27

Nausea and Motion Sickness

It goes by many names—seasickness, car sickness, air sickness—but motion sickness is a single disorder caused by an imbalance in equilibrium. Nausea and motion sickness can leave you feeling miserable and ruin what would otherwise be an exciting occasion or excursion. Fortunately, there are a few helpful foods known for easing both.

What Causes Nausea and Motion Sickness?

During movement, such as in car or airplane travel, the body, the inner ear, and the eyes may feel and see the movement differently. This sends conflicting information to the central nervous system and results in an uncomfortable, sick feeling. For example, imagine that you are on a large boat that is being rocked about by waves. Your body feels the waves but your eyes don't see them, just the stationary inside of the boat. With your eyes saying that there is no motion but your body feeling the rolling of the waves, your brain gets mixed signals. Motion sickness most often occurs in slow, complex movements that involve two different directions at the same time. Nausea, which is the sensation you get when you feel as if you could vomit, is a symptom of motion sickness.

ESSENTIAL

The word "nausea" comes from the Greek *naus*, meaning ship, and refers to seasickness. If the cause of the nausea (motion of the car, boat, plane, etc.) is not removed, the sufferer will likely vomit. However, vomiting as a result of motion sickness does not alleviate the feeling of nausea as it usually does in the case of nausea from an ordinary illness.

Nutrients That Alleviate Nausea and Motion Sickness

The specific nutrients or food components that help to alleviate nausea and motion sickness have not fully been identified. However, drinks with sugar do appear to ease nausea in some people and low-fiber, plain foods are most effective for not further upsetting the stomach when motion sickness and nausea occur. Drinks with sugar and plain foods can be effective whether nausea is due to motion sickness or illness.

Foods That Contain These Nutrients

Ginger is effective at reducing the symptoms of motion sickness, including nausea, in many people. Some research has shown that it is as effective as, or more effective than, over-the-counter medications for motion sickness.

ESSENTIAL

For most people, motion sickness is a minor problem that will stop when the motion stops, but this is not always the case. Some people can be completely incapacitated by the motion sickness and suffer symptoms for days afterward.

Fresh ginger can be grated into soothing drinks, and dried or crystallized ginger can be used as a snack. Dried, ground ginger can also be incorporated into simple baked goods such as breads and cookies.

Ginger Lemon Tea

This soothing tea can be served either hot or cold. The recipe given is unsweetened, but feel free to add some raw sugar or simple syrup if you prefer.

INGREDIENTS | MAKES 1 QUART

2-inch piece of fresh ginger
1 tea bag
¼ cup fresh lemon juice

Citrus Garnish

You can make this tea even when you aren't feeling the effects of an upset stomach. Improve the presentation and make it guest-worthy by thinly slicing oranges or lemons and floating them in the hot tea just before serving.

1. Heat 2 cups of water in a teakettle. Meanwhile, peel and slice the ginger. Put 1 cup of water in a saucepan and add the ginger. Heat to a simmer and cook for about 5 minutes.

2. Place the tea bag in a heatproof bowl and pour the 2 cups of hot water over it. Steep until it reaches your desired strength.

3. Pour the tea, ginger water, and lemon juice into a teapot or pitcher. Add about 1 cup more water. Mix and serve.

PER SERVING Calories: 6 | Fat: 0g | Sodium: 0mg | Carbohydrates: 2g | Fiber: 0g | Protein: 0g

Ginger Baked Apples

*This sweet treat uses a lot of fresh ginger to help reduce motion sickness.
Peeling the apples removes some of the hard-to-digest fiber, which is a good thing when
you are experiencing nausea or motion sickness.*

INGREDIENTS | SERVES 4

4 apples
4 tablespoons muscovado sugar
2 tablespoons fresh ginger, grated
½ teaspoon cinnamon
1 tablespoon unsalted butter

1. Preheat the oven to 375°F. Peel each apple and remove the core. Place the apples in a baking pan.

2. In a small dish, combine the sugar, ginger, and cinnamon. Sprinkle an equal amount into the empty core of each apple. Follow with ¼ tablespoon of butter.

3. Heat ½ cup of water in a saucepan or teakettle and pour into the baking pan with the apples. Bake for 30 to 40 minutes or until tender. Serve warm.

PER SERVING Calories: 127 | Fat: 2g | Sodium: 3mg | Carbohydrates: 30g | Fiber: 2g | Protein: 1g

Gingerbread Oatmeal

This recipe is made with old-fashioned rolled oats.
They can be cooked down easily to make a soft cereal that is easy on the tummy.

INGREDIENTS | SERVES 1

½ cup old-fashioned oats

½ teaspoon cinnamon

1 tablespoon fresh ginger, grated

¼ teaspoon ground cloves

¼ teaspoon ground nutmeg

1 tablespoon maple syrup

1. Combine the oats and 1 cup of water in a saucepan. Bring to a boil, reduce heat, and simmer for 5 to 7 minutes. Stir in the cinnamon, ginger, cloves, and nutmeg.

2. Place the oatmeal in a bowl and top with maple syrup before serving.

PER SERVING Calories: 214 | Fat: 3g | Sodium: 5mg | Carbohydrates: 43g | Fiber: 5g | Protein: 5g

Whole-Grain Cereals

Any whole grain, such as amaranth, steel-cut oats, or millet, can be used with this recipe. Because these grains are high in fiber and don't cook down as easily as rolled oats, it is best to save them for when your stomach feels better.

Ginger Spiced Cookies

These cookies combine ginger with a favorite, comforting dessert.
They include whole-grain flour and minimally refined sugar (and less sugar) for a more wholesome cookie.

INGREDIENTS | MAKES 1½ DOZEN COOKIES

¾ cup unsalted butter, softened

¾ cup muscovado sugar

1 egg

3 tablespoons molasses

1 tablespoon fresh ginger, grated

2 cups white whole-wheat flour

2 teaspoons baking soda

1 teaspoon ground cinnamon

½ teaspoon ground cloves

½ teaspoon ground nutmeg

½ teaspoon salt

1. Preheat the oven to 350°F. With an electric mixer, cream together the butter and sugar. Add the egg, molasses, and ginger and mix well.

2. Sift together the flour, baking soda, spices, and salt. Slowly add the dry ingredients to the wet ingredients. Mix on low until all of the flour is incorporated. Scrape the sides of the mixing bowl with a spatula as you go.

3. Roll the cookie dough into balls to make 18 cookies and place on ungreased cookie sheets. Gently press them down with your fingers or a fork.

4. Bake for 10 to 12 minutes. Cool on the sheets for 2 minutes, then transfer to a cooling rack. Serve warm or at room temperature.

PER 1 COOKIE | Calories: 151 | Fat: 8g | Sodium: 210mg | Carbohydrates: 18g | Fiber: 2g | Protein: 2g

Ginger Banana Bread

The ginger adds a mild spicy note to this sweet banana bread.
Here it is baked as a loaf, but you can easily turn it into muffins as well.

INGREDIENTS | SERVES 10

½ cup demerara sugar

½ cup butter, melted

2 eggs

2 bananas, mashed

¾ cup milk

½ teaspoon vanilla

2 tablespoons fresh ginger, grated

2½ cups white whole-wheat flour

1 teaspoon baking soda

1 teaspoon salt

Selecting and Storing Ginger

Carefully look over the piece of fresh ginger you select and ensure that it is not shriveled or soft, and that no mold is present. If stored in an airtight container in the refrigerator, unpeeled ginger can last about 3 weeks. It can also be stored in the freezer for up to 6 months.

1. Preheat the oven to 350°F. Grease a 8.5" x 4.5" loaf pan.

2. In a mixing bowl, combine the sugar and butter. Stir in the eggs and then add the banana. Mix in the milk, vanilla, and ginger.

3. In a separate bowl, whisk together the flour, baking soda, and salt. Gradually add the dry ingredients to the wet ingredients and stir just until they are combined.

4. Transfer the batter to the loaf pan. Bake for about 25 to 30 minutes or until a toothpick inserted in the center comes out clean. Cool for 5 minutes, then remove from pan and allow to cool on a cooling rack. Slice and serve warm or at room temperature.

PER SERVING Calories: 231 | Fat: 11g | Sodium: 444mg | Carbohydrates: 28g | Fiber: 4g | Protein: 6g

CHAPTER 28

Premenstrual Syndrome

The symptoms of premenstrual syndrome (PMS) and their severity are different for every woman. Research shows that specific nutrients have an influence on these symptoms and relieve the discomfort associated with PMS.

What Is Premenstrual Syndrome?

PMS is a group of varied symptoms that occur one to two weeks prior to the start of a woman's menstrual period. Acne, breast tenderness, fatigue, insomnia, bloating, aches and pains, irritability, and anxiety are all symptoms of PMS. For some women, these symptoms are barely noticeable; for others, they are severe and can affect physical performance and mental focus during this time.

FACT

Approximately 85 percent of women experience the symptoms of PMS. These symptoms usually disappear after a few days without significant impact on the woman. However, for about 2 to 3 percent of women, the symptoms can be so severe they can be debilitating.

Symptoms are thought to be caused by changes in hormone levels and brain chemicals. The symptoms may also be worsened by low vitamin and mineral intake, and alcohol and caffeine intake. In addition, excess sodium can cause water retention and bloating.

Nutrients That Alleviate the Symptoms of PMS

Calcium and magnesium have been found to improve mood and decrease the water retention that leads to bloating. Vitamin B6 has been associated with a decrease in the irritability that accompanies PMS in some studies, as well as reduced depression and breast tenderness. Manganese, when combined with calcium, may also reduce irritability, depression, and tension.

Foods That Contain These Nutrients

Calcium intake can be increased with dairy products such as milk and yogurt, but don't forget about dark leafy greens, including kale and broccoli. For magnesium, try cashews, quinoa, amaranth, and peanut butter. Vitamin

B$_6$ can be found in chickpeas, wild salmon, chicken, and pistachios. Include pineapple, pecans, and raspberries for more manganese.

ESSENTIAL

Risk factors for developing PMS include family history, stress, history of depression, increasing age, high caffeine consumption, a sedentary lifestyle, a diet high in sugar, abuse of alcohol, and having multiple children.

Tips for Incorporating These Foods

Before you begin experiencing PMS symptoms, plan your meals, keeping the key nutrients in mind. Salmon served with dark leafy greens or chicken breast with a pineapple salsa and a side of broccoli are great examples. Snack on nutritious pecans, cashews, fresh raspberries, and pistachios.

Comfort Yogurt Parfait

This parfait can be enjoyed as a breakfast or even a midday snack.
It combines a variety of foods that can help to prevent and relieve the symptoms of PMS.

INGREDIENTS | SERVES 1

8 ounces vanilla Greek yogurt

¼ cup pineapple, diced

1 tablespoon raw cashews, chopped

1 tablespoon raw pistachios

¼ cup fresh raspberries

1 tablespoon raw pecans, chopped

1. Divide the yogurt into 4 equal portions. In a bowl or a dessert cup, add 1 portion of yogurt. Top it with the pineapple.

2. Next add more yogurt, and top it with the cashews and pistachios. Layer with more yogurt and add the raspberries. Finish with yogurt and top it with the pecans. Serve immediately.

PER SERVING Calories: 305 | Fat: 19g | Sodium: 115mg | Carbohydrates: 25g | Fiber: 3g | Protein: 12g

Toasted Chickpeas

When toasted in a hot oven with spices, a simple can of chickpeas becomes a delicious, crunchy snack. This recipe is easy to make and you will have something for munching in about a half hour.

INGREDIENTS | SERVES 4

1 (12-ounce) can chickpeas
2 tablespoons olive oil
½ teaspoon garlic powder
1 teaspoon chili powder
1 teaspoon ground cumin
½ teaspoon salt
½ teaspoon black pepper

1. Preheat the oven to 425°F. Rinse and drain the chickpeas. Place on a clean kitchen towel and dry well.

2. Transfer the chickpeas to a bowl and add the olive oil. Stir to coat. Add the garlic powder, chili powder, cumin, salt, and pepper. Stir gently to coat the chickpeas in the spices, careful not to break them up.

3. Pour the chickpeas onto a baking sheet in a single layer. Bake for about 30 to 40 minutes. Stir gently every 10 to 15 minutes to prevent burning. Remove from the oven when browned and crispy. Serve warm or at room temperature.

PER SERVING Calories: 203 | Fat: 9g | Sodium: 502mg | Carbohydrates: 24g | Fiber: 7g | Protein: 8g

Pecan Chicken Bites

This recipe combines sweet pecans with savory chicken for a quick dinner that is full of vitamin B$_6$ and minerals. You will enjoy this toasted, crunchy topping on chicken.

INGREDIENTS | SERVES 4

12 ounces chicken breast, cut into pieces
½ cup buttermilk
½ cup bread crumbs
½ cup pecans, finely chopped
1 teaspoon salt
½ teaspoon pepper

Appetizer or Main Course

Cut into very small bite-size pieces and serve the cooked chicken at a cocktail party with toothpicks and a honey mustard sauce for dipping. You can also coat whole chicken breasts in the pecans. Serve them with a side of Spicy Sautéed Greens (Chapter 3) or slice them up and serve them over salad.

1. Preheat the oven to 400°F and lightly grease a baking sheet or pan. In a shallow dish or a sealable plastic bag, combine the chicken and buttermilk. Allow the chicken to marinate for 10 minutes while you prepare the other ingredients.

2. On a plate or in a shallow dish, combine the bread crumbs, pecans, salt, and pepper. Remove the chicken from the buttermilk, one piece at a time, and coat in the pecan mixture.

3. Arrange the pieces of chicken on the baking sheet or pan in a single layer. Bake for about 20 minutes, or until the pecans have browned and the chicken has cooked through. Serve warm.

PER SERVING Calories: 253 | Fat: 12g | Sodium: 767mg | Carbohydrates: 13g | Fiber: 2g | Protein: 23g

Hot Tropical Amaranth with Coconut

If you are looking for a change from your daily oatmeal or oat bran, try amaranth.
It cooks up like a porridge for a delicious whole-grain breakfast.
Here, coconut and pineapple add sweetness and tropical flavor.

INGREDIENTS | SERVES 1

½ cup amaranth

1 teaspoon muscovado sugar

2 tablespoons coconut milk

¼ cup fresh pineapple, diced

1 tablespoon unsweetened shredded coconut

Whole Amaranth

Look for whole amaranth in the bulk bin of your health food store, or purchase it online. Just be sure that it is the whole grain and not amaranth flour. Whole amaranth is ideal for hot cereals such as the one featured here. Amaranth flour is finely ground and makes a nutritious addition to bread and muffin batters.

1. Combine the amaranth with 1 cup of water in a medium saucepan over medium-high heat. Bring to a boil, then reduce the heat to simmer. Cook, stirring often, for 20 to 25 minutes or until the water has been absorbed and the grains are tender.

2. Place the amaranth in a bowl and top with the sugar. Stir to incorporate and melt the sugar. Pour in the coconut milk and add the pineapple and shredded coconut. Serve hot.

PER SERVING Calories: 453 | Fat: 14g | Sodium: 9mg | Carbohydrates: 73g | Fiber: 7g | Protein: 14g

Sautéed Broccoli Raab with Cashews

This is a nutty side dish that pairs well with chicken or fish. It is important to limit sodium intake for PMS, so a very small of amount of tamari is used simply to flavor the vegetables and nuts.

INGREDIENTS | SERVES 4

1 pound broccoli raab
1 tablespoon olive oil
1 medium onion, thinly sliced
1 clove garlic, minced
1 teaspoon tamari
½ cup raw cashews

What Is Broccoli Raab?

Broccoli raab is also called rapini or spelled broccoli rabe. It is sometimes used in the cuisines of southern Italy, China, and Portugal. It looks similar to broccoli, is related to the turnip, and is known for having a slight bitter flavor. Boiling before sautéing as suggested in this recipe helps to mellow the bitterness.

1. In a large pot, bring about 6 cups of water to a boil. Add the broccoli raab and cook about 3 to 5 minutes. Remove, chop into pieces, and set aside.

2. In a deep skillet, heat the olive oil over medium-high heat, and add the onion and garlic. Cook for 2 minutes and add the broccoli raab. Sauté for 7 to 10 minutes or until it reaches your desired tenderness.

3. Stir in the tamari and the cashews. Serve warm.

PER SERVING Calories: 151 | Fat: 11g | Sodium: 124mg | Carbohydrates: 11g | Fiber: 4g | Protein: 7g

CHAPTER 29

Psoriasis

Psoriasis is a condition that affects about 7.5 million Americans. It results in red, itchy skin that is both painful and frustrating. Unfortunately psoriasis is a long-term, chronic disease where improvement and worsening of symptoms continually occurs. Some foods can be beneficial in reducing inflammation, improving the condition of the skin.

What Is Psoriasis?

While psoriasis looks like a rash, it is actually a chronic autoimmune disease that is not contagious. It affects a process called cell turnover. Cells usually develop deep in the skin and they rise to the surface over a month's time. With psoriasis, this process happens much more quickly, usually in a few days. This results in dry skin that is patchy, itchy, and red.

FACT

The scaly patches of skin caused by psoriasis are called "plaques." These plaques usually appear on the knees and elbows, but other sites on the body can also be infected, including the scalp, soles of the feet, and genitals. Unlike eczema, which frequents the inner side of a joint (such as the inside of an elbow) where heat sweating can lead to outbreaks, psoriasis is more common on the outer side of joints.

The exact cause for psoriasis is unknown, but it is believed to involve the immune system, which results in the false triggering of the skin to grow new cells. Certain conditions can aggravate psoriasis, including stress, skin injury such as sunburn, and some medications.

Nutrients That Alleviate Psoriasis

Omega-3 fatty acids may help those with psoriasis because of its anti-inflammatory properties. In addition, folic acid may help to combat the nausea caused by psoriasis medications.

ALERT

Some nutrients, such as vitamin D, assist in the regulation of the immune system and may be beneficial for those with psoriasis. However, some medications for the condition already contain high amounts of vitamin D. Talk with your doctor about how nutrients may affect your condition in combination with your medications to avoid consuming too much of a good thing.

Foods That Contain These Nutrients

The best source for omega-3 fatty acids is cold-water fatty fish. Try lake trout, albacore tuna packed in water, and wild salmon.

QUESTION

Should I be concerned about the mercury in fish?
Yes, but don't let that keep you from eating it. High levels of mercury can cause learning disabilities and memory problems in children, making it important for women and children to monitor intake. However, many fish, including those rich in omega-3 fatty acids, are low in mercury. Limit your intake of large fish, including shark, swordfish, and king mackerel.

Plant sources of omega-3 fatty acid can be converted in the body to the same form of omega-3s as that in fatty fish. Some plant sources include walnuts, Brussels sprouts, kale, and spinach. Lentils, pinto beans, papayas, beets, asparagus, and spinach are sources of folate.

Tips for Incorporating These Foods

Incorporate fatty fish into your meals two to three times a week. Make extra when possible and enjoy the leftovers for lunch. Sprinkle walnuts on spinach salad and put fresh kale in your fruit smoothies. Pinto beans and lentils make a hearty, filling base for meatless meals that are full of fiber and nutrients. Experiment with papayas in fruit salad and beets as a side dish if you have never tried them.

Slow-Cooked Pinto Beans

Beans in a slow cooker do take some time, but they require little to no effort during that time. They also provide an inexpensive, nutritious meal. Put them in the pot in the morning, and dinner will be ready when you arrive home from work.

INGREDIENTS | SERVES 6

4 cups dry pinto beans

1 large onion, chopped

3 cloves garlic, minced

2 teaspoons salt

1 teaspoon black pepper

1 teaspoon cumin

1 teaspoon coriander

1. The night before making your beans, place the dried beans in a pan and cover them by at least 1 inch with water. Allow to sit overnight.

2. Put the soaked and drained beans in the slow cooker. Cover with water by about an inch. Stir in the remaining ingredients.

3. Set to high and cook for 8 hours. Serve warm.

PER SERVING Calories: 452 | Fat: 2g | Sodium: 792mg | Carbohydrates: 81g | Fiber: 20g | Protein: 28g

Simple Lentil Soup

A comforting lentil soup is the perfect way to combat a cold or dreary day.
This version is easy to make and packed with nutrients.

INGREDIENTS | SERVES 6

2 tablespoons olive oil

1 medium onion, diced

3 cloves garlic, minced

¾ cup carrot, diced

1 (14-ounce) can diced tomatoes

1 pound lentils, rinsed

6 cups chicken stock

1 teaspoon ground cumin

1 teaspoon smoked paprika

2 cups kale, chopped

1. Heat the oil in a soup pot over medium-high heat. Add the onion and garlic and cook for 1 minute. Add the carrot and cook 2 minutes more. Pour in the tomatoes and heat through.

2. Add the lentils and pour in the chicken stock. Stir in the cumin and paprika. Bring to a simmer and cook, partially covered, for 10 minutes.

3. Stir in the kale and continue to cook until the kale and lentils are tender, about 10 more minutes. Add salt if desired. Serve warm.

PER SERVING Calories: 364 | Fat: 6g | Sodium: 630mg | Carbohydrates: 55g | Fiber: 25g | Protein: 25g

Types of Lentils

There are many different varieties of lentils. Some include red lentils, brown lentils, French green lentils, and black beluga lentils. Each has a slightly different texture and cooking time. Use any type of lentils with this recipe; just test for doneness after the suggested cooking time, and continue to cook if the lentils are not yet tender.

Tuna Melt

The firm texture and rich flavor of albacore tuna will make this sandwich a favorite. It is mixed with herbs, combined with cheese, and served toasted. Feel free to add mayonnaise or your favorite spread if desired.

INGREDIENTS | SERVES 2

1 (5-ounce) can albacore tuna in water, drained

1 tablespoon fresh dill, chopped

2 tablespoons onion, diced

2 tablespoons ricotta cheese

¼ cup sharp Cheddar, shredded

¼ teaspoon salt

⅛ teaspoon black pepper

4 slices whole-grain bread

2 large slices tomato

1. In a small bowl, combine the tuna, dill, onion, ricotta, Cheddar, salt, and pepper. Mix well.

2. Preheat a nonstick skillet, grill pan, or panini press. Divide the tuna mixture and place it on 2 slices of bread. Top each with a slice of tomato and the remaining slice of bread.

3. Transfer sandwiches to the pan or press. Cook until the bread is browned and the tuna is heated through, about 3 minutes on each side over medium heat. Serve warm.

PER SERVING Calories: 259 | Fat: 5g | Sodium: 840mg | Carbohydrates: 26g | Fiber: 4g | Protein: 26g

Open-Face Salmon Sandwich

With spinach, asparagus, and salmon, this open-faced sandwich stacks up all kinds of nutritious ingredients beneficial for psoriasis. If you don't want the lemon dill sauce, feel free to leave it off or substitute your own creation.

INGREDIENTS | SERVES 1

Salt and pepper, to taste

1 (4-ounce) salmon fillet

4 medium asparagus spears

2 tablespoons plain Greek yogurt

1 teaspoon fresh lemon juice

1 tablespoon fresh dill, chopped

1 slice whole-grain bread

½ cup fresh spinach leaves

Sauce Ideas

A good sauce drizzled over an open-faced sandwich makes all the difference. Try mimicking this recipe, but use yogurt with a little mayonnaise, or use sour cream for a twist on flavor. If you like a sweet and salty combination, a spiced fruit chutney goes wonderfully with the savory salmon in this sandwich.

1. Preheat a grill pan on medium-high heat. Salt and pepper the salmon fillet to taste and place on the grill pan. Cook about 3 minutes on each side or until salmon flakes with a fork. Set aside.

2. Prepare an ice bath with about 1 cup of ice in a medium bowl filled with water. Fill a medium-size saucepan with water and bring to a boil.

3. Place the asparagus in the boiling water for about 1 minute. Remove, and immediately place in the ice bath. Remove from the water, dry, and season with salt and pepper to taste. Set aside.

4. In a small dish, stir together the Greek yogurt, lemon juice, dill, and salt and pepper to taste. Place the bread on a plate and top it with the spinach leaves. Drizzle with half of the yogurt.

5. Top with the asparagus and then gently break up the salmon and place it on top of the asparagus. Drizzle with the remaining yogurt sauce. Serve immediately with a fork and knife.

PER SERVING Calories: 238 | Fat: 6g | Sodium: 212mg | Carbohydrates: 17g | Fiber: 4g | Protein: 29g

Papaya Cream

Papaya cream is a traditional dessert in Brazil. You can use your favorite vanilla ice cream or frozen yogurt in this recipe. The traditional recipe calls for a shot of crème de cassis on top, but it is great with or without this addition.

INGREDIENTS | SERVES 2

2 ripe papayas
1½ cups vanilla ice cream

The Right Consistency

Papaya Cream should be at a consistency somewhere between soft serve ice cream and a thick milkshake. It will be slightly melted, but still firm enough to eat with a spoon. If the Papaya Cream is too thin, place it in the freezer for 5 to 10 minutes before serving.

1. Peel the papayas, cut in half, and remove all of the seeds. Cut it into large chunks and place in a blender.

2. Add the ice cream to the blender and pulse until everything is smooth and combined.

3. Pour into 2 dessert cups and serve with a spoon.

PER SERVING Calories: 324 | Fat: 11g | Sodium: 88mg | Carbohydrates: 53g | Fiber: 6g | Protein: 5g

CHAPTER 30

Stress and Anxiety

Stress and anxiety are conditions that are directly related to mental health, but they can affect your physical health, too. Research has identified some nutrients and foods that can influence feelings of stress and anxiety.

What Causes Stress and Anxiety?

Stress is a feeling of frustration that is common in everyday life. Stress is a psychological and physical reaction to pressure placed on an individual by external or internal sources. Pressure can come from the environment outside of you—your home life, relationships, or work life. Pressure also comes from within you, as your desires, urges, and thoughts struggle within you to meet your needs and achieve your dreams. A small amount of stress in your life can be a positive thing. It can motivate you to do your best, such as in meeting a deadline at work. However, when you experience too much stress and are not able to control your stress levels, your mental and physical health can suffer. Stress is a very individual response. One situation may produce stress in one person but not in another.

FACT

Anxiety can also be a symptom of a more serious anxiety disorder that is classified as a psychiatric condition. If you feel that your anxiety is out of your control, consider seeking the guidance of a mental health professional along with incorporating beneficial foods into your diet for mental health and well-being.

Too much stress results in anxiety and such unhealthy coping behaviors as drug or alcohol use. Anxiety is a feeling of fear or apprehension. It can also include physical symptoms—for example, stomach pain, head and muscle aches, rapid heartbeat, and irritability.

Nutrients That Alleviate Stress and Anxiety

According to the National Institutes of Health, low levels of vitamin B_{12} can contribute to feelings of stress and anxiety. Other vitamins play a role in the production and function of neurotransmitters. Some neurotransmitters affect mood, relaxation, and emotions. These include vitamins C, B_6, B_1, B_2, and folate. In addition, the amino acid tryptophan influences the production of serotonin in the brain, which has a calming effect. Low levels of magnesium are also linked to increased and chronic anxiety.

Foods That Contain These Nutrients

Papayas, red bell peppers, basil, and arugula are rich in the nutrients that influence the presence and function of neurotransmitters. Poultry, such as chicken or turkey breast, and milk contain both tryptophan and vitamin B_{12}. Bananas also contain tryptophan. Pumpkin seeds, spinach and Swiss chard, and some beans, including black beans and navy beans, contain magnesium.

ESSENTIAL

The number-one way to beat stress is a method that contains no harmful medications, expensive visits to the doctor, or hours of therapy: it's exercise. When you are stressed, your body is in a fight-or-flight mode, ready for action, and exercise is the exact relief your body needs; exercise gets your body moving and releases the anxiety that stress can build up. Exercise can also help you manage stress before it even begins, as exercise is a proven mood-booster.

Tips for Incorporating These Foods

You can ease stress and anxiety with a simple sandwich that includes chicken or turkey. Bell pepper strips and bananas are ideal for on-the-go snacking. Top muffins with pumpkin seeds before baking and regularly incorporate a large pot of healthful beans into your cooking.

Tropical Chicken Salad

This chicken salad has a sweet twist that also provides nutrients that may reduce stress and anxiety. Eat it served on a bed of lettuce or as a wrap or sandwich.

INGREDIENTS | SERVES 2

1½ cups cooked chicken, shredded

¼ cup celery, diced

¼ cup red bell pepper, diced

½ cup papaya, diced

¼ cup pineapple, diced

¼ cup pecans, chopped

2 tablespoons mayonnaise

2 tablespoons plain Greek yogurt

½ teaspoon salt

¼ teaspoon black pepper

1. In a medium bowl, combine the chicken, celery, bell pepper, papaya, pineapple, and pecans.

2. In a small bowl, mix together the mayonnaise, yogurt, salt, and pepper. Add more salt or pepper to taste. Pour dressing over chicken.

3. Toss all ingredients until fully combined. Refrigerate for at least 30 minutes before serving.

PER SERVING Calories: 390 | Fat: 23g | Sodium: 794mg | Carbohydrates: 14g | Fiber: 3g | Protein: 33g

Grilled Turkey Apple Sandwich with Arugula

The strong, bitter flavor of arugula pairs nicely with the sweet apple in this sandwich. If you are tired of plain whole-grain sandwich bread, try using a whole-grain baguette with this sandwich for variety.

INGREDIENTS | SERVES 2

6 ounces turkey breast, shredded

1 small Granny Smith apple, sliced

⅓ cup Cheddar cheese, shredded

1 cup arugula, chopped

4 slices whole-grain bread

Real Meat

Processed lunch meat has sodium and other preservatives, and very little of the beneficial nutrients found in turkey breast meat. A whole turkey or breast can be worth the investment for your health and pocketbook. Bake it over the weekend and use the meat for soups, sandwiches, and salads throughout your week.

1. For each sandwich, layer half of the turkey, apple slices, cheese, and arugula on a slice of bread. Top with the remaining slice.

2. Preheat a grill pan or panini press. Grill the sandwich on medium-high heat about 3 minutes on each side, or until the bread is browned and the cheese has begun to melt. Serve warm.

PER SERVING Calories: 368 | Fat: 9g | Sodium: 381mg
Carbohydrates: 33g | Fiber: 6g | Protein: 37g

Fresh Red Bell Pepper Dip with Basil

This dip blends sweet red bell pepper, aromatic basil, and tangy yogurt.
It is ideal as a dip for vegetables or as a spread for your favorite sandwich.

INGREDIENTS | MAKES ½ CUP

1 red bell pepper, chopped

1 clove garlic

½ cup fresh basil leaves

½ cup plain Greek yogurt

1 tablespoon lemon juice

½ teaspoon salt

¼ teaspoon black pepper

1. Combine the bell pepper, garlic clove, and basil in a small food processor. Pulse until ingredients are almost puréed.

2. Add the yogurt, lemon juice, salt, and pepper. Blend until all of the ingredients come together into a smooth dip. Add more salt and pepper to taste. Refrigerate 30 minutes before serving.

PER 1 TABLESPOON Calories: 15 | Fat: 1g | Sodium: 153mg | Carbohydrates: 2g | Fiber: 0g | Protein: 1g

Pumpkin Muffins

These spiced muffins topped with crunchy pumpkin seeds are best served warm.
Enjoy them with your favorite cup of coffee or tea for a comforting yet convenient breakfast.

INGREDIENTS | MAKES 12 MUFFINS

½ cup demerara sugar

½ cup butter, melted

2 eggs

¾ cup milk

1 cup puréed pumpkin

2½ cups white whole-wheat flour

1 teaspoon baking soda

1 teaspoon salt

2 teaspoons pumpkin pie spice

1 cup raw pumpkin seeds

Sweet Banana

Mashed ripe banana can add sweetness to your baked goods, allowing you to use less sugar. While the sugar in this recipe has already been reduced, try using banana in your next quick bread or muffin recipe. Reduce the sugar by about ⅓ and add 1 mashed banana. You just might discover a healthier, lower-sugar version of your old favorite.

1. Preheat the oven to 350°F. Grease a 12-muffin tin. In a bowl, whisk together the sugar, butter, and eggs. Stir in the milk and pumpkin.

2. In a separate bowl, combine the flour, baking soda, salt, and pumpkin pie spice. Gradually add the dry ingredients to the wet, stirring just until combined.

3. Divide the batter into the 12 muffin cups. Top each muffin with an equal amount of the pumpkin seeds. Press them down gently into the batter.

4. Bake 20 minutes or until a toothpick inserted into the center comes out clean. Cool in the pan for 3 to 5 minutes; remove to a cooling rack or serve.

PER 1 MUFFIN Calories: 267 | Fat: 15g | Sodium: 272mg | Carbohydrates: 29g | Fiber: 4g | Protein: 8g

Arugula Sun-Dried Tomato Pizza

This flavorful pizza uses very little cheese, but you will never miss it when you taste the sweet and slightly bitter combination of the nutrient-rich arugula and sun-dried tomatoes.

INGREDIENTS | SERVES 4

Dough for 1 (14-inch) pizza crust
⅓ cup mozzarella, shredded
¼ cup Parmesan cheese, grated
½ cup sun-dried tomatoes, sliced
2 cups arugula, chopped

1. Preheat the oven to 400°F. Spread the dough onto a pizza pan and gently prick the surface with a fork in multiple places.

2. Sprinkle on the cheeses and the sun-dried tomatoes. Bake for 10 to 15 minutes, or until the crust is done and the cheese is slightly browned and bubbly.

3. Remove from the oven and immediately spread the arugula on the pizza, allowing it to wilt slightly. Cut into 8 slices and serve.

PER SERVING Calories: 355 | Fat: 9g | Sodium: 829mg | Carbohydrates: 53g | Fiber: 3g | Protein: 16g

CHAPTER 31

Urinary Tract Infections

Urinary tract infections (UTIs) most often occur in the lower part of the urinary system. Once an infection occurs, an antibiotic may be necessary to fight it off; however, there are foods that can help you prevent a UTI from developing.

What Is a Urinary Tract Infection?

A UTI is a bacterial infection of the urinary system. Women are more likely than men to get urinary tract infections, as the bladder and anus are much closer on the female body than the males, thus raising the chances of bacteria entering the urinary tract. Symptoms of a urinary tract infection include:

- A strong persistent urge to urinate
- A burning sensation when urinating
- Urine that appears cloudy
- Passing small frequent amounts of urine
- Strong-smelling urine
- Pelvic pain (in women)
- Rectal pain (in men)
- Pain in the kidneys (signals an infection in the upper urinary tract)
- Urine that appears pink in color (a sign of blood in the urine)

If the infection affects the kidneys, fever and flulike symptoms may also occur, such as chills, shaking, nausea, vomiting, high fever, and upper back and side pain.

FACT

Urine normally contains a mixture of fluids and salt, but it usually does not contain bacteria. When bacteria find their way into the bladder or kidneys (usually by way of sexual intercourse or catheters), they multiply in urine and a urinary tract infection ensues.

Nutrients That Prevent or Alleviate UTIs

Vitamin C can be helpful in two ways when it comes to UTIs. First, it can make the urine more acidic. This acidic environment prevents the growth of bacteria in the urinary system. It is also an antioxidant and supports a healthy immune system. Other unidentified nutrients that come from specific foods are thought to prevent the growth of bacteria leading to a UTI.

Foods That Contain These Nutrients

Cranberries and blueberries contain substances that prevent the growth of bacteria, thus preventing UTIs. The exact method or substance is still under investigation. In addition, vitamin C can be found in red bell peppers, parsley, broccoli, cauliflower, Brussels sprouts, papayas, cantaloupes, and strawberries.

ESSENTIAL

The urinary tract is made up of the kidneys, ureters, urethra, and bladder. Any part of this urinary system can become infected with bacteria and cause a UTI. Most infections infect the lower part of the urinary tract, specifically the bladder and urethra.

Tips for Incorporating These Foods

Dried cranberries and fresh or dried blueberries make an ideal snack and a tangy topping for salads and cereals. You can also drink no-sugar-added cranberry and blueberry juice. Parsley can season any pasta salad, green salad, or breakfast omelet. Broccoli, cauliflower, and Brussels sprouts make perfect, simple side dishes.

Steamed Brussels Sprouts with Cranberries and Parsley

Brussels sprouts are like tiny cabbages. They have a distinct bitter taste that pairs nicely with the sweet, yet tart dried cranberry. You will need a steaming basket or pot for this recipe.

INGREDIENTS | SERVES 4

1 pound Brussels sprouts

1 tablespoon unsalted butter

⅓ cup dried cranberries

2 tablespoons fresh parsley, chopped

½ teaspoon salt

¼ teaspoon black pepper

1. Bring 3 cups of water to a boil in the bottom of a steaming pan. Meanwhile prepare the Brussels sprouts by soaking them in water for about 3 minutes. Carefully cut off the very end of the stems and cut an X in the bottom of each sprout.

2. Place the Brussels sprouts in the steaming basket, reduce the heat of the water slightly, and place the steaming basket over the water. Cover with a lid and steam for 5 minutes.

3. Transfer the Brussels sprouts to a serving bowl. Add the butter, cranberries, parsley, salt, and pepper. Toss gently to mix ingredients and serve warm.

PER SERVING Calories: 105 | Fat: 3g | Sodium: 320mg | Carbohydrates: 18g | Fiber: 5g | Protein: 4g

Cranberry Sauce

This quick cranberry sauce is great as a topping for oatmeal or a spread for a turkey sandwich.
A little added sugar helps to balance the tartness of the berry.

INGREDIENTS | MAKES 1 CUP

1 cup fresh cranberries

¼ cup water

3 tablespoons demerara sugar

1 teaspoon orange zest

¼ cup pecans, finely chopped

Too Tart

If this recipe brings out a little too much of the tartness of the cranberry for your liking, try adding orange juice instead of the water. This will add sweetness and also a stronger citrus flavor to the final sauce.

1. Combine the cranberries, ¼ cup water, and the sugar in a saucepan. Bring to a boil; reduce heat slightly and cook for 10 to 15 minutes, stirring often. The berries should break down and the sauce should begin to thicken.

2. Stir in the orange zest and pecans. Allow the sauce to cool and thicken even further. Store in a sealed container, in the refrigerator, for up to a week.

PER 1 TABLESPOON Calories: 21 | Fat: 1g | Sodium: 1mg | Carbohydrates: 3g | Fiber: 0g | Protein: 0g

Cranberry Orange Drink

This refreshing beverage has the UTI-fighting power of cranberry juice and looks pretty, too. A garnish of fresh orange and cranberries makes it an ideal dinner party drink.

INGREDIENTS | MAKES 2 LITERS

1 orange, sliced
½ cup fresh, whole cranberries
2½ cups unsweetened cranberry juice
1½ cups fresh orange juice
1 liter club soda

1. Place the orange slices and cranberries in a clear glass pitcher.

2. Pour the cranberry juice and orange juice into the pitcher and stir. Carefully pour in the club soda. Serve over ice.

PER ½ CUP SERVING Calories: 32 | Fat: 0g | Sodium: 13mg | Carbohydrates: 8g | Fiber: 0g | Protein: 0g

Berry Tomato Salad

*The sweet flavor of cherry tomatoes goes well with such fruits as blueberries and strawberries.
This salad is packed with vitamin C and other nutrients that help to prevent UTIs.*

INGREDIENTS | SERVES 4

1 cup cherry tomatoes, quartered

½ cup fresh blueberries

½ cup fresh strawberries, diced

½ cup red bell pepper, diced

3 ounces whole-milk mozzarella, cubed

2 tablespoons olive oil

2 tablespoons fresh basil, chopped

Salt and pepper, to taste

Basil Chiffonade

Chiffonade is a way of cutting herb leaves into thin strips. It can be substituted for any chopped basil in this book. Stack the basil leaves, and roll them into a tight bundle like a cigar. Place the bundle horizontally on a cutting board and use a sharp knife to thinly slice the basil. Fluff up and toss on your salad.

1. In a bowl, combine the tomatoes, blueberries, strawberries, and bell pepper. Stir in the cheese cubes and drizzle with olive oil. Toss to coat in the oil.

2. Add the basil. Then add salt and pepper to taste. Serve immediately or refrigerate 30 minutes to 1 hour before serving.

PER SERVING Calories: 156 | Fat: 12g | Sodium: 90mg | Carbohydrates: 7g | Fiber: 2g | Protein: 5g

Rosemary Broccoli and Cauliflower over Brown Rice

This recipe focuses on the flavors of fresh broccoli and cauliflower by cooking it only slightly to maintain crunchiness. The rosemary not only tastes good, but will fill your kitchen with an appetizing aroma.

INGREDIENTS | SERVES 6

1½ cups chicken stock

1 cup brown rice

2 tablespoons olive oil

1 medium onion, thinly sliced

2 cloves garlic, minced

1 head broccoli florets

1 head cauliflower florets

1 teaspoon fresh rosemary, chopped

1 teaspoon salt

½ teaspoon black pepper

1. Combine the chicken stock and rice in a large saucepan. Bring to a boil over medium-high heat. Reduce the heat to low and simmer, covered, for about 45 minutes or until the water is absorbed and the rice is tender. Watch closely toward the end of cooking so the rice does not burn.

2. Heat olive oil in a deep skillet and add the onion and garlic. Cook for about 5 minutes or until onions are softened. Add the broccoli and cauliflower and cook for 3 minutes more, or until the edges begin to brown.

3. Stir in the rosemary, salt, and pepper. Add more to taste if desired. Serve warm over the brown rice.

PER SERVING Calories: 238 | Fat: 6g | Sodium: 594mg | Carbohydrates: 40g | Fiber: 8g | Protein: 9g

CHAPTER 32

Varicose Veins

Not only are varicose veins unsightly, but they can be painful, too. While factors including heredity and weight play a significant role in the development of varicose veins, there are nutrients that can improve leg circulation and decrease the chance of developing these veins.

What Are Varicose Veins?

Veins carry circulated blood back to the heart so that it can be filled with oxygen again and used by the body. To keep blood moving toward the heart, veins have a valve. When this valve becomes weak or damaged, some blood can pool in the veins and swell. These varicose veins are then visible under the skin, most often in the legs. They can cause throbbing, swelling, and itching of the leg, and blood clots can also occur in the vein, which can be painful and dangerous.

FACT

Varicose veins are different from spider veins. Spider veins are smaller and involve the capillaries instead of the veins. They usually show up on the surface of the skin like a spider web and can be blue or red in color. These veins most often occur on the legs, but they can become present on the face as well.

Risk for developing varicose veins increases if you have family members with them, as you age, and for women, especially during pregnancy. Being overweight, standing for long periods without moving around, and sitting with crossed legs can also contribute to the condition.

Nutrients That Improve Circulation and Prevent Varicose Veins

Vitamin C is helpful for circulation and contributes to the structure of the vein wall. Rutin, one of the plant substances called bioflavonoids, may strengthen capillary walls. In addition, the anthocyanins that give some fruits and vegetables their deep red or purple color can tone and strengthen the walls of capillaries, veins, and arteries.

Foods That Contain These Nutrients

Dark-colored berries, such as blackberries and blueberries, and cherries contain anthocyanins and vitamin C, as well as other beneficial nutrients for health. To increase your intake of rutin, eat more asparagus, citrus fruits, apples, and buckwheat.

FACT

Many of the beneficial nutrients of fruits exist in the edible peel. For example, the rutin is found in the apple peel, and the skins of blueberries and cherries contain anthocyanins. In addition, delicate nutrients including vitamin C can be destroyed by heat. Incorporate raw and whole fruits into your diet often for the most health benefit.

Tips for Incorporating These Foods

Snack on berries, cherries, and apples, and if you enjoy fresh juice use these fruits to make your own. Substitute soba noodles made with buckwheat for other pastas and grains in your recipes, or experiment with using buckwheat flour in your breads, cookies, and pancakes.

Asparagus with Orange Ginger Glaze

This recipe will spice up any plain, steamed asparagus.
The citrus and ginger add a pleasant flavor and aroma to the vegetable's distinctive flavor.

INGREDIENTS | SERVES 4

1 pound asparagus spears
½ tablespoon olive oil
Salt and pepper, to taste
1 cup fresh orange juice
1 teaspoon orange zest
1 teaspoon fresh ginger, grated
1 teaspoon tamari

Preparing Asparagus

The top part of the asparagus shoot is the most desirable for eating. Hold one piece of asparagus at the cut end and at a spot halfway up. Allow the end to break at a natural point by bending it gently. Use this piece as a guide for trimming the ends of the rest of the bundle.

1. Preheat the oven to 400°F. Trim the cut ends of the asparagus, wash under running water, and dry. Place the asparagus on a baking sheet in a single layer. Drizzle with the olive oil and sprinkle with salt and pepper. Bake for 10 minutes, until slightly tender.

2. In a saucepan, combine the orange juice, zest, ginger, and tamari. Bring to a boil and cook at a low boil, stirring constantly, for about 10 minutes or until the glaze thickens.

3. Transfer the roasted asparagus from the baking sheet to a serving dish. Pour the glaze over the asparagus and serve warm.

PER SERVING Calories: 66 | Fat: 2g | Sodium: 87mg | Carbohydrates: 11g | Fiber: 2g | Protein: 3g

Apple Cherry Salad

Use a sweet variety of apple to balance the tartness of the cherries and cherry dressing in this salad. Fuji, Gala, or Golden Delicious would be ideal for this recipe.

INGREDIENTS | SERVES 4

1 head romaine lettuce, chopped
1 cup cabbage, finely shredded
2 apples, sliced
1 cup dried tart cherries
½ cup pecans, chopped
½ cup tart cherry juice
1 tablespoon apple cider vinegar
2 tablespoons olive oil
Salt and pepper, to taste

1. In a large bowl, toss together the lettuce and the cabbage. Add the apple slices, dried cherries, and pecans.

2. In a small bowl, whisk together the cherry juice, cider vinegar, and olive oil. Add salt and pepper to taste.

3. Pour the dressing over the salad and toss gently to distribute it over all of the ingredients. Serve immediately.

PER SERVING Calories: 232 | Fat: 17g | Sodium: 10mg | Carbohydrates: 21g | Fiber: 4g | Protein: 2g

Blueberry Water

This recipe can also be called an agua fresca, a refreshing drink of fruit and water common in Mexico and Central America. You can drink this beverage as it is, or add simple syrup or raw sugar to sweeten it a bit.

INGREDIENTS | SERVES 6

1½ cups fresh blueberries

3½ cups water

10 fresh mint leaves

More Fruit Water

Any type of fruit that purées will work for an aqua fresca. Try blackberries, tart cherries, watermelon, or cantaloupe. Prepare in the same way, strain, and pour over ice. For even more refreshing flavor, add lime juice or blend with an herb such as basil.

1. Combine the blueberries, 2 cups of the water, and mint leaves in the blender. Purée until the blueberries are blended and smooth.

2. Strain the pulp through a fine sieve or strainer and collect the drained blueberry water. Transfer the blueberry water to a pitcher and add the remaining 1½ cups water. Stir, serve over ice, and add sugar if desired.

PER SERVING Calories: 22 | Fat: 0g | Sodium: 4mg | Carbohydrates: 6g | Fiber: 1g | Protein: 0g

Buckwheat Blackberry Pancakes

The deep, rich flavor of buckwheat flour goes nicely with blackberries.
Cook some blackberries in your pancakes, but be sure to leave a few extra because they
are equally delicious when served uncooked as a topping.

INGREDIENTS | MAKES 6 PANCAKES

1 egg, beaten
1 cup milk
1 tablespoon muscovado sugar
½ cup white whole-wheat flour
½ cup buckwheat flour
3 teaspoons baking powder
¼ teaspoon salt
2 tablespoons butter, melted
1½ cups fresh blackberries

1. In a bowl, mix together the egg, milk, and sugar. In a separate bowl, combine the flours, baking powder, and salt. Gradually add the dry ingredients to the wet ingredients. Stir in the butter.

2. Heat a nonstick griddle pan over medium heat. Drop the pancake batter by ¼-cup portions onto the hot griddle, working in batches. Press 4 to 5 blackberries into the batter of each pancake.

3. Flip the pancakes once the batter begins to bubble, after about 90 seconds. Cook the same amount on the other side. Serve warm with maple syrup and berries on top.

PER 1 PANCAKE Calories: 162 | Fat: 7g | Sodium: 393mg | Carbohydrates: 23g | Fiber: 4g | Protein: 6g

Cranberry Blueberry Scones

The red, white, and blue color of these scones makes them a fun treat for any patriotic holiday. However, once you try them you will want to make them much more often than two or three times a year!

INGREDIENTS | SERVES 8

1¼ cups white whole-wheat flour
2¼ teaspoons baking powder
3 tablespoons muscovado sugar
½ teaspoon cinnamon
¼ teaspoon salt
¼ cup unsalted butter, cold
⅓ cup dried cranberries
⅓ cup dried blueberries
½ cup milk
3 tablespoons demerara sugar

1. Preheat the oven to 400°F and grease a large baking sheet. In a bowl, stir together the flour, baking powder, sugar, cinnamon, and salt.

2. Cut the cold butter into pieces and add to the dry ingredients. Use 2 knives or a pastry blender to mix until the butter is in small pea-size pieces.

3. Stir in the dried cranberries and blueberries. Add milk a little bit at a time and mix with a fork or spoonula until a cohesive dough is formed. Place the ball of dough on a floured surface and press or roll into a circle about ½ inch thick.

4. Cut the dough into 8 equal triangular pieces. Arrange the pieces on the baking sheet. Top each scone with an equal amount of demerara sugar and gently press the sugar into the dough with your hand.

5. Bake 12 to 15 minutes or until the edges begin to brown. Remove from the baking sheet and cool on a cooling rack. Serve warm or at room temperature.

PER 1 SCONE Calories: 157 | Fat: 6g | Sodium: 210mg | Carbohydrates: 25g | Fiber: 3g | Protein: 3g

APPENDIX A

Print Resources

Bauer, Joy. *Joy Bauer's Food Cures: Treat Common Health Concerns, Look Younger & Live Longer*. (Emmaus, PA: Rodale Books, 2007.)

Bernstein, Carolyn. *The Migraine Brain: Your Breakthrough Guide to Fewer Headaches, Better Health*. (New York: Free Press, 2008.)

Casey, Aggie and Benson, Herbert. *Harvard Medical School Guide to Lowering Your Blood Pressure*. (Columbus, OH: McGraw-Hill, 2005.)

Clough, John. *The Cleveland Clinic Guide to Arthritis*. (New York: Kaplan Publishing, 2009.)

Friedman, Lawrence. *The Sensitive Gut: A Harvard Medical School Book*. (New York: Fireside, 2008.)

Goldberg, Nieca. *Dr. Nieca Goldberg's Complete Guide to Women's Health*. (New York: Ballantine Books, 2009.)

Greene, Bob. *The Best Life Guide to Managing Diabetes and Pre-Diabetes*. (New York: Simon & Schuster, 2009.)

Marwan, Sabbagh. *The Alzheimer's Answer: Reduce Your Risk and Keep Your Brain Healthy*. (Hoboken, NJ: Wiley, 2009.)

Napier, Kristine. *Eat Away Diabetes*. (New York: Prentice Hall Press, 2002.)

Web-Based Resources

"Agricultural Research: Nurture Your Diet, Not Disease," July 2010

This is a web-based document from the U.S. Department of Agriculture that discusses current findings in nutritional research as it relates to diseases including Alzheimer's, heart disease, and diabetes.

www.ars.usda.gov/is/AR/archive/jul10/July2010.pdf

American Cancer Society

This is a resource for current health information about cancers.

www.cancer.org

American Diabetes Association

This is a resource for current health information about diabetes.

www.diabetes.org

American Heart Association

This is a resource for current health information about heart disease and stroke.

www.americanheart.org

Arthritis Foundation

This is a resource for current health information about arthritis and related conditions, such as fibromyalgia.

www.arthritis.org

Linus Pauling Institute, Oregon State University

This is a good source for scientific information about nutrients, health benefits, and food sources.

http://lpi.oregonstate.edu

MedlinePlus

This is a database from the National Institutes of Health where you can find information on foods and nutrition, including nutritional supplements and drugs.

www.nlm.nih.gov/medlineplus/medlineplus.html

National Center for Complementary and Alternative Medicine

This is an excellent resource for learning more about alternative medicine and treatments, as well as the dangers of some supplements.

www.nccam.nih.gov

National Institutes of Health Office of Dietary Supplements

Here you can research specific nutrients, learn about the dangers of deficiency and toxicity, and determine the best food sources.

http://ods.od.nih.gov

University of Maryland Medical Center, Medical References

This is an extensive database of diseases and disorders. It includes information about nutrients for prevention and treatment.

www.umm.edu/medref

The World's Healthiest Foods, The George Mateljan Foundation

This database has research-based nutrition content, information about the origin of healthy foods, and preparation tips.

www.whfoods.org

Index

Acne, 9–16
about: causes of, 10–11; foods to avoid, 10–11; nutrients that may prevent or alleviate, 11
Guava Juice, 14
Kiwi Orange Salad, 13
Red Bell Pepper Spinach Pasta Salad, 12
Roasted Tomato Marinara, 15
Vitamin C Salad, 16
Alcohol, 10, 66, 172, 197, 204, 238, 239
Alzheimer's disease, 17–24
about: foods containing nutrients for, 19; fried fish and, 19; nutrients that may prevent, 18; what it is, 18
Asparagus Chickpea Salad, 21
Cilantro Lime Bean Salad, 20
Grilled Skirt Steak Salad, 24
Simple Lemon Salmon with Dill, 22
Spicy Sautéed Greens, 22
Amaranth
about: whole-grain, 234, 243
Hot Tropical Amaranth with Coconut, 243
Anemia, 25–33
about: iron-deficiency and, 26; nutrients that prevent or treat, 26–27; what it is, 26
Black Bean Quesadilla, 31
Cinnamon Steel-Cut Oats with Berries, 32
Grass-Fed Beef Burgers, 33
Scrambled Eggs with Kale, 30
Spinach Salad with Strawberries and Orange Vinaigrette, 29
Anthocyanins, 6, 37, 140, 141, 156, 157, 188, 270, 271
Antioxidants
absorption of, 97
arthritis and, 36, 37
asthma and, 46
cancer prevention and, 56–57

candida and, 66, 67
cataracts and, 74–75
CFS and, 95
curry and, 5–6
foods with, 37, 46, 47, 57, 67, 95–96, 189
healing power of, 2
high cholesterol and, 188–89
vitamins that act as, 46, 74–75
Apples
about: BRAT diet and, 148; nutrients in peel, 271; varieties of, 153
Apple Cherry Salad, 273
Apple Grape Salad, 160
Ginger Applesauce, 153
Ginger Baked Apples, 233
Apricot and Celery Salad, 184
Arginine, 114, 115
Arthritis, 35–44
about: antioxidants for, 37; curcumin for, 37; foods containing nutrients for, 38–39; nutrients that alleviate, 36–37; omega-3s and omega-6s for, 36–37, 38; types of, 36
Coconut Curry Crusted Trout, 41
Curry Chicken Salad, 43
Fresh Raspberry Salad Dressing, 40
Grilled Plums with Cinnamon Sugar, 42
Roasted Tomato Toasts, 44
Arugula
Arugula Sun-Dried Tomato Pizza, 260
Grilled Turkey Apple Sandwich with Arugula, 257
Asparagus
about: blanching, 136; preparing, 272
Asparagus Chickpea Salad, 21
Asparagus Shrimp Pasta, 136
Asparagus with Orange Ginger Glaze, 272

Grilled Asparagus, 100
Asthma, 45–53
about: environmental risks, 46; foods containing nutrients for, 47–48; nutrients that alleviate symptoms of, 46–47; omega-3s/omega-6s and, 48; sulfites triggering symptoms, 47; what it is, 46
Avocado Banana Salad, 51
"Orange" Juice, 49
Roasted Potatoes and Carrots with Thyme and Rosemary, 53
Sautéed Greens Pizza, 52
Sweet and Spicy Fresh Fruit Salsa, 50
Avocado
Avocado Banana Salad, 51
Avocado Blueberry Salsa, 192
Easy Guacamole, 183

Baked goods, liquid for, 178
Bananas
about: BRAT diet and, 148; diarrhea and, 148; as sweeteners, 259
Avocado Banana Salad, 51
Banana Bread Oatmeal, 200
Banana Rice, 154
Easy Banana Almond Muffins, 223
Ginger Banana Bread, 236
Peanut Butter Banana Smoothie, 198
Basil
about: chiffonade, 267
Fresh Red Bell Pepper Dip with Basil, 258
Pesto, 209
Beans and legumes
about: mashing peas, 207; types of lentils, 249
Asparagus Chickpea Salad, 21
Beef Chili with Lentils, 119
Black Bean Chicken Salad, 120

Black Bean Quesadilla, 31
Cilantro Lime Bean Salad, 20
Easy Bean Dip, 116
Fresh Pesto Pea Salad, 209
Garlic Mashed Potatoes with Lima Beans, 227
Kidney Bean Salad, 206
Lentils and Brown Rice, 146
Mashed Peas, 207
Pumpkin Bean Chili, 210
Simple Lentil Soup, 249
Slow-Cooked Pinto Beans, 248
Toasted Chickpeas, 241
White Bean Tuna Salad, 133
Beef
about: cooking, 57; grass-fed vs. grain-fed, 7
Beef Chili with Lentils, 119
Grass-Fed Beef Burgers, 33
Grilled Skirt Steak Salad, 24
Bell peppers. *See* Peppers
Berries
about: healing power of, 6; nutrients in peel, 271; stocking and freezing, 40; UTIs and, 263
Avocado Blueberry Salsa, 192
Barley Blueberry Almond Salad, 193
Berry Tomato Salad, 267
Blueberry Water, 274
Buckwheat Blackberry Pancakes, 275
Cherry Berry Juice Cocktail, 162
Cranberry Blueberry Scones, 276
Cranberry Orange Drink, 266
Cranberry Sauce, 265
Fresh Raspberry Salad Dressing, 40
Grilled Blueberry Almond Butter Sandwich, 190
Kale Berry Smoothie, 78
Pear, Raspberry, and Walnut Salad, 208
Raspberry Bran Muffins, 127

Steamed Brussels Sprouts with Cranberries and Parsley, 264
Sweet and Spicy Fresh Fruit Salsa, 50
Beta carotene, 94
Beverages
about: fiber from juice, 205; fruit waters, 274; juices without juicer, 175
Blueberry Water, 274
Cherry Berry Juice Cocktail, 162
Cherry Lime Mocktail, 143
Cranberry Orange Drink, 266
Ginger Lemon Tea, 232
Ginger Pineapple Papaya Juice, 175
Ginger Tea, 152
Guava Juice, 14
Kale Berry Smoothie, 78
"Orange" Juice, 49
Peanut Butter Banana Smoothie, 198
Quick Homemade Hot Cocoa, 99
Blanching vegetables, 136
Blood pressure. *See* High blood pressure
Blueberries. *See* Berries
Boron, 212–13
BRAT diet, 148
Breads. *See also* Pancakes; Pizza and calzones; Sandwiches
about: white whole-wheat flour for, 223
Carrot Flaxseed Bread, 217
Cherry Fennel Scones, 178
Cranberry Blueberry Scones, 276
Easy Banana Almond Muffins, 223
Ginger Banana Bread, 236
Nutty Fruit Toast, 166
Pumpkin Muffins, 259
Raspberry Bran Muffins, 127
Roasted Tomato Toasts, 44
Whole-Grain Orange Flax Muffins, 137

Broccoli
about: blanching, 136
Almond Broccoli Salad, 62
Rosemary Broccoli and Cauliflower over Brown Rice, 268
Scallops with Broccoli and Soba Noodles, 202
Broccoli raab
about: what it is, 244
Sautéed Broccoli Raab with Cashews, 244
Brussels Sprouts, Steamed, with Cranberries and Parsley, 264
B vitamins. *See also* Folic acid and folates; Riboflavin
B1, 254
B2, 254
B6, 18, 19, 238, 239, 254
B12, 18, 19, 254, 255
B-complex, 18
foods with, 95–96, 196
insomnia and, 196
stress and, 94, 95–96

Cabbage, in Easy Coleslaw, 124
Caffeine, 10, 149, 196, 197, 204, 238, 239
Calcium
absorption of, 83
absorption of iron and, 27
cold sores and, 115
foods with, 180, 221–22, 238–39
high blood pressure and, 180
magnesium and, 221
menopause, bone loss and, 212
muscle cramps and, 220, 221
PMS and, 238
Cancer, 55–63
about: antioxidants and, 56–57; foods containing nutrients for, 57–58; nutrients that may prevent, 56–57; phytochemicals and, 57, 58; what it is, 56

Cancer—*continued*
  Almond Broccoli Salad, 62
  Garlic Rosemary Thyme Marinade, 60
  Lemon Quinoa Stuffed Tomatoes, 63
  Mushroom Fajitas, 61
  Mushroom Spinach Calzones, 59
Candida, 65–72
  about: foods containing nutrients for, 67–68; nutrients that relieve symptoms, 66–67; what it is, 66
  Cinnamon Spice Almonds, 70
  Grilled Eggplant and Summer Squash, 71
  Lemon Quinoa Stuffed Cucumbers, 68
  Spiced Hot Cereal, 72
  Yogurt Herb Spread, 69
Carbohydrates
  acne and, 10
  compounds, as cancer-fighters, 58
  depression, mood and, 131
  insomnia and, 196, 197
  sources of, 131–32, 196
Carrots
  Carrot Flaxseed Bread, 217
  Roasted Potatoes and Carrots with Thyme and Rosemary, 53
Cataracts, 73–81
  about: causes of, 74; foods containing nutrients for, 75–76; nutrients that may prevent, 74–75; what they are, 74
  Greens and Cheddar Omelet, 77
  Kale Berry Smoothie, 78
  Spinach Pesto and Corn Pasta, 80
  Whole-Grain Pancakes with Berries, 81
  Zucchini, Corn, and Green Bell Peppers, 79
Cauliflower

Cauliflower and Toasted Walnuts, 125
  Rosemary Broccoli and Cauliflower over Brown Rice, 268
Celery
  Almond Stuffed Celery, 182
  Apricot and Celery Salad, 184
Celiac disease, 83–91
  about: foods containing nutrients that increase symptoms, 84–86; nutrients that increase symptoms of, 84; tips for avoiding foods that increase symptoms, 85–86; what it is, 84
  Baked Sweet Potatoes, 87
  Herbed Black Rice, 90
  Potato Chive Pancakes, 89
  Quinoa and Summer Squash, 91
  Simple Green Salad, 88
Cereal. *See* Grains
Cheese
  about: adding to salads, 12, 29; blue cheese appetizer option, 225; fresh grated Parmesan, 12; quality of, 52
  Black Bean Quesadilla, 31
  Blue Cheese Almond Stuffed Prunes with Honey, 225
  Cherry Feta Grain Salad, 142
  in Egg dishes. *See* Eggs
  Ricotta Stuffed Plums, 158
Cherries
  about: anthocyanins in, 6; buying, 141; healing power of, 6; varieties of, 141
  Apple Cherry Salad, 273
  Cherry Berry Juice Cocktail, 162
  Cherry Fennel Scones, 178
  Cherry Feta Grain Salad, 142
  Cherry French Toast, 161
  Cherry Lime Mocktail, 143
Chicken
  about: grilling, 218

Black Bean Chicken Salad, 120
  Cashew Chicken Stir-Fry, 102
  Curry Chicken Salad, 43
  Curry Chicken with Pineapple, 159
  Lemon and Sage Grilled Chicken, 218
  Pecan Chicken Bites, 242
  Pineapple Chicken with Ginger, 177
  Tropical Chicken Salad, 256
  Ultimate Chicken Soup, 111
Chickpeas. *See* Beans and legumes
Cholesterol. *See* High cholesterol
Chronic fatigue syndrome (CFS), 93–102
  about: antioxidants and, 95; B vitamins and, 94–95; essential fatty acids and, 95; foods containing nutrients for, 95–97; minerals and, 95; nutrients that alleviate, 94–95; what it is, 94
  Cashew Chicken Stir-Fry, 102
  Grilled Asparagus, 100
  Melon Salad with Mint, 98
  Quick Homemade Hot Cocoa, 99
  Roasted Pumpkin Smoked Cheddar Risotto, 101
Cilantro Lime Bean Salad, 20
Cilantro substitutions, 120
Cinnamon Spice Almonds, 70
Cinnamon Steel-Cut Oats with Berries, 32
Citrus
  about: lemon garnish for tea, 232
  Asparagus with Orange Ginger Glaze, 272
  Cherry Lime Mocktail, 143
  Cranberry Orange Drink, 266
  Ginger Lemon Tea, 232
  Kiwi Orange Salad, 13
  Lemon and Sage Grilled Chicken, 218
  Lemon Quinoa Stuffed Cucumbers, 68

Lemon Quinoa Stuffed Tomatoes, 63

"Orange" Juice, 49

Orange Sesame Shrimp and Vegetables, 201

Orange Vinaigrette, 29

Whole-Grain Orange Flax Muffins, 137

Cocoa, in Quick Homemade Hot Cocoa, 99

Coconut oil, 194

Cold and flu, 103–11

    about: foods containing nutrients for, 105–6; nutrients that prevent or alleviate, 104–5; symptoms and causes of, 104

    Grilled Veggie and Mushroom Burger, 110

    Mashed Sweet Potatoes, 108

    Sautéed Kale with Sunflower Seeds, 109

    Ultimate Chicken Soup, 111

    Vegetable Couscous, 107

Cold sores, 113–20

    about: foods containing nutrients for, 116; granola and, 117; nutrients that prevent or alleviate, 114; what they are, 114

    Beef Chili with Lentils, 119

    Black Bean Chicken Salad, 120

    Easy Bean Dip, 116

    Parmesan Crusted Cod Fillets, 118

    Quick Yogurt Parfait, 117

Constipation, 121–28

    about: foods containing nutrients for, 123; nutrients that alleviate, 122; what it is, 122

    Cauliflower and Toasted Walnuts, 125

    Easy Coleslaw, 124

    Homemade Muesli with Wheat Bran, 126

    Raspberry Bran Muffins, 127

Roasted Root Vegetables, 128

Cooking healing foods, 7–8

Corn

    about: fresh, 79

    Spinach Pesto and Corn Pasta, 80

    Zucchini, Corn, and Green Bell Peppers, 79

Couscous, 107

Cramps. See Muscle cramps; Premenstrual syndrome (PMS)

Cranberries. See Berries

Cucumbers, Lemon Quinoa Stuffed, 68

Curcumin, 5–6, 37–38, 156, 157

Curry

    about: healing power of, 5–6

    Coconut Curry Crusted Trout, 41

    Curry Chicken Salad, 43

    Curry Chicken with Pineapple, 159

Cyclooxygenase-1 and -2 (COX-1 and COX-2), 37, 156

Dairy, grass-fed vs. grain-fed cows and, 7. See also Cheese; Eggs; Yogurt

Dementia, 18. See also Alzheimer's Disease

Demerara sugar, 62

Depression, 129–37

    about: foods containing nutrients for, 131–32; nutrients that prevent or alleviate, 130–31; what it is, 130

    Asparagus Shrimp Pasta, 136

    Herbed Quinoa Pilaf, 134

    Savory Barley Salad, 135

    White Bean Tuna Salad, 133

    Whole-Grain Orange Flax Muffins, 137

Desserts

    Comfort Yogurt Parfait, 240

    Ginger Spiced Cookies, 235

Papaya Cream, 252

Quick Yogurt Parfait, 117

Diabetes, 139–46

    about: foods containing nutrients for, 141; nutrients that control or prevent, 140; types of, 140; what it is, 140

    Autumn Oatmeal, 145

    Cherry Feta Grain Salad, 142

    Cherry Lime Mocktail, 143

    Cherry Vinaigrette, 144

    Lentils and Brown Rice, 146

Diarrhea, 147–54

    about: causes of, 148; foods containing nutrients for, 148–49; foods to avoid, 149; nutrients that prevent or alleviate, 148

    Banana Rice, 154

    Buttered Noodles, 151

    Garlic Broth Soup, 150

    Ginger Applesauce, 153

    Ginger Tea, 152

Dips and spreads

    about: making spreads into dressings, 69

    Easy Bean Dip, 116

    Easy Guacamole, 183

    Fresh Red Bell Pepper Dip with Basil, 258

Drinks. See Beverages

Eggplant

    Grilled Eggplant and Summer Squash, 71

Eggs

    about: frittata substitutions, 170; pastured vs. farm-raised chickens and, 7

    Cherry French Toast, 161

    Cremini and Chard Frittata, 170

    Egg Panini with Spinach, 167

    Greens and Cheddar Omelet, 77

Eggs—*continued*
    Scrambled Eggs with Kale, 30
    Tex-Mex Breakfast Baked Potato, 186
Electrolytes, 220, 221

Fajitas, 61
Fats
    absorption of fat-soluble nutrients and, 97
    acne and, 10
    heartburn, cooking and, 173
Fatty acids. *See* Omega-3 fatty acids; Omega-6 fatty acids
Fiber
    constipation and, 122–23
    diarrhea and, 148, 149
    foods with, 3, 123, 205
    high cholesterol and, 188, 189
    IBS and, 204, 205
    natural vs. isolated fiber, 4
    soluble, 188, 189
Fibromyalgia, 155–62
    about: foods containing nutrients for, 157; nutrients that prevent or alleviate, 156; what it is, 156
    Apple Grape Salad, 160
    Cherry Berry Juice Cocktail, 162
    Cherry French Toast, 161
    Curry Chicken with Pineapple, 159
    Ricotta Stuffed Plums, 158
Fish and seafood. *See also* Salmon
    about: canned tuna, 133; cooking scallops, 202; mercury in, 247; omega-3 fatty acids and, 247; trout, 41
    Asparagus Shrimp Pasta, 136
    Coconut Curry Crusted Trout, 41
    Orange Sesame Shrimp and Vegetables, 201
    Parmesan Crusted Cod Fillets, 118
    Scallops with Broccoli and Soba Noodles, 202

Tuna Melt, 250
White Bean Tuna Salad, 133
Flavonoids, 6, 140, 188, 189, 270
Flaxseed
    about: ground vs. whole, 137
    Carrot Flaxseed Bread, 217
    Pumpkin Flax Pancakes, 215
Folic acid and folates, 7, 18, 19, 130–31, 132, 246, 247, 254
Food
    cooking and eating, 7–8
    healing with. *See* Healing power of food; *specific maladies*
    local, 6–7
    organic, 6
    selecting, 6–7
French toast, 161
Fruit. *See also specific fruit*
    about: cataracts and, 75; choosing fresh, 47; fruit sauces, 13; fruit waters, 274; stocking and freezing, 40; sulfites and, 47, 51
    Sweet and Spicy Fresh Fruit Salsa, 50
"Functional foods," 3

Garlic
    about: antimicrobial nature of, 148; cancer prevention and, 57; candida and, 67; diarrhea and, 148, 149; healing power of, 3, 5
    Garlic Broth Soup, 150
    Garlic Mashed Potatoes with Lima Beans, 227
    Garlic Rosemary Thyme Marinade, 60
    Mushroom, Garlic, and Spinach Pizza, 169
Ginger
    about: antioxidants in, 37; as blood thinner, 38; diarrhea and, 148, 149; heartburn and, 172, 173; nausea/motion sickness and,

231; reducing inflammation, 67, 172; selecting and storing, 236
    Curry Chicken with Pineapple, 159
    Ginger Applesauce, 153
    Ginger Baked Apples, 233
    Ginger Banana Bread, 236
    Gingerbread Oatmeal, 234
    Ginger Lemon Tea, 232
    Ginger Pineapple Papaya Juice, 175
    Ginger Spiced Cookies, 235
    Ginger Tea, 152
    Orange Ginger Glaze, 272
    Pineapple Chicken with Ginger, 177
Gluten-free foods, 67, 84–86
Grains. *See also* Breads; Oatmeal; Pancakes; Quinoa; Rice
    about: celiac disease and, 84–86; cooking with bulgur wheat, 199; flavoring, 63; gluten-free, 67, 84–86; iron absorption and, 27; serving muesli, 126; soaking whole grains before cooking, 27; sweetening cereals without sugar, 145; types of barley, 193; wheat bran and constipation, 123; wheat germ, 75–76; white whole-wheat flour, 223; whole-grain cereals, 234
    Barley Blueberry Almond Salad, 193
    Easy Trail Mix, 168
    Homemade Muesli with Wheat Bran, 126
    Hot Tropical Amaranth with Coconut, 243
    Savory Barley Salad, 135
    Spiced Hot Cereal, 72
    Turkey Salad with Bulgur Wheat, 199
    Vegetable Couscous, 107
Grapes, in Apple Grape Salad, 160
Greens. *See also* Kale; Salads; Swiss chard

about: adding to juices, 49; cataracts and, 75; plating, 22
Greens and Cheddar Omelet, 77
Sautéed Greens Pizza, 52
Spicy Sautéed Greens, 22
Grilling indoors, 71
Grilling temperatures, 218
Guava
about: Vitamin C content, 11, 14
Guava Juice, 14

Headaches, 163–70
about: foods containing nutrients for, 164–65; migraines, 164, 165; nutrients that alleviate, 164; types of, 164
Cremini and Chard Frittata, 170
Easy Trail Mix, 168
Egg Panini with Spinach, 167
Mushroom, Garlic, and Spinach Pizza, 169
Nutty Fruit Toast, 166
Healing power of food. *See also specific foods and specific maladies*
about:: overview of, 1
food as medicine, 2
"functional foods" and, 3
historical perspective, 2
isolated nutrients vs., 3–4
medical conditions and, 8
nutrition research, 3, 5
popular foods, 4–6
science validating, 2, 3, 5
selecting foods, 6–7
Heartburn, 171–78
about: foods containing nutrients for, 172–73; foods to avoid, 173; nutrients that alleviate, 172; waiting to lie down after eating and, 172; what it is, 172
Cherry Fennel Scones, 178
Ginger Pineapple Papaya Juice, 175

Grilled Pineapple, 174
Pineapple Chicken with Ginger, 177
Tropical Oatmeal, 176
Herbs and spices, 53, 90, 120
Herpes. *See* Cold sores
High blood pressure, 179–86
about: foods containing nutrients for, 181; nutrients that prevent or reduce, 180–81; as risk factor for other conditions, 179; what it is, 180
Almond Stuffed Celery, 182
Apricot and Celery Salad, 184
Easy Guacamole, 183
Mustard Potatoes Salad, 185
Tex-Mex Breakfast Baked Potato, 186
High cholesterol, 187–89
about: cholesterol levels, 188; foods containing nutrients for, 189; nutrients that prevent or control, 188; what it is, 188
Almond Crusted Salmon, 191
Avocado Blueberry Salsa, 192
Barley Blueberry Almond Salad, 193
Carrot Cake Oat Bran, 194
Grilled Blueberry Almond Butter Sandwich, 190

Insomnia, 195–202
about: foods containing nutrients for, 196–97; nutrients that alleviate, 196; what it is, 196
Banana Bread Oatmeal, 200
Orange Sesame Shrimp and Vegetables, 201
Peanut Butter Banana Smoothie, 198
Scallops with Broccoli and Soba Noodles, 202
Turkey Salad with Bulgur Wheat, 199

Iron
absorption of, 27, 28
anemia and, 26–28
foods with, 27–28
heme vs. nonheme, 26–27
Irritable bowel syndrome (IBS), 203–10
about: foods containing nutrients for, 205; foods to avoid, 204; nutrients that alleviate, 204; what it is, 204
Fresh Pesto Pea Salad, 209
Kidney Bean Salad, 206
Mashed Peas, 207
Pear, Raspberry, and Walnut Salad, 208
Pumpkin Bean Chili, 210
Isoflavins, 212, 213

Kale
about: adding to juices, 49; types of, 109
Kale Berry Smoothie, 78
Sautéed Kale with Sunflower Seeds, 109
Scrambled Eggs with Kale, 30
Spicy Sautéed Greens, 22
Kiwi
Kiwi Orange Salad, 13
Vitamin C Salad, 13

Lemon. *See* Citrus
Lentils. *See* Beans and legumes
Local foods, 6–7
Lysine, 114–15

Magnesium
calcium and, 221, 238
CFS and, 95
foods with, 95, 164, 181, 221–22, 238–39, 255
head pain and, 164
high blood pressure and, 180

Magnesium—*continued*
    muscle cramps and, 221
    PMS and, 238–39
    stress, anxiety and, 254
Medical conditions, 8
Medications
    food complications and, 38
Melons
    about: choosing, 98; ripeness of, 98
    Melon Salad with Mint, 98
Menopause, 211–18
    about: foods containing nutrients
        for, 213; nutrients that alleviate
        symptoms of, 212–13; what it is,
        212
    Carrot Flaxseed Bread, 217
    Lemon and Sage Grilled Chicken,
        218
    Pumpkin Flax Pancakes, 215
    Sweet Soy Grilled Tofu, 214
    Tofu Vegetable Stir-Fry, 216
Muscle cramps, 219–27
    about: foods containing nutrients
        for, 221–22; nutrients that pre-
        vent or alleviate, 221; types and
        causes of, 220–21
    Blue Cheese Almond Stuffed
        Prunes with Honey, 225
    Breakfast Potatoes with Spinach,
        224
    Easy Banana Almond Muffins, 223
    Garlic Mashed Potatoes with Lima
        Beans, 227
    Spinach Salad with Almond Butter
        Dressing, 226
Mushrooms
    about: as cancer-fighters, 59; wash-
        ing, 110; white button, 59
    Cremini and Chard Frittata, 170
    Grilled Veggie and Mushroom
        Burger, 110
    Mushroom, Garlic, and Spinach
        Pizza, 169

Mushroom Fajitas, 61
Mushroom Spinach Calzones, 59

Nausea and motion sickness, 229–36
    about: causes of, 230; foods con-
        taining nutrients for, 231; nutri-
        ents that alleviate, 230
    Ginger Baked Apples, 233
    Ginger Banana Bread, 236
    Gingerbread Oatmeal, 234
    Ginger Lemon Tea, 232
    Ginger Spiced Cookies, 235
Neurotransmitters, 130–31, 156, 254,
    255
Nutraceuticals, 3
Nutrition
    isolated nutrients vs. real food, 3–4
    research validating, 3, 5
Nuts and seeds. *See also* Flaxseed;
    Pumpkin (and seeds)
    about: adding to salads, 29; choos-
        ing almond butter, 182; head
        pain and, 164–65
    Almond Broccoli Salad, 62
    Almond Butter Dressing, 226
    Almond Crusted Salmon, 191
    Almond Stuffed Celery, 182
    Cauliflower and Toasted Walnuts,
        125
    Cinnamon Spice Almonds, 70
    Easy Banana Almond Muffins,
        223
    Easy Trail Mix, 168
    Grilled Blueberry Almond Butter
        Sandwich, 190
    Nutty Fruit Toast, 166
    Peanut Butter Banana Smoothie,
        198
    Pear, Raspberry, and Walnut Salad,
        208
    Pecan Chicken Bites, 242
    Whole-Grain Orange Flax Muffins,
        137

Oatmeal
    about: celiac disease and, 84;
        creamier, 200; oat bran, 194;
        whole-grain cereals, 234
    Autumn Oatmeal, 145
    Banana Bread Oatmeal, 200
    Carrot Cake Oat Bran, 194
    Cinnamon Steel-Cut Oats with Ber-
        ries, 32
    Gingerbread Oatmeal, 234
    Tropical Oatmeal, 176
Omega-3 fatty acids
    Alzheimer's disease, memory and,
        18, 19
    arthritis and, 36–37, 38
    asthma and, 47
    CFS and, 95
    depression and, 131
    foods with, 7, 19, 36–37, 96, 131,
        189, 247
    high cholesterol and, 189
    method of raising animals affecting
        amount of, 7
    omega-6s and, 48, 97. *See also*
        Omega-6 fatty acids
    psoriasis and, 246, 247
    salmon and, 5
    tips for incorporating into diet,
        38
Omega-6 fatty acids, 36–37, 38, 47, 48,
    95, 97
Onions, candida and, 67
Orange. *See* Citrus
Organic foods, 6
Oxalates, 8, 27

Pancakes
    Buckwheat Blackberry Pancakes,
        275
    Potato Chive Pancakes, 89
    Pumpkin Flax Pancakes, 215
    Whole-Grain Pancakes with Ber-
        ries, 81

Papaya
    about: beta carotene in, 94; heart-
        burn and, 172, 173; psoriasis and,
        247; stress, anxiety and, 255
    Ginger Pineapple Papaya Juice, 175
    Papaya Cream, 252
    Tropical Oatmeal, 176
Parsnips, in Roasted Root Vegetables,
    128
Pasta
    about: choosing, 80
    Asparagus Shrimp Pasta, 136
    Buttered Noodles, 151
    Red Bell Pepper Spinach Pasta
        Salad, 12
    Scallops with Broccoli and Soba
        Noodles, 202
    Spinach Pesto and Corn Pasta, 80
Pear, Raspberry, and Walnut Salad,
    208
Peas. See Beans and legumes
Peppers
    Fresh Red Bell Pepper Dip with
        Basil, 258
    Red Bell Pepper Spinach Pasta
        Salad, 12
    Zucchini, Corn, and Green Bell Pep-
        pers, 79
Phthalides, 181
Phytates, 27, 96
Phytochemicals, 3, 5, 6, 37, 46, 57, 58,
    74, 140, 188
Phytoestrogens, 212–13
Pineapple
    about: heartburn and, 172, 173
    Grilled Pineapple, 174
    Pineapple Chicken with Ginger, 177
    Tropical Oatmeal, 176
Pizza and calzones
    Arugula Sun-Dried Tomato Pizza,
        260
    Mushroom, Garlic, and Spinach
        Pizza, 169

Mushroom Spinach Calzones, 59
    Sautéed Greens Pizza, 52
Plums
    Grilled Plums with Cinnamon
        Sugar, 42
    Ricotta Stuffed Plums, 158
Polyphenols, 27, 37
Potassium, 180, 181, 220, 221–22
Potatoes
    about: baked, blood pressure and,
        181; baking for mashing, 227
    Breakfast Potatoes with Spinach,
        224
    Garlic Mashed Potatoes with Lima
        Beans, 227
    Mustard Potatoes Salad, 185
    Potato Chive Pancakes, 89
    Roasted Potatoes and Carrots with
        Thyme and Rosemary, 53
    Roasted Root Vegetables, 128
    Tex-Mex Breakfast Baked Potato,
        186
Premenstrual syndrome (PMS),
    237–44
    about: foods containing nutrients
        for, 238–39; nutrients that alle-
        viate, 238; risk factors for, 239;
        what it is, 238
    Comfort Yogurt Parfait, 240
    Hot Tropical Amaranth with Coco-
        nut, 243
    Pecan Chicken Bites, 242
    Sautéed Broccoli Raab with
        Cashews, 244
    Toasted Chickpeas, 241
Proteins
    Alzheimer's disease, memory and,
        19
    complete, combining foods for, 132
    depression, mood and, 130, 131–32
    free radicals and, 74
    insomnia and, 196, 197
    sources of, 19

Prunes, in Blue Cheese Almond
    Stuffed Prunes with Honey, 225
Psoriasis, 245–52
    about: foods containing nutrients
        for, 247; nutrients that alleviate,
        246; what it is, 246
    Open-Face Salmon Sandwich, 251
    Papaya Cream, 252
    Simple Lentil Soup, 249
    Slow-Cooked Pinto Beans, 248
    Tuna Melt, 250
Pumpkin
    Pumpkin Bean Chili, 210
    Pumpkin Flax Pancakes, 215
    Pumpkin Muffins, 259
Pumpkin (and seeds)
    about: antifungal properties of
        seeds, 67; roasting, 101; seeds
        and head pain, 164–
        65
    Easy Trail Mix, 168
    Roasted Pumpkin Smoked Cheddar
        Risotto, 101

Quinoa
    about: affordable, 68; rinsing,
        91
    Herbed Quinoa Pilaf, 134
    Lemon Quinoa Stuffed Cucumbers,
        68
    Lemon Quinoa Stuffed Tomatoes,
        63
    Quinoa and Summer Squash, 91

Raspberries. See Berries
Resources
    print, 277
    web-based, 279–80
Riboflavin, 164, 166
Rice
    about: BRAT diet and, 148
    Banana Rice, 154
    Herbed Black Rice, 90

Rice—*continued*
Lentils and Brown Rice, 146
Roasted Pumpkin Smoked Cheddar
Risotto, 101
Rosemary Broccoli and Cauliflower
over Brown Rice, 268
Rutin, 270, 271
Salads
about: adding cheese and nuts
to, 29; flavored vinegars for, 88;
serving to avoid sogginess, 160
Almond Broccoli Salad, 62
Apple Cherry Salad, 273
Apricot and Celery Salad, 184
Asparagus Chickpea Salad, 21
Avocado Banana Salad, 51
Barley Blueberry Almond Salad, 193
Berry Tomato Salad, 267
Black Bean Chicken Salad, 120
Cherry Feta Grain Salad, 142
Cilantro Lime Bean Salad, 20
Curry Chicken Salad, 43
Easy Coleslaw, 124
Fresh Pesto Pea Salad, 209
Kidney Bean Salad, 206
Kiwi Orange Salad, 13
Melon Salad with Mint, 98
Mustard Potatoes Salad, 185
Pear, Raspberry, and Walnut Salad,
208
Red Bell Pepper Spinach Pasta
Salad, 12
Savory Barley Salad, 135
Simple Green Salad, 88
Spinach Salad with Almond Butter
Dressing, 226
Spinach Salad with Strawberries
and Orange Vinaigrette, 29
Tropical Chicken Salad, 256
Turkey Salad with Bulgur Wheat,
199
Vitamin C Salad, 16
White Bean Tuna Salad, 133

Salmon
about: best sources for, 38; healing
power of, 5
Almond Crusted Salmon, 191
Open-Face Salmon Sandwich, 251
Simple Lemon Salmon with Dill, 22
Sandwiches
about: paninis without press, 167;
processed lunch meat vs. real
meat for, 257; sauces over, 251
Egg Panini with Spinach, 167
Grilled Blueberry Almond Butter
Sandwich, 190
Grilled Turkey Apple Sandwich
with Arugula, 257
Open-Face Salmon Sandwich, 251
Tuna Melt, 250
Yogurt Herb Spread for, 69
Sauces, salsas and dressings
about: flavored vinegars, 88; fruit
sauces, 13; making spreads into
dressings, 69; marinating, 60
Almond Butter Dressing, 226
Avocado Blueberry Salsa, 192
Cherry Vinaigrette, 144
Cranberry Sauce, 265
Fresh Raspberry Salad Dressing, 40
Garlic Rosemary Thyme Marinade,
60
Orange Ginger Glaze, 272
Orange Vinaigrette, 29
Pesto, 209
Roasted Tomato Marinara, 15
Spinach Pesto, 80
Sweet and Spicy Fresh Fruit Salsa, 50
Yogurt Herb Spread, 69
Seeds. *See* Nuts and seeds
Selecting healing foods, 6–7
Sodium intake, canned foods and, 210
Soups and stews
Beef Chili with Lentils, 119
Garlic Broth Soup, 150
Pumpkin Bean Chili, 210

Simple Lentil Soup, 249
Ultimate Chicken Soup, 111
Soy products, menopause and, 213.
See also Tofu
Spinach
Breakfast Potatoes with Spinach, 224
Mushroom, Garlic, and Spinach
Pizza, 169
Mushroom Spinach Calzones, 59
Red Bell Pepper Spinach Pasta
Salad, 12
Spinach Pesto and Corn Pasta, 80
Spinach Salad with Almond Butter
Dressing, 226
Spinach Salad with Strawberries
and Orange Vinaigrette, 29
Spreads. *See* Dips and spreads
Squash
about: winter, 128
Grilled Eggplant and Summer
Squash, 71
Quinoa and Summer Squash, 91
Zucchini, Corn, and Green Bell Pep-
pers, 79
Stress and anxiety, 253–60
about: causes of, 254; exercise and,
255; foods containing nutrients
for, 255; nutrients that alleviate,
254; out of control, 254
Arugula Sun-Dried Tomato Pizza,
260
Fresh Red Bell Pepper Dip with
Basil, 258
Grilled Turkey Apple Sandwich
with Arugula, 257
Pumpkin Muffins, 259
Tropical Chicken Salad, 256
Sugar and sweeteners
bananas as sweeteners, 259
demerara sugar, 62
fruits as sweeteners, 145
less-refined cane sugars, 42
Sulfites, 47, 51

on Anything!

...ing® list spans a wide range of subjects, with more than 500 titles covering 25 different categories:

...ess	History	Reference
...eers	Home Improvement	Religion
...hildren's Storybooks	Everything Kids	Self-Help
Computers	Languages	Sports & Fitness
Cooking	Music	Travel
Crafts and Hobbies	New Age	Wedding
Education/Schools	Parenting	Writing
Games and Puzzles	Personal Finance	
Health	Pets	

Supplements. *See also specific vitamins and minerals*
 absorption and toxicity issues, 3–4
 fat-soluble, absorption of, 97
 limited benefit of, 4
 real food vs., 3–4
Sweet potatoes
 about: microwaving, 87; spiking
  with liqueurs, 108
 Baked Sweet Potatoes, 87
 Mashed Sweet Potatoes, 108
 Roasted Potatoes and Carrots with
  Thyme and Rosemary, 53
Swiss chard
 about: head pain and, 164, 165;
  stress, anxiety and, 255
 Cremini and Chard Frittata, 170

Tofu
 about: menopause and, 213; press-
  ing, 214
 Sweet Soy Grilled Tofu, 214
 Tofu Vegetable Stir-Fry, 216
Tomatoes
 about: adding spices to, 15; BPA in
  canned, 119; varieties of, 44
 Arugula Sun-Dried Tomato Pizza,
  260
 Berry Tomato Salad, 267
 Lemon Quinoa Stuffed Tomatoes, 63
 Roasted Tomato Marinara, 15
 Roasted Tomato Toasts, 44
Tryptophan, 130, 131, 196, 197, 254, 255
Turkey
 about: processed lunch meat vs.
  real meat, 257
 Grilled Turkey Apple Sandwich
  with Arugula, 257
 Turkey Salad with Bulgur Wheat,
  199
Turnip greens, 11, 19, 47, 48, 75, 95,
 123. *See also* Greens
Turnips, in Roasted Root Vegetables, 128

Tyramine, 165
Tyrosine, 130

Urina

Cra
Rosem
 over Br
Steamed Brus
 Cranberries a

Varicose veins, 269–76
 about: foods containing nut
  for, 271; nutrients that impro
  circulation and prevent, 270;
  what they are, 270
 Apple Cherry Salad, 273
 Asparagus with Orange Ginger
  Glaze, 272
 Blueberry Water, 274
 Buckwheat Blackberry Pancakes,
  275
 Cranberry Blueberry Scones, 276
Vegetables
 about: blanching, 136; cataracts
  and, 75
 Grilled Veggie and Mushroom
  Burger, 110
 Orange Sesame Shrimp and Veg-
  etables, 201
 Roasted Root Vegetables, 128
 Tofu Vegetable Stir-Fry, 216
 Vegetable Couscous, 107
Vinaigrettes. *See* Sauces, salsas and
 dressings
Vinegars, flavored, 88
Vitamin B. *See* B vitamins

b
 7
cancer p
cataracts an
cold/flu and, 1
foods with, 11, 47, 5
 high cholesterol and, 1
Vitamins and minerals. *See* S
 ments; *specific vitamins and
 minerals*

Wheat germ, 75–76

Yogurt
 about: Greek, 127
 Comfort Yogurt Parfait, 240
 Quick Yogurt Parfait, 117
 Yogurt Herb Spread, 69

Zucchini. *See* Squash

We Have
EVERYTHING®
on Anything!

The Everything® list spans a wide range of subjects, with more than 500 titles covering 25 different categories:

Business	History	Reference
Careers	Home Improvement	Religion
Children's Storybooks	Everything Kids	Self-Help
Computers	Languages	Sports & Fitness
Cooking	Music	Travel
Crafts and Hobbies	New Age	Wedding
Education/Schools	Parenting	Writing
Games and Puzzles	Personal Finance	
Health	Pets	

Supplements. *See also specific vitamins and minerals*
  absorption and toxicity issues, 3–4
  fat-soluble, absorption of, 97
  limited benefit of, 4
  real food vs., 3–4
Sweet potatoes
  about: microwaving, 87; spiking with liqueurs, 108
  Baked Sweet Potatoes, 87
  Mashed Sweet Potatoes, 108
  Roasted Potatoes and Carrots with Thyme and Rosemary, 53
Swiss chard
  about: head pain and, 164, 165; stress, anxiety and, 255
  Cremini and Chard Frittata, 170

Tofu
  about: menopause and, 213; pressing, 214
  Sweet Soy Grilled Tofu, 214
  Tofu Vegetable Stir-Fry, 216
Tomatoes
  about: adding spices to, 15; BPA in canned, 119; varieties of, 44
  Arugula Sun-Dried Tomato Pizza, 260
  Berry Tomato Salad, 267
  Lemon Quinoa Stuffed Tomatoes, 63
  Roasted Tomato Marinara, 15
  Roasted Tomato Toasts, 44
Tryptophan, 130, 131, 196, 197, 254, 255
Turkey
  about: processed lunch meat vs. real meat, 257
  Grilled Turkey Apple Sandwich with Arugula, 257
  Turkey Salad with Bulgur Wheat, 199
Turnip greens, 11, 19, 47, 48, 75, 95, 123. *See also* Greens
Turnips, in Roasted Root Vegetables, 128

Tyramine, 165
Tyrosine, 130

Urinary tract infections (UTIs), 261–68
  about: foods containing nutrients for, 263; nutrients that prevent or alleviate, 262; symptoms of, 262; urinary tract parts and, 263; what they are, 262
  Berry Tomato Salad, 267
  Cranberry Orange Drink, 266
  Cranberry Sauce, 265
  Rosemary Broccoli and Cauliflower over Brown Rice, 268
  Steamed Brussels Sprouts with Cranberries and Parsley, 264

Varicose veins, 269–76
  about: foods containing nutrients for, 271; nutrients that improve circulation and prevent, 270; what they are, 270
  Apple Cherry Salad, 273
  Asparagus with Orange Ginger Glaze, 272
  Blueberry Water, 274
  Buckwheat Blackberry Pancakes, 275
  Cranberry Blueberry Scones, 276
Vegetables
  about: blanching, 136; cataracts and, 75
  Grilled Veggie and Mushroom Burger, 110
  Orange Sesame Shrimp and Vegetables, 201
  Roasted Root Vegetables, 128
  Tofu Vegetable Stir-Fry, 216
  Vegetable Couscous, 107
Vinaigrettes. *See* Sauces, salsas and dressings
Vinegars, flavored, 88
Vitamin B. *See* B vitamins

Vitamin C
  acne and, 11
  as antioxidant, 46, 74–75, 105
  asthma and, 46
  boosting immune system, 115
  cancer prevention and, 57
  cataracts and, 74–75
  CFS and, 95–96
  circulation, varicose veins and, 270–71
  cold/flu and, 104–5
  cooking reducing value of, 7–8
  foods with, 11, 16, 28, 47, 57, 75, 95–96, 255, 263, 270
  iron absorption and, 27
  stress, anxiety and, 254, 255
  UTIs and, 262, 263
  Vitamin C Salad, 16
Vitamin D, 4, 18, 19, 246
Vitamin E
  acne and, 11
  as antioxidant, 46, 74–75, 188
  asthma and, 46, 47
  boosting intake with wheat germ, 75–76
  cancer prevention and, 57
  cataracts and, 74–75
  cold/flu and, 104, 105
  foods with, 11, 47, 57, 75, 105, 189
  high cholesterol and, 188–89
Vitamins and minerals. *See* Supplements; *specific vitamins and minerals*

Wheat germ, 75–76

Yogurt
  about: Greek, 127
  Comfort Yogurt Parfait, 240
  Quick Yogurt Parfait, 117
  Yogurt Herb Spread, 69

Zucchini. *See* Squash